SECRETS, PLOTS & HIDDEN AGENDAS

What You Don't Know About Conspiracy Theories

Paul T. Coughlin

InterVarsity Press
Downers Grove, Illinois

InterVarsity Press
P.O. Box 1400, Downers Grove, IL 60515
World Wide Web: www.ivpress.com
E-mail: mail@ivpress.com

InterVarsity Press® *is the book-publishing division of InterVarsity Christian Fellowship/USA*®, *a student movement active on campus at hundreds of universities, colleges and schools of nursing in the United States of America, and a member movement of the International Fellowship of Evangelical Students. For information about local and regional activities, write Public Relations Dept., InterVarsity Christian Fellowship/USA, 6400 Schroeder Rd., P.O. Box 7895, Madison, WI 53707-7895.*

ISBN 0-8308-1624-0

Printed in the United States of America ♻

Library of Congress Cataloging-in-Publication Data

Coughlin, Paul T.
    Secrets, plots & hidden agendas: what you don't know about
conspiracy theories / Paul T. Coughlin.
        p. cm.
    Includes bibliographical references.
    ISBN 0-8308-1624-0 (pbk.: alk. paper)
    1. Conspiracies.   I. Title.   II. Title: Secrets, plots, and
hidden agendas.
    HV6275.C67   1999
    364.1—dc21   98-29822
                                                                       CIP

20	19	18	17	16	15	14	13	12	11	10	9	8	7	6	5	4	3	2	1
16	15	14	13	12	11	10	09	08	07	06	05	04	03	02	01	00	99		

Acknowledgments

Numerous people and organizations helped to make this work possible. This book might not have come to be without the help of Quentin Schultze. Thank you for helping someone you have never met. May we someday fish the Rogue. Special thanks to Perry Atkinson, a special person who is living proof that the best man doesn't always get the job. Additional thanks go to Craig Black, Bill Moore, Dee (Virginia) Strock, Sue Schneider, Lee Lanphier, Hope Russell, Bill Haas, Bob Hunter, the late Garrett Miller, Joe Robinson, B. J. Oropeza, Tim King, Tom Coughlin, Betty Coughlin, Rikki Coughlin, Laura Coughlin and Tom Jr., the archenemy of flabby thinking.

Thank you to the excellent staff at InterVarsity Press, the Phelps family of Evangel Family Bookstores, *The Mail Tribune* and the reference staff at the Jackson County Library.

Finally and most important, a very hearty thank-you to Sandy and our tribe, who encouraged their husband/father to work in a square, cold van on the driveway when all the while they wanted him to come inside and wrestle on the floor by the fire.

1

Conspiracy Theories Are Everyone's Business

I deeply regret not taking the information that I had to the police.
I put myself first in spite of a sea of grief and sorrow experienced by bombing victims.
I am so completely ashamed that I did not come forward with my knowledge right away. . . .
[The bombing victims'] stories are so horrifying, so heartbreaking,
so full of human suffering that I cannot bear them.
I feel as though my mind would break.
**Michael Fortier, after receiving his sentence of twelve years in prison
for his role in the Oklahoma City bombing**

I have nightmares of my daughter calling out for me from the rubble of the building.
The hardest thing a mother will ever [have] to do is bury her child.
Marsha Kight, mother of Frankie Merrell, bombing victim

While taking a much-needed vacation, I woke up on the morning of April 20, 1995, to headlines of a hit-and-run war. Photos showed victims and rescuers covered in a macabre paste composed of blood and coarse concrete dust. The story documented with cool detachment how an explosion carved a deep scar into a stout rectangular-shaped building reminiscent of the cratered structures of World War II. Testimonies of Oklahoma City residents punctuated the story with hysteria and fear that the perpetrator was still at large.

My family and I had been so busy playing in the wilds of the Pacific Northwest that we hadn't heard as much as an incomplete sentence about the bombing attack. With my elbows propped on a honey-pine breakfast table, I read the suspicions rippling through Associated Press and other wire stories regarding the identity of the bomber or bombers. The main suspects were misidentified as Middle Eastern terrorists.

While I waded through accounts that wrestled with specific questions—What kind of bomb was it? How many might still be buried inside the concrete and rebar rubble? Who did it and for what motive?—I felt as if I were suffocating in heavy wool blankets. Breaking television news stories fulfilled my suspicions—and my prediction made more than a year previous on my daily radio talk show.

I had predicted on *The Paul Thomas Show* that some form of violence would be executed against the U.S. government, because I took seriously the anger expressed by callers against the federal government for its alleged and deliberate "murder" of religious extremists at Waco and Ruby Ridge. My callers believed that these "planned executions" were part of a "New World Order" conspiracy.

But not all of my callers agreed as to who was or wasn't part of the conspiracy. Many, such as John, believed that there was a concerted effort on the part of the elitist media to propagate liberal political and social agendas calculated to pull America from its "godly foundation." He was thankful that talk show hosts such as Rush Limbaugh were there to balance the score every weekday.

Scott, however, believed that Limbaugh was part of the conspiracy, as was nearly every U.S. president, especially if a member of the Masonic Lodge. Scott believed that the U.S. government carried out the Oklahoma City bombing in an attempt to restrict the Second Amendment right to bear arms.

Callers such as Mark argued emphatically that the national debt was being deliberately increased to turn control of the country over to evil international bankers who would destroy America's sovereignty and erect the New World Order. He also believed that most churches and influential church leaders, such as Billy Graham, James Dobson, Chuck Colson, the late Walter Martin, but especially the pope, were leading the world toward this New World Order (see chapters two and three).

Other callers, such as seventy-something Will, believed in all these conspiracies and more. They were convinced that Jews were behind them all, just as Will's hero, Henry Ford, had "exposed" earlier in the century.

Though their intensity varied, all were convinced that we are living in what the Bible refers to as the "last days" or "end times." This unprecedented epoch will feature not only the return of Christ to earth but will also include a network of nefarious conspiracies. Proof, they claimed, is found in today's headlines, which they believe fulfill essential Old and New Testament prophecies. Many callers who adhered to these conspiracy theories spoke of horrific apocalyptic scenarios and claimed that they had lived for more than a generation in the grip of a vast and sinister conspiracy controlled by Satan, the embodiment of evil.

Apocalyptic Expectations on the Rise

The Trends Institute, a nonreligious organization in Albany, New York, has noticed an increase in apocalyptic, end-times expectations. This establishment, which tracks modern trends via news reports and public-opinion polls, predicted that the arrival of the year 2000 would spread apocalyptic visions throughout some Christian circles. "Some Christians will regard the turn of the century as the approach of the apocalypse because the Bible's Book of Revelation predicts that Jesus Christ will reign on Earth for one-thousand years."

A poll taken in late 1997 indicated that 66 percent of Americans, including a third of those who never attend church, say they believe that Jesus Christ will return to earth someday. This was a 5 percent increase over a poll taken just three years earlier.

There is no official roster of Christian conspiracy believers. Some have fled society, so it is impossible to cite with certainty their number. However, the rising number of fast-selling apocalyptic books that claim to prove we are living during the last days implies that their ranks are impressive and increasing.

It takes fewer than a hundred thousand sales for a book to make the U.S. bestseller list. Yet many books about conspiracy theories garner far greater sales. Among them are *En Route to Global Occupation, The New World Order: The Ancient Plan of Secret Societies* and *Hidden Dangers of the Rainbow.* Five million copies of *None Dare Call It Conspiracy* are in print, and six million copies of *None Dare Call It Treason* sold in just eight months. *New World Order* was a *New York Times* bestseller and has been quoted by militia leaders as yet more proof that God himself has foretold their fears of government tyranny.[1]

Some of these bestsellers quote anti-Semitic authors, such as those published in *Spotlight,* a weekly newspaper produced by the Liberty Lobby, as reliable sources. *Spotlight* claims to expose many of the same conspiracies written about by Christian authors. It boasts 100,000 paid subscribers. In the early 1980s, the publication claimed a circulation surpassing 300,000. *Personal UPDATE,* published by leading Christian conspiracy theorist Chuck Missler, claims a circulation of more than 200,000 Christians each month.

Christian radio is another medium of the Christian conspiracy message. The largest provider of these theories is *Point of View* with Marlin Maddoux from Dallas, Texas. More than three million people listen to his daily two-hour talk show.[2] Leading Christian conspiracy theorist Don McAlvany is another who has used the radio waves to spread these theories. He says that in one year alone more than six million "concerned Americans listened to or read" his warnings as "America's #1 geo-economic privacy expert."[3]

Some have mistakenly argued that Christian conspiracy theorists, and the militia they help produce, inhabit only certain regions of the United States. After one of my shows devoted to the topic of Christian conspiracy theories born from popular end-of-the-world preaching, I asked my guest, Frank Beckwith, a noted Christian writer and speaker, if he believed that Christian conspiracy theorists were geographically isolated. Beckwith, a professor of philosophy who has been a guest on numerous other radio talk shows, is startled by their numbers. "They're everywhere," he said.

I have interviewed pastors, youth pastors, Christian realtors and contractors, financial advisers and business owners who believe in the same conspiracies that the militia and the ultraconservative John Birch Society warn against but who belong to neither. They do not wear fatigues but dress the same as most people. They go to evangelical churches and praise the Lord of the universe. But they believe that an elite and evil group controls world events and that such evil control is the fulfillment of Bible prophecy. They do not walk around with a far-off look in their eyes, nor are they dumb or uneducated. Some own successful businesses or have received prestigious scholarships. These theories have become an addendum to their faith.

Dean Compton, the compelling cofounder of the National Alliance of Christian Militia, is another example of how prevalent such theories have become within the church. He says that about 90 percent of the people within the militia movement are Christian (see chapter four). "Ninety-nine percent of the people in the Christian patriot movement per se would fit well in a Calvary Chapel or Baptist church."[4]

These conspiracy theories within the church are connected to other more remarkable theories found within the culture at large. Americans have grown increasingly skeptical of the truthfulness of their government but increasingly credulous that aliens are out there and possibly among us. Antigovernment conspiracy theories are a cash crop, especially for Hollywood (see chapter seven).

Chris Carter, conspiracy theorist and creator of the foreboding *X-Files,* airs on his weekly television series a laundry list of earthly and paranormal conspiracies. They include how high-ranking government officials assassinated both John F. Kennedy and Martin Luther King Jr. Carter, through his paranormal version of *Dragnet,* has succeeded in topping filmmaker Oliver Stone, in part because Carter has tapped into a cultural vein that purports, in the words of the concluding credits of *X-Files,* that "The Truth Is Out There."

Independence Day, a movie in which America's secretary of state all but admits that the U.S. government is involved in a conspiracy to conceal alien encounters, was the seventh highest grossing movie ever. According to *Books in Print* there are almost as many books about UFOs (more than 250), in which the common thread is some kind of government conspiracy theory, as there are books about the Kennedy family. A 1997 poll reveals that 65 percent of Americans believe a UFO crash-landed near Roswell, New Mexico, in 1947 and that 80 percent believe the U.S. government is involved in some type of conspiracy to conceal the existence of aliens.

Such UFO conspiracy theories have taken on increasing validity within the church—so much so that popular Christian conspiracy theorist Chuck Missler expects "the Antichrist, when he shows up, to either be an alien or be connected with one." He writes that this supposed alien connection "would be consistent from what else we can infer from Scripture."[5]

Why Now?

Since the Oklahoma City bombing and the conviction of antigovernment conspiracy theorists Timothy McVeigh, his cohort Terry Nichols and accomplice Michael Fortier, millions of Americans have been exposed, perhaps for the first time, to an antigovernment view that has created for them more questions than answers. One of those questions is, why now?

Now, at the turn of the century, is a time in the minds of many (including non-Christians) that will usher in hell on earth. Indeed, Christians within the militia movement have been told for more than twenty-five years that they have been living during this period.

This mixture of religious and secular speculation results in part from a dovetailing of two contemporary movements. The first came in the fifties with the founding of the anticommunist, ultraconservative and conspiracy-prone John Birch Society (JBS). The second came in 1970 with the release of the bestselling book of that decade *The Late Great Planet Earth* by Hal Lindsey and the much-forgotten C. C. Carlson. This worldwide bestseller captured the minds of millions, both inside and outside the church, and is revered today as the work that began the modern-day end-times prophecy movement.

These two worldviews have been married by men such as Don McAlvany, who adheres to the JBS's ultraright political views, which are often saturated with conspiracy theories, and who preaches an end-times message similar to Hal Lindsey's. The political lenses through which McAlvany and others view current events are the same events that they believe prove we are living in the last days. According to militia leader Dean Compton, these are the people who constitute much of the militia movement—people who also believe that botched government standoffs with religious extremists at Ruby Ridge and Waco are signposts of the last days.

Lindsey predicted that the tribulation would begin in 1981. When it didn't, he and others revised their end-times calendar. Now they argue that the last generation to inhabit this present earth was the one that witnessed the 1967 war, when Israel took over all of Jerusalem. Add forty years (which, according to Lindsey, is a biblical number for a generation) subtract seven for the tribulation, "and the result is 2000 A.D., a seemingly perfect year to begin a millennium."[6] This is one prediction that has fueled the race toward the apocalypse.

A second prediction comes from what was the bestselling book in the world for part of 1997: Michael Drosnin's *The Bible Code.* Drosnin claims to show how "hidden text in the Old Testament reveals the future."[7] He asserts that the assassinations of Anwar Sadat, John and Robert Kennedy and former Israeli prime minister Yitzhak Rabin can all be found in the Old Testament by using his complicated code. "I did check for the death of [Princess] Diana the day after she was killed. And, in fact, it was encoded quite clearly within a few verses of the book of Exodus."[8]

But the predictions of these deaths pale when compared to Drosnin's bombshell forecast of nuclear holocaust. During an Internet interview or "chat," he wrote that "the most terrible warning encoded in the Bible is that we might face a nuclear world war. . . . The words 'atomic holocaust' and 'world war' are encoded in the Bible."[9] Drosnin says that they are encoded with the same year: 2000. "I think that might be the real Armageddon." (Drosnin also lists the year 2006 for this scenario and believes that "we can prevent it from happening," but given the rise in apocalyptic literature at the turn of the century, it's likely that the second date will be discarded.)

Warner Brothers has announced that it will make a movie based on Drosnin's book. Leading Christian conspiracy theorist Chuck Missler in his *Personal UPDATE* newsletter advertised similar Bible code books, as well as a series of articles defending the accuracy of such a hitherto hidden code.

Emerging technologies have often been suspected of playing a dominant role in end-times apocalyptic scenarios. Some argued that a large and powerful computer located in Europe was the beast described in the book of Revelation. That theory has been debunked by even Christian conspiracy theorists. The latest technological horror, however, that has the ear of many fundamentalist/evangelicals is the "millennium bug" or Y2K (Y=Year and K=1000, making Year 2000). This computing problem originates from an error on the part of computer designers. The year in which the "date field" was recorded in computers was assigned only two digits (such as 99) instead of allowing for four digits (such as 1999). Tests show that without costly intervention, once we reach the year 2000 computers will reset to the year 1900.

This could create some real and disturbing problems, since so many industries, such as national defense, air traffic control, and banking rely so heavily on computers. Some believe that such a scenario will create internal conflicts within computer networks, causing them to lock up or even shut down completely. Some conspiracy theorists believe that there will be no better time in America's history for agents of the New World Order to attack. For the millions who dogmatically believe that they are living during the last, or "terminal," generation, these are slippery and precarious times.

The Internet

It would be reactionary and inaccurate to blame the rise in conspiracy theories on the increase in the use of the Internet and the World Wide Web. Blaming new technologies for the ills of a society is a favorite pastime among conspiracy theorists. But the Internet has helped to foster its rise for some obvious reasons.

The information revolution and the availability of home computers have re-created the way people do business—and revolution. Because of this new technology the militia movement is perhaps the first U.S. movement to become equipped and organized through nontraditional media. The militia community has embraced it with open arms: "The Internet is a marvelous tool never before available to the mass of Mankind in our search for Truth."[10]

The Internet's ability to disseminate conspiracy theories into the homes of numerous Americans hit its apex with the deception of seasoned journalist Pierre Salinger. His long career as a trusted ABC newsman will likely be eclipsed by his role as the journalist who, via information gleaned from the Internet, gave credence to the belief that the fatal explosion of TWA flight 800 on July 17, 1996, was the work of the U.S. Navy. The information he claimed to receive from unnamed sources in "French security" was later discovered to be one of a legion of conspiracy theories bouncing throughout cyberspace. More than a year after his report, Salinger still contends that the fatal crash was the result of friendly fire.

Via the Internet radical messages can be disseminated with very little cost and with blinding speed. Newsletters, with their expensive printing and mailing, are giving way to the Internet, which is postage and toll free. The monopoly that major networks held on raw information no longer exists, and the Christian conspiracy community is eager to help its demise, since they believe that the established news media are part of the New World Order conspiracy (see chapter six).

The Internet is quick and inexpensive. It is an ideal venue for spreading the conspiracy theorists' message, since most newspapers or book companies are unlikely to publish their ideas. This quick and easy system is a perfect medium for what one person calls a "leaderless resistance."

Racist and former Ku Klux Klan leader Louis Beam wrote that his fellow brothers in arms should form small groups with no official leader who could be caught and thus pull others down with him: "All individuals and groups operate independently of each other, and never report to a central headquarters or single leader for direction or instruction."[11] He encourages his readers to plot and carry out acts of domestic terrorism. Writes one militia group: "THE FUNDAMENTAL RULE GUIDING THE ORGANIZATION OF THE FREE MILITIA IS GENERALIZED PRINCIPLES AND PLANNING BUT DECENTRALIZED TACTICS AND ACTION."[12]

The Internet is their ideal decentralized but accessible meeting place, a virtual militia bunker. It is a clearinghouse for antigovernment manifestos and e-mail, a clearinghouse of inspiration for Timothy McVeigh and others who believe that the U.S. government is guided by evil intentions. The Internet, though an excellent place to receive data, has often been mistaken as a source of reliable news.

The Internet has also become a militia shopping mall. "They're doing a great job of exploiting the new media opportunities," says Raymond Franklin of the Maryland Police and Correctional Training Commission.[13] Web sites do not have to reveal who the operators are or where they are located, so their 250 Web sites are attractive because they preserve the anonymity of militia members.

Some of the home pages that claim to expose various conspiracies present a detailed Bible study explaining how today's international affairs fulfill Old and New Testament prophecies. These Bible studies are advocated by Christian patriots, the same patriots who warn that warfare with America's evil federal government, the whore of Babylon as described in Revelation, probably cannot be avoided.

Another reason conspiracy theories in general have become so prevalent is that they are a symptom of a greater ill. Blaming entire groups for a nation's political and economic woes is becoming increasingly common in America, and Jews are a common target (see chapter five).

Selling Christian conspiracy theories has become a cottage industry. It is a gold mine for those who believe that conspiracies are being implemented and who know how to market their message to a welcoming crowd. A whole industry of selling gold coins to worried conspiracy disciples has also emerged, since gold is heralded as the answer to a collapsing monetary system.

Being a former program director, I know that selling fear (or what is called in the industry "crisis radio") makes for a fast way to boost a station's male audience. Since Christian radio traditionally draws more women than men, it is smart business to include radio programs such as *Point of View* in a station's daily programming. It attracts a large number of men across various demographics, which looks good to potential advertisers. Programmers know that end-times Christian conspiracy theories grab and hold an audience.

But not all Christian conspiracy theorists write books and promote those books on Christian radio stations in order to get ahead. Many are true believers living deliberate lives. They are painfully serious about living, about rearing responsible children and about improving society for the betterment of all. They love unborn children and their neighbors. But as chapter eight shows, the deeper they delve into end-times conspiracy theories, the more their lives take on characteristics they never would have predicted.

Legitimate Concerns

When discussing Christian conspiracy theories during my talk show, I found myself stumbling over the same truth so often that I eventually had to stop, concede, then proclaim it: *Conspiracies, plans made in secret with harmful intent, do in fact occur.*

The words for *conspiracy/conspire/conspirator* occur in almost thirty biblical passages.[14] Some of the situations described are notable: Absalom conspired against his father, David (2 Samuel 15:12); a conspiracy, revealed through the prophet Jeremiah, included men of Judah and some in Jerusalem (Jeremiah 11:9); a conspiracy among prophets in Israel was described as "a roaring lion tearing the prey" (Ezekiel 22:25 NASB); Jews formed a conspiracy against Paul, saying they would neither eat nor drink until he was killed (Acts 23:12). Though the term is not used to describe the genocidal plot of Haman against the Jews (recorded in the book of Esther), no one would deny that it was a conspiracy.

Yet even in light of such genuine and disturbing conspiracies, the Bible admonishes us not to call a conspiracy what is commonly called a conspiracy. It admonishes us not to fear conspiracies or even rumors of them. Instead, we are to fear God (Isaiah 8:12-13). Even so, from Genesis, with its fundamental account of creation, to Revelation, with its electrifying explanation of events yet to be, the Bible reveals that, like turbulence to an airliner, a war between good and evil affects believers. And this war is intensified and fueled by real and troubling conspiracies.

This book can examine only a portion of the conspiracies recorded in history, as well as their offspring—cover-ups. The U.S. government alone has been involved in enough conspiracies to provide sufficient fuel for some of today's paranoia. According to *U.S. News & World Report,*

The FBI did spy on a host of radical but nonviolent domestic groups like Vietnam Veterans Against the War as part of its Cointelpro effort. The CIA has worked hand in hand with a gallery of liars, thieves, and drug traffickers. The U.S. Public Health Service did allow some 400 African-American men with syphilis to go untreated while it observed them for 40 years in the Tuskegee study—for which the federal government did not apologize [until 1997].[15]

Cover-ups at Waco and Ruby Ridge, where an FBI executive pleaded guilty to obstruction of justice, have also stoked conspiracy thinking. But the Christian conspiracy community is not concerned with just any conspiracy. It is consumed only by those conspiracies they believe fulfill prophecies concerning the end of the world, such as a global government, or what Christian conspiracy theorists call the New World Order (see chapters two and three).

One of the main advocates of the New World Order is Strobe Talbott. This former *Time* editor and deputy secretary of state within the Clinton administration believes that nationalism, with its predisposition toward feuds and world wars, is an antiquated governing structure. What modern people really need, according to Talbott, is a global perspective that will include global laws superseding national laws: "I'll bet that within the next hundred years . . . nationhood as we know it will be obsolete; all states will recognize a single, global authority. A phrase briefly fashionable in the mid-20th century—'citizen of the world'—will have assumed real meaning by the end of the 21st."[16] This is troubling rhetoric, whether or not you belong to a militia.

Talbott believes what the best minds in the world have asked rhetorically: "Is national sovereignty such a great idea after all? It has taken the events in our own wondrous and terrible century to clinch the case for world government."[17] *National Review* writer Martin Sieff compares Talbott to Edward Frederick Lindley Wood, "one of the two prime architects of the catastrophic policy of appeasement toward Adolf Hitler":[18]

Nearly sixty years after a catastrophic series of blunders by clever fools and principled cowards gave us what Churchill called "the unnecessary war" that killed 50 to 80 million people, the same mindset has emerged in control of United States foreign policy.... Halifax was obsessed with coming to an understanding with Hitler's Germany. He thought nothing of serving up entire countries, such as Czechoslovakia, which stood in the way of his grand design.... Talbott has similarly pursued a policy of Russia first, adamantly refusing to "endanger" the relationship by threatening retaliation for Moscow's open military aggression against the new neighboring republics of Moldova, Azerbaijan, and Tajikistan. ... Talbott has systematically opposed any concrete moves to expand NATO into Central Europe.[19]

To Sieff and others who are not members of a militia, Talbott's rhetoric and actions are the latest manifestations of a utopian philosophy that has plagued humankind ever since the Tower of Babel. Conservatives such as Sieff know that such Star Trek notions of human cooperation are utopian pipe dreams that surmise human goodness while neglecting its depravity.

But Christian conspiracy theorists do not believe that such rhetoric fumes from pipe dreams. They believe that Talbott and his colleagues within the United Nations, the World Constitution and Parliament Association, and the Council on Foreign Relations, and others within the Clinton administration, have the power and will to destroy American democracy, setting the stage for the antichrist, just as they believe that the Bible forewarns when it speaks of a seven-year tribulation. As Christian conspiracy theorist Gary Kah contends,

Decent people tend to find it difficult to believe that there could be individuals so evil in nature as to actually try to take control of the world on behalf of Lucifer (Satan). . . . However, as difficult as it may be to believe, this effort to create a Luciferic New World Order, I discovered, was, and is, for real.[20]

Kah and other Christian conspiracy theorists believe that such evil is possible in part because the last days will include global oppression and concentration camps for true Christians, which is one reason militia cells appear to them as paramilitary havens against encroaching and systematic evil. Armageddon will conclude this period of time, giving way to Christ's second coming. But numerous Christians, including many within the militia, believe that they will not be spared this tribulation. They will be forced to endure it. Even worse, they will be hunted down and killed for Christ's sake.

Yet despite its heightened rhetoric, the patriot/conspiracy community harbors legitimate concerns. Montana Senator Max Baucus has understood these concerns and warns that America must listen to the frustrations of ordinary people who find themselves turning to the conspiracy/militia community for help. He quotes Montana rancher Tom Breitbach, who said that when people feel increased economic pressure, they grow desperate and will resort to desperate measures. Baucus claims that "most casual militia members are not Nazis or criminals. But they are angry. Angry about slow income growth, economic pressure on working families, and some of Washington's decisions on bread-and-butter issues."[21]

Christian conspiracy theories born from end-times scenarios do not materialize from thin air. They grow around grains of truth, which on the one hand makes them attractive but on the other makes it difficult to sift the chaff from the wheat. As I investigate the claims of conspiracy theorists in this book, I will be attempting the challenging task of sifting the chaff from the wheat.

Chapters one and two focus on the New World Order conspiracy believed to be alive and well not only in America but on all of planet earth. Chapter four considers the impact of religious ideas and convictions on the patriot movement in America, which is a hotbed for conspiracy theories. Chapters five, six and seven examine the legitimacy of conspiracy theorists' assumptions about who the conspirators really are. In chapter eight I argue that a healthy, balanced view of prophecy does not require the existence of satanic conspiracies, and in chapter nine I discuss why conspiracy theories are so attractive to so many people. The final chapter focuses on what people can do to keep conspiracy theories from getting blown out of proportion.

Finding out the truth about conspiracies, where they come from and what they mean for all of us should concern us greatly, for Oklahoma City showed that bombs made of common fertilizer and racing fuel are equal-opportunity destroyers. They do not discriminate between old and young, government and nongovernment employees, educated and uneducated, religious and nonreligious. A report released several years after the Oklahoma City bombing shows that its victims include not only those who were killed and injured but the rescue workers as well. "Five of the rescue workers have killed themselves since the bombing, the divorce rate among the city's firemen is up nearly 300 percent and there's been an increase in family violence among the city's police force."[22] Clearly, conspiracy theories and a response to them are everyone's business.

2

The *Global* Not-So-New World Order Conspiracy

Belief in a group of global conspirators is hundreds of years old. Yet the groups accused of vying for global control vary from century to century and from decade to decade. This dynamic and ever-changing theory of global control, what Christian conspiracy theorists call a New World Order, stems from the latest twists and turns of international affairs that are believed to be the fulfillment of end-times prophecy.

Those entities accused today of constructing the New World Order, thus carrying out Satan's will, include United Nations global operations, the government of the former Soviet Union and international ecumenical movements.

Difficult to Define

The term *New World Order,* which gained popularity during the late 1980s and early 1990s, carries with it as many different definitions as there are disparate political views. Consequently the New World Order has no singular definition, goal or motive. But since the group that has poured the most passion and certainty into its definition has been the Christian conspiracy community, its members are credited with defining the phrase and keeping it alive years after most world leaders have dropped the term from their speeches.

They define the New World Order as a secret organization of key financial, government, military, academic, religious and media leaders whose ultimate goal is to control the entire social, political and economic structure of the planet. Those who include alien beings in their theories believe that this control extends to our moon and nearby planets as well.

Theories about how these leaders take control vary, though they follow a common scenario. Theorists believe that the conspirators will ruin the nuclear family through the corrupting forces of the media and public education, which are controlled by New Age religious leaders and secular humanists. Then Marxist/Freemasons, who created America's economic structure with inherent and fatal weaknesses, will, at the appointed time, bring the entire house of cards tumbling down. This economic collapse will force America, and indeed the world, into global chaos. Once mired in misery, the world will go crawling to global organizations such as the United Nations to beg for relief.

The New World Order conspirators will then be able to unleash their final plan: complete planetary control. It is commonly believed that this final stage will include foreign troops, since American troops are considered unlikely to slaughter fellow Americans—hence the reports of unmarked black helicopters, Hong Kong police or Gurkhas, U.N. troops and others, such as Japanese pilots, training on American soil. The first to be rounded up and put into regional concentration camps will be born-again, patriotic and armed fundamentalist Christians.

Christian conspiracy theorists believe that this lust for control goes beyond mere human ambition and greed. They maintain that the conspirators are following the will of their master, Satan, thus fulfilling end-times Bible prophecy. The satanic conspirators will force Christians to receive the mark of the beast as described in Revelation, for otherwise Christians would not be able to buy or sell goods and services. Attempts have been made to link this mark to the universal product code and various credit cards.

Other Definitions

But not all who have talked about the New World Order assign to it this evil intent. Former president George Bush argued that the New World Order meant global cooperation for the betterment of humanity without the creation of a draconian global government. In a speech delivered on September 16, 1990, he said that the New World Order would create a place where the "rule of law supplants the rule of the jungle. A world in which the nations recognize and share responsibility for freedom and justice." For him the New World Order was a collection of ideals that could create a kinder, gentler world.

Powerful political animals, such as Strobe Talbott, long for a global government, but Bush is a prime example of a person who can promote a collection of ideals by which nations should govern without advocating an international governing body that supersedes national governments. Bush's new order was seen by some as consistent with the teachings of Christ, who reminds all that they are their brother's keeper. Bush's rhetoric shows that not all who talk about this vague and relativistic phrase favor a global government.

Liberals have hailed the term as part of an increasing global consciousness. This includes ecological stewardship, global relief from famine and major diseases, and global peace-affirming operations, such as U.N. efforts in the former Yugoslavia and other troubled regions.

Conservatives such as former Prime Minister Margaret Thatcher deny that global cooperation can ever exist at a meaningful level. Believing that the human heart cannot be officially mended by utopian political decree, many conservatives believe that the term *New World Order* is the stuff that earns speech writers another week's vacation for a good performance.

Nothing New Under the Sun

The belief that elite, evil forces control the world has a long and varied history, beginning nearly a thousand years ago. In 1186, rumors and prophecies of a New World Order were circulated by astrologers during the Third Crusade in a document called the "Letter to Toledo."[1] After Charles I, king of England, was beheaded in 1649, his countrymen spoke of a "new order" free of his tyrannies.[2] Speeches given by Woodrow Wilson through the League of Nations mirror today's new-order platitudes.[3] Hitler used similar language to describe his party's sinister thousand-year reign,[4] but it lasted only twelve years and four months.

Among the oldest groups believed to be behind the New World Order is the Illuminati Order. *Proofs of a Conspiracy,* a 304-page book published nearly two hundred years ago and used to attack presidential candidate Thomas Jefferson, outlines how this foreign cabal is planning to take over America. It depicts leading political figures as dupes at best and co-conspirators at worst in a devilish scheme devised by godless, liberal intellectuals from overseas. Though published early in the nineteenth century, such rhetoric is reminiscent of today's Christian conspiracy community.

The Illuminati ("Enlightened Ones") Order was founded on May 1, 1776, by Adam Weishaupt (1748-1830), a disgruntled professor of canon law in the conservative state of Bavaria.[5] The late Walter C. Utt, chairman of the department of history at Pacific Union College, maintained that "the Illuminati program . . . [was] long on naive and utopian talk about moral and social regeneration but short on concrete programs. Its most clear-cut concept was a fierce hatred of clericalism as a perversion of the pure principles taught by Christ."[6]

Scot John Robison helped bring the Illuminati conspiracy theory, now with a Freemason twist (odd, since Robison was once a member of a British lodge), to America by means of his 1797 treatise.[7] But "his laborious data scarcely supported his fevered conclusion that the Illuminati made and directed the French Revolution."[8]

Robison's Illuminati conspiracy, however, grabbed the attention of Jedidiah Morse (1761-1826), a Boston preacher and orthodox Calvinist. Morse and other New England preachers devoted numerous sermons to this alleged conspiracy. But, as many do today, he adjusted the conspiracy to fit his circumstances and political allies. "Robison's book stressed the Masonic connection, but Morse prudentially muted the sound of his trumpet on this point, showing he well knew what he was about, for most of the leaders of his own party were Masons—Washington, Hamilton, Jay, Revere, to mention a few."[9]

The Civil War sired similar conspiracy theories, this time centered on Catholics, Irish and Mormons. When Jewish immigration increased after 1870, theories about their conspiratorial control were revived. The Russian Revolution also revived long-standing anti-Semitic conspiracy theories, as did World War I. Throughout the 1930s Jews were connected to the Masonic lodge through various symbols. Some argued that the "Jewish Illuminati" arranged the crucifixion of Christ. Many of today's anti-Semitic conspiracy theorists refer to the New World Order as the "Jew World Order."

In his 1965 book *The Paranoid Style in American Politics* the late historian Richard Hofstadter wrote that America is now full of citizens who view history as "a vast and sinister conspiracy, a gigantic and yet subtle machinery of influence set in motion to undermine and destroy a way of life."[10]

Today the John Birch Society and numerous Christian authors have resurrected concerns about an Illuminati conspiracy. According to Walter Utt, "Catholic, Masonic, and Jewish components have been dropped or muted and the combo of revolutionists and world financiers remains. Today's conspiracy is seen as a survival of the Illuminati and asserts a direct line of descent from Weishaupt through Marxism to the Western financiers, who orchestrate the entire world scene."[11] Part of this control supposedly originates from international organizations.

The United Nations

According to most Christian conspiracy theorists, the group that helps orchestrate this evil control is the United Nations. In a video series titled *America in Peril,* which can be rented from John Birch Society bookstores, Mark Koernke warns that the United Nations has already launched an invasion of the United States.

Koernke claims that U.N. troops are in America, bivouacked in secret military camps. He also maintains that Crips, Bloods and other urban gangs are being "trained, equipped and uniformed" by the federal government. Koernke believes that the United States has been divided into ten regions and that U.N. troops and the Federal Emergency Management

Agency (FEMA) plan to lock up born-again Christians in forty-three regional "detention camps." He says with a dry and sober tone that the processing center for detainees in the western half of the United States is in Oklahoma City.

This video, the first of three that would catapult him to the top of the patriot speaking circles, was made *before* the Oklahoma City bombing. Therefore Koernke gives America reason to worry about another possible strike when he says, "We do not know what the [detainee processing] location is for the eastern seaboard; however, by all indications Fort Drum [New York] will be the control point for [detainees] in the eastern half of the United States." Callers into *The Paul Thomas Show* have recommended Koernke as a reliable source.

A close friend of Koernke confirms that his end-times interpretation fuels his belief that the New World Order is the fulfillment of Bible prophecy. Ramon Martinez, who was Koernke's best man, said that Koernke believes that the book of Revelation showed him that he is living at the threshold of Armageddon.[12]

As is often the case, many conspiracy theories contain some legitimate concern. For instance, Philip Lawler, editor of *Catholic World Report,* an international monthly news magazine, describes the world that some in the U.N. wish to create. In a commentary for the *Wall Street Journal,* which some associate with the New World Order, Lawler recounts how the United Nations World Conference on Women, held in Beijing, China, in 1995, aimed to create an entirely new gender order. "In the 'Draft Program for Action' that formed the basis for the Beijing discussions, the dominant theme [was] not concern for welfare of women, but an amorphous new concept called 'the gender perspective.'"[13] This included at least five distinct possibilities of "heterosexual men, heterosexual women, lesbians, homosexuals and bisexuals."

The term *gender* was never actually defined in the document, and U.N. officials denied that the meeting attempted to redefine the term. They argued that the term meant nothing more than what is has always meant. But during one preparatory meeting, a delegate from Latin America said that the U.N. was attempting to redefine what it meant to be male and female. The delegate submitted that the term *gender* should mean "the existence of women and men as the two sexes of the human being." This definition was rejected.

Though the document was technically a draft, the drafters clearly planned to redefine what it meant to be a man or woman. Rough drafts may not be the final product, but they are a type of road map that points in a general but definite direction. Therefore the drafters of this road map wanted to keep away from the conference those who held to a traditional view of gender. Lawler says, "More than 40 conservative groups—including Concerned Women for America, by far the largest women's membership organization in the U.S.—were initially denied credentials to attend"[14] some of the preparatory meetings.

This U.N. strong-arm tactic was followed by another attempt to move the conference down its new-order path. In August 1995 the U.N. "convened an unprecedented meeting to expunge all proposed amendments from the working draft, thereby producing a clean new document (with the Orwellian title 'non-paper')."[15] This became the main focus of the more popular discussions.

Lawler and others rightly chastise the U.N. conference for its radical goals and strong-arm politics. But unlike the Christian conspiracy community, he did not make of the event more than it was. "Of course the result of the Beijing conference will be just one more U.N. document, with no real enforcement mechanism to support it. But the language of the document cannot be dismissed as irrelevant, because it will become the standard against which foreign aid grants, World Bank loans and IMF programs are judged."[16]

The United Nations became the main enemy of the Christian conspiracy community after the Soviet Union collapsed. With their worldview in trouble, conspiracists moved quickly to find another entity they could weigh down with the responsibility of the New World Order's planetary domination. The United Nations fit the bill. It has been described as all-powerful, having its roots in demonic occultism and religions. Christian conspiracy theorists believe that it is able to carry out what hitherto no other group of conspirators has accomplished. A closer look, however, supports a different view.

With Europe in ruins and Japan facing defeat, diplomats met more than fifty years ago in San Francisco to create the United Nations "to save succeeding generations from the scourge of war." Now 185 nations are members of an organization that has been characterized by corruption, mismanagement and an inability to fulfill its charter mission.

While the United Nations was trying to keep peace in Somalia, $3.9 million vanished from its headquarters in Mogadishu. The cash, lying inside a cabinet with a faulty lock, was stolen in what investigators called an inside job. Administrators of the U.N.'s Children's Fund disclosed that its Kenya operation had lost as much as $10 million to fraud and mismanagement by employees. These incidents reveal some glaring truths about the U.N.'s inability to manage itself. One longtime official described the operation as containing "appalling inefficiencies and back-biting and corruption."[17]

Former U.N. ambassador Madeleine Albright likened the organization to a "business with 185 members of the board; all of them with strong and contradictory opinions, coming from every conceivable culture, speaking every conceivable language—and each with a brother-in-law who is unemployed."[18]

Former U.N. secretary general Boutros Boutros-Ghali admitted that if member countries, especially the United States, do not pay back dues, the world body will be forced to shut down. "There is not enough cash to do what we're being asked to do," he said. Seventy nations are behind in payment, owing a total of $3.25 billion. The U.S. owes $1.4 billion, and some Republicans in Congress advocate that the U.S. should not pay until the U.N. stops sponsoring conferences such as the one in Beijing. Other members of Congress say that they will be willing to pay back dues when the U.N.'s bureaucracy is trimmed to a satisfactory level. Such opposition to U.N. programs contradicts the claim made by Christian conspiracy theorists that the Republican Party is part of the New World Order.

Though globalists are drawn toward groups such as the United Nations, that does not mean the U.N. has the power to implement their plans. It is true that some globalists meet in private, behind closed doors, as at the "Renaissance Weekend." Described as an "informal house party," this secret meeting in January 1993 was a place where a thousand like-minded and powerful people discussed policy and personal issues, says the Associated Press. "Some members of the press [were] invited to the event on the condition that they not breathe a word about what transpires, or else not be invited back."[19] Among the people who attended the event were Strobe Talbott and David Gergen of *U.S. News & World Report*. But groups of like-minded people have always met in secret, including the militia, Christian Coalition and Concerned Women for America. Secrecy is no measure of ability or, for that matter, conspiracy.

In light of the U.N.'s current budget problems and lack of support for some of its programs, the next few years could see the end of the U.N. as we know it, which raises the question: If it has as much power as its critics charge, why is it suffering from the ailments it admits to? Certainly the "evil Western financiers," the same ones who supposedly created the former Soviet Union and both world wars, would have the ability to keep the organization healthy. Also, if the U.N. were so unilateral, why would it allow the United States, Russia, Britain, France and China the power of veto within the Security Council?

But perhaps the greatest contradiction for the Christian conspiracy community about the United Nations is that it chartered the founding of Israel in 1948. Due largely to the writing of Hal Lindsey, the founding of Israel is seen by most Christian conspiracy theorists as the start of the final countdown toward the end of this present world. Most Christian conspiracists believe that the Hebrews are still God's chosen people. If so, why would the forces of Satan, which allegedly work through the United Nations, give God's chosen a homeland once again?

Soviet Union

Before the fall of the former Soviet Union, Christian conspiracy theorists argued that the world's most powerful communist country was the mastermind behind the New World Order, so upon the Soviet rock they built their theories. There was no questioning such belief, for most pop Bible prophecy writers believed, and still do, that the U.S.S.R. was

Gog and Magog, Israel's enemy from the north as described in Ezekiel 39. So confident was this belief that leading Christian conspiracy theorist Don McAlvany wrote that the Soviet Union could never fall:

> The communist nations will not fail economically, because (as Lenin recognized) greedy, shortsighted Western business and financial interests will not let them fail—they will finance and prop them up just as they did Nazi Germany in its rise to power in the 1930s. . . . Gorbachev has found a way to save Russia economically (at Western expense) . . . and set the stage for world domination in the mid to late 1990s.[20]

Not only have McAlvany's predictions fallen under the weight of their own extremes, he also contradicts his own statements about having access to secret and exclusive information. One of the many promotional flyers in his monthly newsletter explains: "Why Over 6 Million Concerned Americans Took Heed to What Don McAlvany Said Last Year Alone. . . . With a background in undercover intelligence, he remains closely connected with the international intelligence community, as well as with an exclusive network of highly-placed officials in financial political circles." To be sure, McAlvany is not the only conspiracy theorist to make such large statements. But given all his "exclusive information" and ties to the "intelligence community," especially regarding the former Soviet Union, his being in the dark about the imminent Soviet collapse is baffling.

McAlvany, like many conspiracists since the fall of the Soviet Union, was forced to a play his most extreme hand ever: he denied that the fall ever happened. In the September/October 1991 edition of the *McAlvany Intelligence Advisor* (MIA) the headline reads, "The Rebirth of an Empire: What Is Really Happening in the Soviet Union." McAlvany asserts that the Soviet "scriptwriters" fooled the entire world into thinking that the country collapsed. The twenty-four-page newsletter, the longest in MIA history, is the writing of a man covering his tracks and shoring up a house of political and theological cards. When the Berlin Wall began crumbling, so did McAlvany's reputation. Like liberal revisionists, McAlvany and other Christian conspiracists were left with no alternative but to rewrite history to their liking.

McAlvany's influence on many within the Christian community is impressive. They devour his newsletters, highlighting entire pages, circling key paragraphs again and again. They are a loyal and captive audience who, if told often enough, will believe that the former Soviet Union never fell and that false information to the contrary is the work of the "evil secular press," hit men of the New World Order (see chapter six).

The New World Order's Cross-Denominational Conspiracy

International ecumenical movements are viewed as part of New Age religion's ability to pervert the church. They prove that the church is increasingly apostate, thus fulfilling end-times prophecy.

For example, when Chuck Colson accepted the Templeton Prize at the ecumenical Parliament of World Religions in 1993, he used the opportunity to preach a pure and simple Christian message, including how salvation comes through no one else but Christ. Colson's acceptance speech was one of the most insightful, faith-inspiring and at times haunting speeches given in the 1990s. Consequently it has been one of the most requested shows for *The Paul Thomas Show* and has been aired numerous times. Nowhere was there a hint of New Age compromise. But Texe Marrs, creator of *Flashpoint* newsletter, suggested that Colson was a wolf in sheep's clothing, a "born again New Ager disguised as an evangelical Christian."[21]

The parliament was supposed to have launched a New Age conspiracy at this 1993 event, which was to culminate in the year 2000 by bringing all religions together. Such a conspiracy is unlikely in the extreme, for even while the parliament was meeting, a Hindu group heckled a couple of speakers, Greek Orthodox members pulled out, and four Jewish groups walked out because racist Louis Farrakhan of the Nation of Islam was one of the speakers.[22] Furthermore, how is the World Council of Churches going to unify all religions when it still does not admit Jehovah's Witnesses and Mormons?

Conclusion

The New World Order is a pliable and malleable piece of political and theological work. It must be so in order to accommodate the changing face of those accused of carrying out Satan's will. Today the primary international enemy of the Christian conspiracy community is the New World Order agenda of the United Nations. But if the U.N. falters or collapses, don't expect the Christian conspiracy community to break camp.

Before the United Nations the great enemy was the Soviet Union, whose collapse oddly fueled the Christian conspiracy community's resolve. Though these theories are specific, they are just vague enough to reappear with a new twist on an age-old theme just when it seems they are down for the count. Like evolutionists in search of Lucy, conspiracists sift and brush through current events. But they piece together only the stories that support their treasured conspiracy theories.

3

The *American* Not-So-New World Order Conspiracy

We are viewed by the government as . . . enemies.
They already know all they need to know about you.
You are the enemies of [America].
Do my words shock or alarm you? They shouldn't.
Those in government who have labored over the years to build the road
that leads to the New World Order at this time are beside themselves with joy.
We pledge that those last few miles will be paved,
not just with the bloods and bones and hearts of the patriots,
but they will be paved,
that road will be paved with tyrants' bloods and tyrants' bones.
Conspiracy theorist Louis Beam

International conspiracy theories, ranging from crude to sophisticated, have circled the globe for hundreds of years in an age-old attempt to blame specific groups for the world's problems. American conspiracy theorists have taken these theories and cross-pollinated them with events and organizations that are uniquely American. The result is a crop of hybrid theories that have motivated domestic terrorists such as Timothy McVeigh. The organizations and events that domestic conspiracy theorists say are running America's role in the New World Order include the economic policies prescribed by the Federal Reserve, the educational decisions handed down by a nefarious and anti-Christian public school system, and an unholy trinity of conspiracies at Waco, Ruby Ridge and

Oklahoma City—events so notorious they have come to be known simply by their bloodied soil.

The Federal Reserve

Christian conspiracy theorist James Wardner sums up the domestic fears of many of his colleagues:

> I am here to tell you that the declining American standard of living has been PLANNED from the beginning . . . at the highest levels of American government—a plan to fail, a plan to create insecurity and uncertainty, a plan to make the American people serfs in the New World Order.[1]

John McManus of the John Birch Society believes that the national debt has been deliberately increased in order to ruin America, making Americans serfs to international bankers. These conspirators include the Federal Reserve under the leadership of Alan Greenspan, who was a protégé of the late Ayn Rand and accepts libertarian economic theory— neither of which fits into a New World Order globalist philosophy.

Of all the entities accused of promoting the New World Order, however, the Federal Reserve (the Fed) has some sticking power—if only on the surface. Congress created it in 1913 in an attempt to stabilize the economy, and it does possess commanding control over our banking system and our money supply. At the top of the Federal Reserve System is the Board of Governors, all of whose members are appointed to fourteen-year terms by the president with the advice and consent of the Senate. The president also appoints a governor to serve as the Federal Reserve chairman for a four-year term.

The mission of the Federal Reserve is to promote a healthy economy, which is innately controversial given the multitude of economic theories. It regulates the rate of interest that commercial banks pay when they borrow money from it, it buys and sells government bonds, and it tells commercial banks how much of their assets can be held in the Federal Reserve. The Fed tries to balance two economic indicators—inflation and interest rates. It has the power to raise or lower either one, which is bound to hurt one industry or another, creating natural fuel for various conspiracy theories.

The Fed is sometimes considered a fourth branch of government because it is composed of a powerful group of national policymakers freed from the usual restrictions of governmental checks and balances. Since it is self-financing, Congress has little if any influence over its budget, making the Fed relatively free from partisan political pressure.

One Christian conspiracy theorist told me that prior to the Gulf War the Federal Reserve was planning to increase the prime interest rate so much that few would be able to afford to buy a home. This, he said, was an attempt to restrict private ownership of land so that people would be more accustomed to New World Order socialism. But what really happened? Interest rates soon hit their lowest point in twenty-five years, allowing many across the country to purchase even more private property.

The belief that America's monetary system is rigged dates back to well before the founding of the Federal Reserve. Many conspiracy theorists argue that the common dollar bill is exhibit A that our government has been part of an evil New World Order conspiracy since its founding. They point to the symbol with the pyramid and eye called the Great Seal. The seal is mainly for diplomatic purposes. It is affixed to treaties, commissions and letters from the president to foreign leaders. The Continental Congress adopted the design on June 20, 1782, and the U.S. Congress did so on September 15, 1789.

The side of the seal in question is the thirteen-step pyramid, topped with an eye—supposedly the eye of God—within a triangle. Over the triangle are the words *Annuit Coeptis,* "He has favored our undertakings." On the base of the pyramid are the Roman numerals MDCCLXXVI, or "1776." The Latin words *Novus Ordo Seclorum,* "New Order of the Ages," also appear. This translation, however, does not satisfy Christian conspiracy theorist Dwight Kinman. In the front of his book *The World's Last Dictator* he states that it really means "The New World Without God Order."

The seal incorporates Masonic symbolism, though many Christian conspiracy theorists believe that they are actually satanic symbols, which reveal Satan's control over America's monetary system. But the founding fathers, many of whom were apparently Christians and Freemasons both, were influenced by Masonic imagery. It is only logical that from this imagery they would design a seal to symbolize a new nation with new dreams and a "new order." The founding fathers produced a system of such supreme checks and balances that it arguably merited such prophetic language. But as is often the case within the Christian conspiracy community, symbols are interpreted through an antihistorical framework to fit a particular end-times theology.

Masonic symbols only *represent* reality—they are not reality itself. Their meaning, like words, changes with time. Contemporary culture's use of the cross is a good example. The understanding of the cross has changed to fit certain lifestyles and perceptions; it is no longer used exclusively to symbolize Christ's redemptive work through his death and resurrection. (Pop star Madonna managed to use the sacred symbol as a sexual ornament by draping it across her bare stomach and navel.)

The Public School System

The New World Order is credited with controlling America by way of the Constitution, which some Christian conspiracy theorists believe was written by devil-worshiping, humanist Freemasons. They believe that Freemasons are connected to pagan New Age religion through various associations, mostly through its secretive fraternal ceremonies and oaths, which carry heavy religious meaning. Freemasons are allegedly connected to the Illuminati Order, which is believed to be a resurrected pagan humanist order dating back to the days of ancient Rome. What is odd about this pairing of pagan New Age religious leaders and secular humanists is that many secular humanists regard New Age religion as foolish and their leaders as charlatans.

According to many callers to *The Paul Thomas Show,* this New Age/humanist connection is found in the public school system, which is conspiring to dumb down America's children in order to make them docile, compliant workers of the New World Order. They believe that this is being accomplished through programs such as "outcome based education." Also called OBE or Goals 2000, its proponents say that it is designed to give schoolchildren marketable skills in an increasingly complex job market, especially those students who do not go on to complete college. Critics of the plan believe that it is yet another step toward globalism.

There is good reason to cross swords with public education and the Education Department. Critics such as former secretary of education William Bennett have presented a compelling argument that public education in America needs to be reformed. In addition, it is quite possible that the Education Department has engaged in a conspiracy by holding illegal meetings. The department may have violated federal law by holding such meetings in an attempt to thwart innovative changes within public education that many Americans support, such as a voucher system, or what has been called school choice.

Writing in *The Christian Science Monitor,* former presidential candidate Lamar Alexander accused the Education Department of holding secret sessions that violated the Federal Advisory Committee Act, which governs how a federal department can conduct meetings with outside parties. By law these meetings must be announced in the Federal Register. "That hasn't occurred for these sessions," he said.[2] This is the same statute under which the secret meetings of President Clinton's health-care task force were successfully challenged.

But what the Christian conspiracy community fails to consider is the influence of societal factors that have led to the decline of test scores. They do not concede other contributing factors, such as divorce and the breakdown of the nuclear family, cramped and oversized classes, unstable revenue sources, the burden of increasing social agendas, the numbing increase in television and computer-game consumption. It has been my observation that children who do not like to read and who find education "boring" have parents who rarely read more than *TV Guide* and who are also not interested in learning. Are these parents willing partakers in the New World Order as well?

Christian conspiracy theorists argue that the New Age is monolithic, wielding power in every major political and cultural institution. Again, there is some truth to this assessment. Writes Christian author and political aide Bruce Barron, "New Age devotees are often among the most avid supporters of the goal of one-world government."[3] Yet as Barron warns, Christian conspiracy disciples employ "innuendo, false logic and speculation to create a sensationalistic thesis that liberal policy makers, [and] New Agers . . . are working together to establish a new world order."[4]

Unholy Trinity: Ruby Ridge, Waco and the Oklahoma City Bombing

Conspiracists contend that U.S. federal enforcement agencies, such as the Federal Bureau of Investigation (FBI), the Central Intelligence Agency (CIA) and the Bureau of Alcohol, Tobacco and Firearms (ATF), have been subverted by agents of the New World Order. Among their prime objectives is the restriction and eventual repealing of the constitutional right to bear arms. Once Americans are disarmed, New World Order troops will be able to make quick work of America, the last enclave of individual freedom and liberty.

Christian conspiracy theorists believe that the federal government has deliberately murdered fellow Americans during violent standoffs in order to sway public opinion against gun ownership. That is what they believe happened at Waco, Texas (with the Branch Davidians), and at Ruby Ridge, Idaho (with the Weaver family). Both the Davidians and the Weavers adhered to apocalyptic, antigovernment conspiracy theories, which explains in part the Christian conspiracy community's instinctive rush to their defense.

They believe that the bombing in Oklahoma City took this scheme even further. With antimilitia sentiment steadily rising in America, conspiracy theorists believe that the federal government, not Timothy McVeigh and Terry Nichols, blew up the Alfred P. Murrah Building in Oklahoma City on the second anniversary of the tragic Waco disaster. They believe that the bombing was designed to turn public opinion into a deathblow against the militia, which is all that stands between America and New World Order concentration camps.

Ruby Ridge. Whenever truth is shrouded by cover-ups, such as at Ruby Ridge, conspiracy theories rush in to enlighten the public. Cover-ups at Ruby Ridge delayed justice, and when justice is delayed, it is often denied.

When justice is slow, it allows conspiracy theories to breed and multiply. That is what happened as a result of Ruby Ridge. Those who believed that Ruby Ridge was a kind of New World Order weather balloon argued that it was designed to determine if patriotic Americans had the will to resist overt government tyranny.

Much like Waco, Ruby Ridge convinced many Christian patriots that the American government had declared war on gun-owning religious Americans. Timothy McVeigh visited Ruby Ridge to conduct his own investigation. McVeigh concluded that the government intentionally killed two of the Weavers. Even years after the tragedy KDOV radio received passionate phone calls insisting that Congress investigate the abuses and conspiracy behind Ruby Ridge.

While the rest of the nation was talking about Whitewater, Bosnia and who would run for president in 1996, conspiracists kept their focus on an event that had passed from interest. On the surface, it seemed to involve only a few people who seemed to be in the wrong place at the wrong time. But Christian conspiracy theorists stuck to their guns and would not let the event and its cover-ups get swept under the rug. They could not forget what happened on a remote ridge in northern Idaho.

In the August heat of 1992, in the northern arm of Idaho, conspiracy theorist, survivalist and white supremacist Randy Weaver knew that something was clearly wrong with his mountaintop world. The confrontation began when federal agents staked themselves out below the cabin on August 21 because Randy Weaver had failed to appear in court on illegal gun sale charges. (A jury would later find him innocent on the basis of entrapment.)

For eighteen months, knowing that the government was out to arrest him, Weaver rarely left his hilltop cabin. One reason the standoff lasted as long as it did was that the Weavers believed that if they surrendered they would be put in AIDS-infested institutions and other horror camps of the New World Order. August 21 would have been like all the other days that authorities hid in the woods to collect information if it hadn't been for the family dog, Striker. The yellow lab presumably picked up the scent of the agents and barked continually, increasing the concern of

Randy, his son Sammy and family friend Kevin Harris.

All were armed when they investigated down the hill. Randy Weaver encountered a federal agent and was ordered to freeze. Instead, he ran back to the cabin and yelled for his son and family friend to do the same. A shoot-out followed, leaving fourteen-year-old Sammy dead with a bullet in the back. U.S. marshal William Degan of Boston lay dead as well, shot in the chest. In a later incident Vicki Weaver would be killed by a government sniper, who said he never saw her but was instead shooting at Kevin Harris.

Initially, when the Treasury Department released its report regarding the ATF's role in the Weaver tragedy, it found no wrongdoing. Reports like this and the ones to follow led conspiracy theorists, many within the militia, to beat plowshares into swords. The infamous standoff with federal agents even became a made-for-television movie.

That federal agencies moved with such crushing power against a handful of religious extremists troubled many Americans. The killing of Vicki Weaver haunted men such as John Trochmann, one of the founders of the Militia of Montana. He stood at the foot of Ruby Ridge protesting the attack. "We witnessed the tyranny of government. It was a devastating event for me."[5] Though he has believed in conspiracies since he was nine years old, Ruby Ridge redefined his life, fueling his opposition to the "shadow government" he has sworn to fight.

Attorney General Janet Reno established a Justice Department task force to investigate the events. It concluded in a 1994 report that the FBI's hostage rescue team overreacted to the threat of violence. The report also stated that the agency's shoot-on-sight policy violated the bureau's guidelines and Fourth Amendment restrictions on police power, a point conspiracy theorists had pounded home ever since the standoff ended. In addition, FBI director Louis J. Freeh said that the rules of engagement "were poorly drafted, confusing, and can be read to direct agents to act contrary to law and FBI policy."[6]

In his opening statement before the Senate Subcommittee on Terrorism, Technology and Government Information, Freeh spoke with refreshing candor: "Indeed, for the FBI, Ruby Ridge was a series of terribly flawed law enforcement operations with tragic consequences. We know today that law enforcement overreacted at Ruby Ridge." In his nine-page opening statement Freeh said that although he was not the acting director of the FBI during the standoff, he was "sincerely disappointed with the FBI's performance during the crisis and especially in its aftermath." As a result Freeh said that he has "changed almost every aspect of the FBI's crisis response structure and modified or promulgated new policies and procedures to address the flaws and shortcomings apparent from the FBI's response. I am committed to ensuring that the tragedies of Ruby Ridge never happen again."

Though he readily admitted the mistakes of his agency, Freeh also made a compelling argument on behalf of law enforcement, which stands as an antidote to the forces of conspiracy thinking, especially when it is fortified by end-times speculation:

> We rely upon the men and women of law enforcement to do their best job under very difficult circumstances. In return for protecting us, we vest them with a measure of discretion and ask them to use the best judgment. Sometimes, as human nature tells us, that judgment may be imperfect and mistakes will happen. As long as we ask them to be in the arena, to be ready in the middle of the night to take cover behind a tree or a mailbox, to put their lives and the well-being of their families in the line of fire, we must show some empathy and compassion for their human fallibility. This is particularly true as we judge with the calm, well-lighted knowledge of hindsight, far from what the Supreme Court calls "split-second judgments" in circumstances that are tense, uncertain and rapidly evolving.

A government task force's 543-page report about Ruby Ridge offers a thorough review of the events and includes specific recommendations for avoiding future Ruby Ridges. Keep in mind that Christian conspiracy theorists claim that all major political parties and arms, including the judicial, legislative and executive branches, are part of the conspiracy. But if so, why would a Senate subcommittee lead such a damaging review of another government agency that is supposed to be part of the same conspiracy? Also, if the press were part of the same conspiracy, why would it release damaging information that has increased suspicions about the government's activities and power?

Contrary to claims by the Christian conspiracy community, the government has admitted wrongdoing at Ruby Ridge. In October 1996, FBI executive E. Michael Kahoe admitted in federal court that he had destroyed an internal FBI report criticizing the bureau's handling of the affair. He agreed to help prosecutors discover whether other FBI officials were involved in the cover-up. Kahoe could receive a sentence of up to ten years in prison and a $250,000 fine. But his conviction came four long years after the fatal standoff, allowing antigovernment conspiracy theories to flourish.

The U.S. Justice Department decided in 1994 against prosecuting Lon Horiuchi, the FBI sharpshooter who killed Vicki Weaver. But in August 1997, Boundary County prosecutor Denise Woodbury filed a charge of involuntary manslaughter. If convicted, Horiuchi could face ten years in prison.

In light of these admissions and developments, it is difficult to understand how Ruby Ridge was part of the New World Order conspiracy. Is embarrassing the Justice Department, the FBI and other federal agencies part of advancing their global agenda? The federal government gave the Weaver family $3.1 million, which, short of a formal admission, implied wrongdoing. Is it a goal of the New World Order to make millionaires out of hitherto unknown citizens? If Randy Weaver was just a God-fearing American who became a victim of an unprovoked attack by agents of the New World Order, why did he admit in court that he was not without blame in the tragic affair? To date, there has been plenty of evidence that mistakes and cover-ups were committed on Ruby Ridge. But there has been no evidence that the government, as part of a New World Order, intentionally tried to kill the Weavers.

Waco. On February 28, 1993, before the final and fatal raid on April 19, which was shown live on CNN as more than eighty followers of cult leader David Koresh perished, another attempt to serve David

Koresh a search warrant failed. The attempt to serve a warrant for illegal weapons possession turned into an hour-and-a-half gun battle, leaving four federal agents dead, twenty people injured, and six Davidians dead. That set the stage for a fifty-one-day standoff that would later lead to a campaign for better rules of engagement between federal agencies and extremist organizations. To this day, Davidians such as Amo Bishop Roden refer to the Davidian way of religion as the true "End-Time church."

America's worst homegrown terrorist, Timothy McVeigh, whose face resurfaces throughout the world of far-right conspiracy theories that are propagated within the church, made a pilgrimage to Waco, an event that fed his rage against the federal government, for he also believed that the government intentionally killed the Davidians. This fact surfaced during an interview he gave while in Waco as well as when FBI agents seized photos that McVeigh had taken at the burned-out complex.

Democrats, who then controlled Congress, were not eager to launch a probe that might embarrass an already troubled administration. There was not a huge clamoring from Republicans either. Both parties fell down on the job, feeding the conspiracy community's belief that both were part of the conspiracy. Later, some lawmakers, including Senator John McCain, Representative Bill McCollum and Majority Leader Bob Dole, would call for public hearings.

Waco led many to question the government's competency when dealing with religious extremists. Alan A. Stone, professor of psychiatry and law at Harvard University, said, "The further I get away from Waco, the more I feel that the government stonewalled. . . . It would be better if the government would just say, 'Yes, we made mistakes, and we've done this, this and that, so it won't happen again.' And to my knowledge, they've never done it."[7]

But to the Christian conspiracy community, Waco was no mistake. Don McAlvany spoke for many when he wrote that Waco, like Ruby Ridge, was more than an operation gone horribly bad: "Operation Waco was the beginning of religious persecution of unpopular, non-mainstream religious groups. . . . Since the American people (including Christians) did not protest one peep over the destruction of the Branch Davidian sect, the attacks will now begin to accelerate."[8]

Timothy McVeigh agreed with McAlvany. While on his antigovernment pilgrimage to Waco, McVeigh told then journalism student Michelle Rauch of Southern Methodist University that the "government is afraid of the guns people have because they have to have control of the people at all times. Once you take away the guns, you can do anything to the people."[9] McVeigh also said that the disaster at Waco was "just the beginning" and that people should expect more such attacks.

Texas Representative Steve Stockman presented the conspiracy theory that the Clinton administration raided Waco on April 19 in an attempt to win support for stronger gun control.[10] Numerous callers echoed this theory and also quoted one of the militia's leading female figures. Linda Thompson argued in her video *Waco, the Big Lie* that the government deliberately set the compound on fire that fateful day, knowing that they would be killing the followers of Koresh and their innocent children in a raging inferno.

Thompson's video, which has been recommended by Christian conspiracy theorists such as Chuck Missler, does make a graphically deceptive case if taken at face value. The videotape, taken from actual footage that made its way onto *Nightline*, appears to show a tank setting the building on fire. But none of the nine Bradley Fighting Vehicles, two Abrams tanks or five M728 combat engineering vehicles (modified M60 tanks) were equipped with the ability to throw flames. What was seen in the video was light bouncing off the tank's barrel.

Thompson, who believes that she and her family have been regularly followed by black helicopters, wrote this in a letter posted on the Internet: "The holes were bashed in the sides of the building, not to introduce CS gas, so much as to make sure the house was well ventilated, so that the fire would spread rapidly. I have received reports from no less than 15 people across the country who saw on the TV footage, two men in black uniforms, wearing gas masks, set the fire."[11] Yet photos that detect heat show that the fire began inside, set by Davidians.

Other theories about the failed raid contend that the tanks knocked over

fuel cans, sparking the flames. But a team of independent arson investi-
gators from fire departments in Houston, Los Angeles, San Francisco and
Pittsburgh concluded that the Davidians started the fire by using flamma-
ble fuels in three separate locations. However, the book *Out of the Ashes:
Making Sense in Waco,* a collection of essays, articles, editorials and
letters that contain troubling accounts of the raid, maintains that the
"independent" arson team was far from independent. It argues that the
head of the arson team spent eight years on a joint task force with the
ATF's Houston office.

But this criticism is not corroborated by another independent study by
two experts from the University of Maryland. They came to the same
conclusion as the first group of experts. In addition, three surviving
Davidians reported hearing shouts from their colleagues to "start the fire."
FBI listening devices, some of which had been inserted into the skin of
milk cartons, overheard Davidians making statements such as "Spread
the fuel."[12] Videotapes of the blaze also show that the first fire broke out
on the second floor, which tanks did not penetrate. According to autopsy
reports, some of the Davidians' clothing contained lighter fluid and other
fire-causing agents.

Conspiracy theorists are undaunted by these facts and continue to insist
that the Davidians were deliberately murdered, in part by the government's use of tear gas, or more specifically, CS gas. They argue that the
chemical was used for two possible reasons: to asphyxiate the Davidians
and to help set the structure ablaze. But according to Nizam Peerwani,
chief medical examiner for the Tarrant County Medical Examiner's
District in North-central Texas, the cause of death among the ashes at
Waco was not so simple.

Of the thirty-three bodies found within the compound's bunker,
twenty-five were children. "Most of them had died as a result of smoke
inhalation or suffocation. And a couple of them had died as a result of
blunt trauma due to collapsing debris."[13] At least three kids had been shot
to death, and one was stabbed to death. But most were found next to their
mothers, curled under what were once wet blankets. Further, Peerwani
says that there was no gas residue on the bodies:

We looked for the gas there. . . . We looked for the parent compound
in all the victims that we had tissues and blood to examine. We also
looked for the metabolite of the drug. Specifically, the o-chloroben-
zaldehyde and malononitrile, which had two byproducts of the CS
gas. And we didn't detect any in any of the cases.[14]

The chief examiner professes no doubt that there was exposure to the gas,
but not the type needed to kill. "CS gas has an extremely short confine,
five to 10 minutes. It is rapidly eliminated from the body."[15]

Conspiracy theorists argue that the use of CS gas is illegal and has been
banned, though they conveniently do not say by whom. At the time of
Attorney General Janet Reno's testimony before the Senate, the Chemical
Weapons Convention, signed in January 1993 by 159 nations, including
the United States, prohibited the development, production, stockpiling or
use of chemical weapons. But, as Reno testified, though the treaty had
been ratified by twenty-nine nations, it needed to be ratified by sixty-five
to become law. Therefore the use of the gas did not violate international
law. As is often the case, when international accords can be used to support
their theories, conspiracy disciples employ them without noticing how it
contradicts their belief that international agreements are part of the New
World Order conspiracy.

The decision to use CS gas became one of the most hotly debated points
of the entire investigation. It persists today in the conspiracy community
as proof that Janet Reno, with her pro-gun-control position, is an agent
of the New World Order.

The Christian conspiracy community reacted so forcefully to the failed
raid in part because the Davidians had stockpiled weapons, including
illegal automatic machine guns and hand grenades. Some Christian
conspiracy theorists are also well armed, and they feared they could be
next. Combine this fear with Attorney General Reno's pro-gun-control
rhetoric, and Reno slips effortlessly into the end-times, New World Order
timetable.

Those close to Reno emphasize that to understand why the government finally raided the Davidian compound, it is important to understand

the events that made her an advocate of children. Reno's childhood was marked by embarrassing events surrounding her parents' alcohol abuse, by her father's quick and unexplained exit from the family and by an eccentric mother who once needed to be picked up because she passed out drunk on the sidewalk. "My mother was not 'somewhat difficult.' My mother could be extremely difficult," says Janet's sister Maggy. Janet has often said, "Mother loved us hard and spanked us hard."[16]

Her rough childhood and meager beginnings bred in Reno a rescuer's mentality. She earned a staunch reputation for protecting children as the state attorney in Florida's Dade County. It was the desire to rescue children, some say, that prompted Reno to finally give into FBI demands to raid the compound the second time.

According to a Justice Department report, Reno's decision to approve the tear-gas attack upon the Davidians after denying the request to do so numerous times was partly influenced by the belief that children were being abused inside the compound. During one meeting, someone alleged that Koresh was beating babies. Reno and others would later say they remember the comment but couldn't recall with certainty who said it.

Koresh's abuse of children was well known. He was a polygamist who believed that girls in their young teens were potential wives, and once a girl was of the proper age to become his wife she received a plastic Star of David. Koresh also advocated spanking children until their buttocks bled. "[The child's] bottom was hit so much that the skin was raw. It's not like a scrape. It's just where the skin is hit so much that it bruises and can't take anymore and bleeds," said follower Robyn Bunds. Another follower confessed, "Yeah, I spanked [my child]. I'm not proud of it. . . . I'm sorry I did that. There's no way to take it back. But I was told to. . . . Vernon [Koresh's real first name] said that even if a child died from a spanking they would go to heaven."[17] Another Davidian said that she watched Koresh beat her eight-month-old girl for forty minutes because she did not sit on his lap. He kept beating the child because she wouldn't stop crying.[18]

However, Christian "patriots" claim that other Justice Department reports state that since Koresh was wounded in the February 28 shootout, he was unable to abuse children. Bruce Perry, chief of psychiatry at Texas Children's Hospital, evaluated the twenty-one children released from the compound. He concluded in his report that the children had not been sexually abused. But as the spanking examples reveal, abuse can be more than sexual. Still, says one observer, "the FBI maximized things [such as accusations of child abuse] they knew would ring a bell with [Reno]."[19]

Federal agencies have been properly criticized for the failed raid. ATF director Stephen Higgins was forced into early retirement, and five other ATF supervisors were fired as well. Clint Van Zandt, one of the chief negotiators in the failed raid, was among the first to criticize the way the FBI handled the affair. He told me that the tension between negotiators and FBI tacticians who surrounded the building made it impossible to establish a proper degree of trust with Koresh and his right-hand man, Steve Schneider. Van Zandt, along with FBI director Louis Freeh, who acknowledged that procedures at Waco were "inadequate," would later help draw up new rules of engagement against religious extremists. These new rules helped to bring about a peaceful resolution in the case of the Freemen of Jordan, Montana.

Americans may never know for sure the exact events surrounding the Waco massacre. The real world is a complex place full of complicated decisions. Reports clearly show, however, that Reno, who was not eager to attack the Davidians, may have received selective reports from the FBI designed to secure her approval. There were also cover-ups, but not the kind led by a soulless, high-ranking U.S. attorney general in cahoots with the devil to remove guns from every American's home so that United Nations storm troopers, the National Guard and gang members could more easily launch the New World Order.

The Oklahoma City bombing. Soon after the Oklahoma City bombing on April 19, 1995, the worst terrorist attack on U.S. soil, which killed 168 people, including nineteen children, and injured hundreds, the conspiracy community said it knew who was *really* responsible. Some theorists, such as James Bo Gritz, argued that Timothy McVeigh and Terry Nichols were fall men set up by the federal government to take the blame for the bombing of the Alfred P. Murrah Federal Building.[20]

Christian conspiracy disciples called in to *The Paul Thomas Show* saying that President Clinton arranged the bombing in order to encourage passage of strict gun-control laws cloaked as antiterrorism legislation. They said he used the event to divert attention from Whitewater investigations and to boost his ratings by showing that he too can be tough on crime. People who held to this position quoted polling data as proof, which is remarkable since they believe that the press and its polls are part of the New World Order conspiracy. Belying the Christian community's claim that the government is the real culprit behind the bombing is that even some within the antigovernment press conceded that the government's case against McVeigh and Nichols was solid.

Why bombers bomb is a puzzle Lawrence W. Myers plans to solve. It's the subject of a book he's been shaping for a number of years. Every bomber, including McVeigh, he says, has had a conspiracy theory pushing him along the path to retaliation. When Myers talks about these complex theories, he rattles off facts, statistics and observations about the bombing as if he were an official hotline into the mind of those who did it. Though he is the chief investigative reporter for *Media ByPass* magazine, an impartial reader might wonder how he ever got the job.

Myers, in a cover story titled "A Closer Look" (at the Oklahoma City bombing), refers to the slew of conspiracy books, tapes and special reports as a "cottage industry." He believes that the bulk of conspiracy material is produced to make money.[21] Yet each issue of *Media ByPass* carries ad after ad that supposedly reveals numerous conspiracies and how a certain tape, video or book proves it. "Conspiracy lovers, our catalog's for you," says one ad.

Media ByPass is so sympathetic to beliefs about a New World Order conspiracy that Timothy McVeigh in June 1998 sent the publication an essay that seemed to offer justification for the Oklahoma City bombing. Writes McVeigh: "I have chosen Media Bypass as a possible forum for this piece because, frankly, I realize that it is quite provocative . . . and . . . doubt that any mainstream media would touch it."

Myers also believes the government's claim that McVeigh's single fertilizer bomb was powerful enough to destroy the Murrah building.

During one talk show, Myers refuted the belief common among conspiracy disciples that such destruction required two bombs. This argument assumes that one bomb made from ordinary fertilizer could not possibly have created so much damage. Christian conspiracy theorists, such as Don McAlvany, claim that seismographic readings show two distinct bombs, more proof that the government is guilty of a cover-up and is possibly the real culprit.

But even Stephen Jones, McVeigh's court-appointed attorney, who has received more than twenty-one thousand witness statements, more than four hundred hours of videotapes, and photographs from more than twenty different sites in Oklahoma and Kansas that were taken by intelligence agencies, did not include in his multiheaded conspiracy theory the belief that two bombs exploded in Oklahoma City that fateful day.

This wasn't Myers's first attack on the belief that the federal government bombed its own building. In the November 1995 issue of *Media ByPass* Myers wrote that the government's case against the two suspects was solid, which was why the jury moved to indict them. It included three key pieces of evidence: phone records, explosives and fingerprints. He also points out that McVeigh sold *The Turner Diaries,* a racist diatribe, during tours of midwestern gun shows.[22] The similarities between the *Diaries* and the Oklahoma City bombing are remarkable, including some components used to create the bomb, the time of day and the bombing of a fictional federal building similar to the Oklahoma blast. A photocopied passage from the novel was found glued to an envelope in the getaway car used by McVeigh, which was pulled over soon after the bombing during a routine traffic stop.

Overall, Myers's article refutes many claims made by the conspiracy community, which is remarkable given how his publication is prone to conspiracy thinking. So it's no wonder that a reader from Winnipeg, Manitoba, chose not to renew his subscription. "I am very disappointed with your coverage of several important news stories, especially the OKC bombing." The Canadian conspiracy theorist instead recommended Christian conspiracy theorist Texe Marrs's "excellent" article in the July issue of *Flashpoint.* "Your magazine *[Media*

ByPass] has ignored the real story behind the bombing." Myers's profile of McVeigh is "nothing more than government propaganda," he said.[23]

The unhappy Manitoba subscriber said that the building was blown up from inside by "several demolition charges, not by a so-called fertilizer bomb." He asserted that everyone knows that McVeigh is a patsy and a scapegoat. "The real OKC terrorists are the same jackbooted thugs who burned down a church and murdered 90 people in Waco, Texas."[24]

A number of other theories surround the bombing. McVeigh's attorney, Stephen Jones, contended that McVeigh and Nichols were pawns in a global conspiracy so large that Jones said he was not sure where it ended. This was the premise of his book *Others Unknown.* He argued that the conspiracy could include Middle Eastern terrorists, German nationalists and U.S. supremacists and could even expand to areas such as Asia and Mexico. Yet McVeigh himself discounted such theories, and the federal judge presiding over the case would not allow this Pandora's box of a theory to be introduced into court due to its lack of evidence.

Jones's vast conspiracy theory, reminiscent of that amassed by O. J. Simpson's skilled defense team, shows just how far a crafty defense attorney will go to turn unresolved questions into reasonable doubt in the minds of potential and real jurors. As with attorney Johnnie Cochran's convincing closing statement on national television in defense of O. J. Simpson, it is the job of a defense attorney to feed suggestive questions. By suggesting but never proving such a global conspiracy, Jones tried to have his way in court in a culture predisposed to conspiracy thinking (see chapter seven).

But perhaps the most damning information about McVeigh's guilt came from his own lips. According to confidential defense reports obtained by the *Dallas Morning News,* McVeigh described to his defense team how "he bombed the Oklahoma City federal building, saying the daytime attack left a 'body count' intended to get a point across to the government." McVeigh's lead attorney, however, denied knowing about any such document.

Days after releasing the information, the *Dallas Morning News* decided not to release any additional information from the confidential report, citing concern for McVeigh's right to a fair trial. McVeigh's statements, culled from summaries of several 1995 interviews with a defense team member at the El Reno Federal Correctional Institution in Oklahoma, validated key elements of the prosecution's case, such as how McVeigh and Nichols committed robbery and burglary to obtain money and materials to complete the bombing.

Conclusion

In America, a land rich with domestic conspiracy theories, this true confession by America's most notorious homegrown terrorist is unlikely to sway staunch conspiracy theorists. They still believe that a host of domestic organizations such as the Federal Reserve and the public school system, as well as an unholy trinity of murder at Waco, Ruby Ridge and the Oklahoma City bombing, are exhibits A through E that show America's willing role in the New World Order. Defending America from the New World Order is the prime objective of the militia, which must be understood in light of its religious views, the topic of the next chapter.

4

The Militia's
Religious Impulse

The patriot movement across the United States is probably ninety percent Christian. . . .
Ninety nine percent of the people in the Christian patriot movement per se
would fit well in a Calvary Chapel or a Baptist church.
Dean Compton, cofounder, National Alliance of Christian Militia

[The Freemen's] political philosophy is based on their religious philosophy.
And in that respect, they are very similar to the young man
who was just convicted of murdering the prime minister of Israel.
They're similar in the depth of their convictions to Hamas.
Jim Page, *Soldier of Fortune* magazine

Numerous groups adhere to conspiracy theories. Yet the groups that
have been the most aggressive and belligerent toward the federal government and other supposed agents of the New World Order are found on the
far-right end of the political spectrum. This is no accident. The anger of
patriots and related conspiracy theorists, such as many of the late Davidians, toward alleged conspirators has been fueled by a complex religious
underpinning, a condition usually absent in other parts of the political
spectrum. This religious underpinning has the ability to push people into
armed confrontation because they believe that their enemies are also the
enemies of God.

For many self-described patriots and their kin, these enemies are the
product of apocalyptic end-times speculation and tragic standoffs between armed citizens and the federal government. According to the leader
of the National Alliance of Christian Militia, this religious connection has
convinced many to "lock-n-load" in the militia nearest them.

Dean Compton

Militia leader Dean Compton, cofounder of and spokesperson for The National Alliance of Christian Militia, has his beliefs deeply rooted within the Christian end-times community. Compton was the architect of "Operation Protect America," designed to thwart illegal immigration and the smuggling of illegal drugs across the U.S.-Mexican border by calling for armed patriots to monitor the entire border twenty-four hours a day. Compton said that key government agencies express little interest in stopping this flow and that some might even be profiting from it.

His concerns were validated when *U.S. News & World Report* devoted a front-page story to the same problem. The cover story explains how drug cartels have already bought up the Mexican government and have now turned their attention north.[1] The article explains that Mexico is the conduit for 70 percent of the cocaine and one-quarter of the heroin that reaches America, that thirty-two law enforcement officials have been indicted for border-related drug corruption and that eighteen have been convicted.[2]

Compton's plan for border control, however, never materialized. While discussing his operation during a radio interview in September 1995, Compton did not advocate violence against the Mexican people or against the American government. Rather, he remained calm during the interview, only occasionally flaring up with passion, which is often mistaken for anger. During my face-to-face interview with him, he never expressed the fury and hostility that have come to characterize much of the militia.

In front of the militia's volatile backdrop stands Dean Compton. His less strident message makes him likely to be challenged by extremists who scapegoat other races. In fact, Compton and other nonracist patriots are considered by extremists to be part of the "Jewish problem" that must be erased. The *National Christian News,* a Christian Identity publication, argues that true patriots should not "let phony 'Patriot' organizations tell you, 'See, the conspiracy is not Jewish.'"[3]

I interviewed Compton at a quiet restaurant in Ashland, Oregon. He stands six feet two inches tall, and I would guess some high-school football or basketball coach would have been happy to have him on his team. The father of three wore a black, Stetson-style hat, the same one he has on in the photo accompanying the November 1994 *Time* article written about him and his cofounder, Bruce Ballard.

Compton is the type of militia member who forces opponents of militias, such as Morris Dees of the Southern Poverty Law Center, to admit that within the movement there are people with nonracist motives. Compton, a man in his middle thirties, possesses a down-home charm and a sometimes youthful enthusiasm for his cause.

Why a "Christian" militia? Compton says that at least ten to fifteen million people participate in the militia movement. "There are more than ten thousand people in the militia in northern California," Compton says, and at least that many in southern Oregon. But he says that the Christian militia lives by different standards. "For instance, a patriot guy may think it's okay if the end justifies the means to take your life. Christians can't go out and commit murder. God says I can't go out and violate the law."

Compton says that he and others within his organization conduct their opposition to the federal government differently. "The Bible says you can't hate anybody. So you can call yourself a patriot and I call myself a patriot," but those other patriots can also hate anyone they want. "The gospel of Jesus Christ says I can't hate anybody. And I really don't want to associate with people who hate men or women or hate the Jews or hate blacks. We don't want to be lumped in with those people."

Compton says that only about 2 percent of the total patriot movement is motivated by hate. "The patriot movement across the United States is probably 90 percent Christian. Most of the people within the patriot movement believe this nation was founded on the gospel of Jesus Christ; that's what the Supreme Court said. And they are willing at least to adhere to those basic principles."

He does realize, however, that there are people who use the "Christian" label. "They used to be called the Ku Klux Klan, the Aryan Nation. But they said 'You know, we aren't getting very far with [these names], we aren't raising any money, so let's take this other title from these people who have been minding their own business for two hundred years."

Compton does not attend an organized church. "My church won't take me," he says, and the reason is multifaceted. "Churches are licensed by the state . . . and their tax-exempt status says they can't get involved in any of this stuff. We won't talk about it, but people are saying, 'Whoa, if there is truth, I want to hear the whole truth.' That's why you're seeing a lot of people come out of what are considered mainstream churches and say, 'Look, how come you won't talk about the global government that is coming? How come you won't talk about this one-world monetary system that even the president's talking about? How come you won't talk about the consequences of globalism? How come you won't talk about what it means to be buying rugs from China who are using seven-year-old little kids chained to the machine? How come they won't talk about this stuff?' Because they have a tax-exempt status that they're worried about." To Compton, the church's reluctance to speak out on these issues is just one example of how the church is becoming increasingly apostate, a signpost of the coming apocalypse.

Another reason many Christian patriots do not attend church is that "the Bible says that you have no need for man to teach you anything, but the Holy Spirit that was given unto man will teach you all things." He is not without fellowship, however. He says that some of his militia meetings draw more than 250 people. "You would call that a congregation. I could have a thousand there, and if I gave it a week's notice, we could have ten thousand." Compton says that everyone has a race to run, and none should forsake assembling together in fellowship. "I don't have to sit in a [church] building to be charitable. I don't have to sit in that building to tithe."

Compton says there is a group of people across the country, usually mature Christians who join the militia, who see America dissolving before their eyes. "They want to do something about it, not for themselves because it's not popular what we're doing." They want to make a difference for their kids, but many churches are opposed to such action. "With my church they said, 'We'll allow you to come, as long as you don't talk about any of that stuff.' Yeah, they want me to lie. The Bible says if I do not speak out to persuade a man from his evil ways that God will hold him accountable for his sin but me accountable for his blood. And you want me to shut up? I don't think so."

Compton says that his testifying put him at odds with some in the church, which brought division. It was best that he break away, as did Paul and Barnabas. He says that he and his partner use some meetings within the patriot community as a witnessing tool.

Theology. Compton says that the theological perspective of those within his Christian militia is very much in line with orthodox Christianity. With A. W. Tozer as his hero, the militia leader says that he is "not into the charismatic stuff" but rather adheres to "basic, fundamental teaching which says God is holy, man is not. God is perfect, I'm never going to be. I don't have to work my way to heaven, but because of the fruits of the Spirit I will have certain things in my life that will manifest what Jesus did for me."

His theology, fortified by the writings of Hal Lindsey, also includes the belief that Christ's return is real and imminent. "Based on what I can see, documents I have seen, these people that are running this government right now are trying to set up a system that they said would [happen] by the year 2000. I can prove this to anybody. I have had not one person, believer or nonbeliever, when [I] sit down and lay all the documents out" say that the conspiracy is not real.

Though he believes that today's events do fulfill Bible prophecy, he says they may "take a thousand years" to be fulfilled. "I do believe, based on what God says, that when we as a culture do the things that we're doing that God is going to judge us. . . . If I'm wrong, amen. If I'm right, amen. What can you say if you're not ready? 'If Dean's right, oh s—t!' If he's not right, you don't lose anything."

He can see the New World Order coming, and it is an anti-God government. "I have a responsibility to oppose this evil or get out of its way. If we the people decide we want this evil, I just want to be on the sideline when God starts burning things. If we can change things by informing people, and that's the stage we're in, let's do this."

Such a belief highlights a troubling dichotomy within the Christian conspiracy community. On the one hand they view today's events as the fulfillment of the end times—the one-world government they believe exists today as part of God's divine plan. Yet on the other hand they believe they can thwart this plan through their opposition. But Compton looks at it another way: "Based on what I can read in the Bible, you and I were never given the power or authority, nor the responsibility, to make changes in the outcome of the world. You and I were given a specific individual thing, and that's to run the race. God is going to look at it and say 'By faith—by faith! Noah did this, by faith Abraham did this . . .' So this is what I do. I say, 'God, I don't know what's going to happen tomorrow. But based on what I see and what you said, I have a responsibility to react to [the one-world government] in a certain way.' "

This includes being ready, similar to Noah. "God didn't tell Noah, 'It's going to rain eighteen days and fifty-six minutes and four hours. . . .' He said, 'Noah, it's going to rain.' He said build a boat." Part of this Noah-like readiness includes preparing for the approaching political war. "My job is to occupy till he comes. . . . If [the conspirators] don't pull this thing off right now, if they give me another five years of saying what I'm saying, it's going to be a thousand years from now. If this global government is going to happen, they have a window of opportunity. David Rockefeller said the same thing. He said 'I've got a short period of time to do this. We have the technology.'

"And I swear, if God will allow me the strength, this global anti-God government is never going to come and raise my children. That's what they say they're going to do; they're trying it right now in the schools." He says that the conspirators plan to "kill people like you and raise your children to worship this new angel of light, this one-world global Buddha Buddha. That ain't acceptable to me. If there were another island to go to, for Christians to go to worship God and worship him only, I'd go. But they've pushed us off the side of the earth and said, 'You will take this kind of crap or we won't allow you to live.' . . .

"Christians believe in a conspiracy because the Bible says that there is a one-world government coming. That's what Jesus taught. There is a global system coming that is anti-God, anti-Christian and follows the line of Lucifer. . . . Now, do I believe that there are six Jewish people running the whole world? No." He says only about 1 to 2 percent of those within the patriot movement believe in such a Jewish conspiracy. "Most mainstream people in the patriot movement are guys who go to work for a living and don't hate anybody."

Compton says that the majority of Christians within the militia believe we are living in the end times. "A predominant amount of people within the militia believe that it is possible that there is a short amount of time left. Most men that I see, they may not have the biblical" understanding of the end times, but they have a feeling in their gut that something is very wrong in the world, and they don't know exactly why. He implies heavily that this feeling is coming from the Holy Spirit stirring inside them.

This notion of evil being discerned intuitively by Christians in the last days is present in Pat Robertson's *The End of the Age.* In it Robertson portrays the antichrist, Beaulieu, as a charming and "warm person with a ready wit."[4] But says one Christian about Beaulieu, "I felt it. It was cold and icy. It was evil. There is something very disturbing, something sinister about this guy."[5] Compton says these are the same people, once they realize that evil is increasing, who are heartbroken that they have been asked to leave their local church.

Norman Olson

In June 1995 Norman Olson, at that time the regional militia commander from northern Michigan, gave a strident testimony before the Senate Subcommittee on Terrorism, Technology and Government Information. Perhaps for the first time America saw a clear connection between the militia and a unique Christian perspective that has circulated within evangelicalism/fundamentalism for nearly thirty years. The meeting was assembled after the shock and horror of the Oklahoma City bombing in an effort to fathom the militia mindset.

Olson said that he could understand why someone would commit the Oklahoma City bombing. He told the committee, chaired by Arlen Specter of Pennsylvania, that the government had not allowed for areas of refuge, presumably for angry conspiracy theorists, as outlined in the Old Testament. Olson accused the federal government of being the enemy of the average citizen, part of the New World Order that he and many others believe is predicted in the book of Revelation. He professed that he is not opposed to using violence against the government: "We're talking about a situation where armed conflict may be inevitable if the country doesn't turn around."[6]

The fifty-year-old father of three was removed as head of the Michigan Militia and pastor of Calvary Baptist Church after he said that Japanese officials with the aid of the U.S. government were responsible for the Oklahoma City bombing. He later reorganized as the commander of the Northern Michigan Regional Militia, saying his old group had been taken over by moderates. He sells slim-line Bibles in the same glass display case in which he sells guns and survivalist weapons.

In late 1995 Olson preached in an auction barn in Wolverine, Michigan, to thirty militia members.[7] "Hey, they need the Lord Jesus Christ," he told *Christianity Today.* "One young man received the Lord that day." This self-professed "pistol-packin' preacher" has a Jewish grandmother. He is dispensational, a Calvinistic evangelist and a former pastor in the General Association of General Baptists. He was once a Christian-school principal. Olson sees himself in a long line of Christian militia leaders who he says helped overthrow the British during the American Revolution.[8]

End-times writer John Walvoord, chancellor of Dallas Theological Seminary, agrees with Olson about a coming one-world government. But he disagrees about the rapture: "The world government that is going to come in the future is going to be during the Great Tribulation. [Militia leaders] just ignore the Rapture completely."[9] This is a comforting thought to many—but not to all—dispensational Christians. Some believe that the tribulation has already begun and that believers will not be raptured from it. Olson speaks for many Christian militia members when he says, "Where do we get this idea that we are supposed to sit down and let a corrupt government get worse and worse? Our Lord told us to contend for the faith and occupy until he comes."[10]

Holy Wars
Although Compton and other Christians within the militia movement say

that only a minute percentage of the patriot movement is motivated by racism, news accounts from across the country tell another, more troubling story. Militia leaders may claim that they are law abiding and do not promote violence, but acts of violence—and plans for violence that were halted before realization—show that some militia members are making preemptive strikes against the whore of Babylon and a cast of other end-times demons.

In fairness, it is the racist "patriot" who warrants the most concern. Of the more than 400 militia and approximately 350 allied patriot groups in our country, at least 130 have ties to racist groups such as Aryan Nations or the Ku Klux Klan. Just as Malcolm X and other radical followers of Elijah Poole laughed at the civil rights movement under the leadership of the late Martin Luther King Jr., today's racist conspiracy theorist laughs at the nonracist militia. Nonracist patriots are a joke to dangerous supremacists such as Louis Beam, LeRoy Schweitzer and Dale Jacobi, all of whom are Christian Identity leaders.

Norman Olson and fellow militia leader Ken Adams will talk to the FBI, but supremacist patriots will not. They believe that the FBI is an agent of ZOG, the Zionist Occupied Government, an international Jewish conspiracy. To the racist theorist, the nonracist is soft, shortsighted and easily fooled by the grand conspirators. Speaking with the FBI and testifying before Congress constitute fraternizing with the enemy. They will have no part in that, and they disdain those who do.

Freemen
They call themselves "Freemen," a tax-protesting, antigovernment, racist organization that believes, for now, that a paper revolution is the best way to attack the New World Order and other enemies of God. The most famous group of Freemen settled in Jordan, Montana, where they declared a sovereign and separate country based on racist Aryan beliefs. Wanted for nearly $2 million worth of illegal financial transactions and for threatening the life of a federal judge, the Freemen of Justice Township engaged in an eighty-one-day standoff with the FBI in the spring of 1996, enduring the longest federal siege in modern U.S. history.

To the relief of the small town and indeed much of the nation, it was resolved peacefully—so peacefully that Montana militia leader John Trochmann, who once had a bounty put on him by the Freemen, paid authorities a sober, backhanded compliment: "If we look at the federal agencies and their actions with Randy Weaver and at Waco, they have not acted like that this time. Perhaps they've learned something." FBI director Louis Freeh seemed to lend credibility to Trochmann's assessment when he said the day of the surrender, "I think the American people can take great comfort that the law was enforced and that it was done in a way that did not do harm to anyone. . . . We tried a fundamentally different approach."[11]

As do other conspiracy theorists, some Freemen believed that if they surrendered they would be injected with cancer cells and "no brain" drugs while in jail, which would really be a New World Order concentration camp. Speaking about a fellow Freeman, Edwin Clark told Senator Charles Duke of Colorado during a taped conversation, "When he went to Missouri, a man, a doctor from New York City come in and told Leroy . . . , 'You'll never see the light of day.' And he says, 'I'll guarantee you before you leave here I'm gonna inject you with a, with a deadly . . . dose of cancer.' "

Clark maintains that the government has tried to kill other jailed Freemen. "I know of two of them, one of them at least. He was as healthy as a . . . horse when he went in there, and he came back . . . There was another one, I can't remember his name, they, they give him a lethal dose of 'no brains' when he come back."

The Freemen had enough brains to mount an illegal paper revolution, which they taught to at least eight hundred other people in seminars. It included issuing outlandish lawsuits and other bogus legal documents designed to clog the legal system. Will Hutchison, chief of the Montana Justice Department's Agency Legal Services Bureau, says the Freemen of Justice Township have filed so many actions against the government that the cases have made up more than half of the division's caseload. "We've had tremendous amounts of pleadings, literally volumes. Some inches thick."[12] Local resident and former county attorney Vicki

Knudsen is more blunt: "Once a court accepts one of these asinine Freemen things, it's in the system. Everybody named in it becomes involved [and] has to respond. It's not funny. It's not romantic. It's scary."[13]

Montana attorney general Joseph P. Mazurek says that Freemen followers come from the agricultural community. "When they get into financial trouble and can't pay back their loans, they blame it on government, saying the money's no good since we went off the gold standard."[14]

Jailed Freeman LeRoy Schweitzer, whose arrest along with another Freeman began the standoff, conducted seminars on how to dupe the government as well as average citizens—something the authorities label "crime classes." During the taped seminars that were later leaked to the authorities, Schweitzer tells the attendees that the information he is about to share "might look complicated" but they will quickly catch on. But where do these people get the authority to write bad checks and issue phony money orders against people who are not part of the government, some of whom are also in dire financial straits? Schweitzer has an answer: "When you are born, you are the state, under God's law. . . . We are the new Federal Reserve. We are competing with the Federal Reserve—and we have every authority to do it."

A student of Schweitzer, who labeled him a "great American," took the Freemen's tactics to another level. M. Elizabeth Broderick of Palmdale, California, wrote more than $100 million in bad checks. How this puts a dent in the grand conspiracy, especially when bogus checks are written on the accounts of average Americans trying to make a living, has never been adequately explained by the Freemen or Broderick.

The Reverend Jerry Walters

The Reverend Jerry Walters met Montana Freemen leader Randy Skurdal, then a forty-three-year-old former Marine, in 1994 during his weekly visits to the Mussel Shell County Jail. "We could instantly tell that our worldviews were very far apart. He thought I was a duped Aryan." By *duped* Skurdal meant that the Lutheran minister did not realize that he was a true Israelite by virtue of his race.

"It is not helpful to hurl Scripture quotations at these people. They read the same Scriptures that Christians do, but their hermeneutics are different."[15] Hermeneutics is the science and methodology of scriptural interpretation. It is the consistent application of certain interpretive principles when reading or studying Scripture. It is the lens through which people read Scripture. For most Christians this lens includes themes of God's unconditional love, grace and forgiveness. To the Freemen it encompasses something different.

Walters had received a letter from Skurdal before meeting him, when Walters moved to Roundup on his first assignment in the ministry. Skurdal's letter sheds light on his July 1998 conviction for threatening to kill U.S. District Judge Jack Shanstrom. It also reveals Skurdal's disdain for the judicial system, such that before his trial began he asked U.S. Magistrate Richard Anderson to remove himself from the case. Anderson refused.

In the letter Skurdal welcomes Walters to Roundup and explains that he was baptized as and grew up as a Lutheran. But he wastes no time getting to the heart of the letter when he asks if Walters will teach about which race is the true Israel. A traditional church background is common among far right conspiracy theorists. Often they are asked to leave or they leave these churches in disgust, believing that their church preaches only what is transitory and popular rather than all of God's truth.

Skurdal reveals another tendency among far-right religious conspiracy theorists when he tells the minister, "I have not attended any churches for the past fifteen years," due to the teaching of Christian churches that the Jews are God's chosen people. Skurdal considers such teaching "contrary to the teachings of My Lord and King, JESUS, in John 8." He then takes advantage of a disturbing fact from church history when he appeals to the writings of the "Honorable DR. Martin Luther, who understood the hatred the jews had toward us, Israel." Luther (1483-1546), from whom Lutherans initially derived their name and theology, actively opposed the anti-Semitism of his day until in older age he succumbed to the scapegoating of European Jews.

Skurdal soon reveals why he thinks Jews hate his race. He believes that the white race are direct descendants of Adam, the real Israelites of the Bible. (As explained later, Freemen believe that Jews are descendants of

Satan who share his evil will.) Evil Jews have taken over America's judicial system, so it is likely that in Skurdal's mind disparaging a magistrate as illegitimate in his trial was not meant as grandstanding. The magistrate and the U.S. judicial system are bastard children of a sweeping and nefarious Jewish conspiracy. Specifically he argues that Congress acts upon an ill-defined "Noahide law," which is contrary to the Freemen's twisted interpretation of the Bible and instead is based upon the "Babylonian Talmud, jewish laws." Worse, this Noahide law was adopted by Congress without the knowledge and consent of "Israel, the American People." Under this Jewish law, Skurdal believes, "Christian People Under the Word of God, would be considered 'guilty' of violating" laws that would subject them to "capital punishment by decapitation" for worshiping the triune God.

Skurdal asks Walters if he plans to teach these truths. Skurdal is clear on this point: "I do not wish to attend any more judeo-Christian churches that do not know the Word of God." He signs the letter claiming he is "from the Tribe of Dan."

Matthew 5:10—"Blessed are those who are persecuted because of righteousness, for theirs is the kingdom of heaven"—is drawn upon for comfort by Skurdal and other religious conspiracy theorists who acknowledge that their views are frequently met with hostility and scorn. Through Skurdal and the Freemen we see that how one views truth rests upon certain premises, and we can note how precarious such assumptions can be. When a person accepts the premise, born from tortured hermeneutics, of righteousness by birthright (which appeals to pride) and not by grace and faith (which requires humility), that person negates responsibility for the harms caused by a sordid ego and sordid appetites.

Walters has been a guest on every major television network and has given interviews to many major newspapers during and since the Montana standoff. He is considering writing a book about his experiences, which have earned him a $100 billion lien. Because he disagreed with the Freemen publicly, Walters was slapped by the Freemen common law court with this lien for crimes of treason, slander, perjury and related charges. They were determined that Walters "was going to answer to them." He was presented with a twenty-eight-page document justifying the lien. In this document Skurdal shows the fury and swirling logic behind Freemen legalese.

The document is a blitzkrieg of non sequiturs, straw-man arguments and guilt by association. Walters becomes an "agent of 'Satan,'" part of "four hundred and fifty prophets of Baal" connected to Congress. Terms such as "color of law" and "laws of the alien" are melded with religious significance in nearly the same breath. Congress, he says, "could not consume the bull for burnt offering back then" nor can it today, because it worships "false gods, Baal, i.e., Satan." Skurdal concludes with the impossible statement, "Judicial Notice is taken of this fact."

The logic of such writing cannot be followed, and perhaps this is the intent: to drag the world into their convoluted interpretation of jurisprudence. Law in the United States has become so complicated that lawyers and judges dare not practice all of it, deciding instead to specialize. The Freemen thus take advantage of the loss of a common grip on law by connecting their racist rules to legal jargon. After all, who knows enough about contemporary law to find them guilty? Law, the Freemen have discovered, is a natural frontier in the conspiracy wars.

Conspiracy theorists have long done the same thing to antiquity. Few people have a clear understanding of history and current events, so mainstream culture can barely muster a rebuttal when false (or "alternative") views of history are unleashed. The John Birch Society has done this for decades through books and magazines. Hollywood continues the tradition of historical deceit through the work of people like Oliver Stone and Chris Carter. (See chapter seven.)

The document continues with a theological explanation for the Freemen belief that all whites are descendants of Seth, the third son of Eve. Freemen believe that Seth was the first pure Aryan and that Aryans are the true Israelites, God's chosen people. According to their view of the Genesis creation story, Eve had intercourse with Satan, who had taken the shape of a serpent or possibly a type of serpent-man. The result was Cain, the spawn of Satan, the first "evil Jew." Proof of such evil is found in the slaying of his brother Abel. All other races are described in Genesis as two-legged "beasts of the fields." Cain mingled with these people, spreading Satan's seed.

Walters says that such theology creates an "incarnational dualism," where the two seeds—that of Adam producing Seth and righteous Aryans, and that of Satan producing Cain, who later spread the satanic seed to all other pre-Adamic races—are portrayed as two racial groups pitted against each other in an end-times battle between good and evil.

This two-seed interpretation influences how the Freemen read all other Scripture. "When they read the New Testament, they do not believe Jesus was a Jew. He couldn't be. They believe he was an Israelite," from the house of David, who was not a Jew but was an Israelite.

Since they are God's chosen people, meant to rule over all creation, they are individual and sovereign kings—hence the term *Freemen*. They are the law by way of skin color and birth, which means they don't need a driver's license, for instance, but other races do. So when Freemen say they are the new Federal Reserve, it is not meant as a rhetorical ploy to justify the economic rape of others. They create new currency because doing so is the prerogative of kings.

They are strict constitutionalists because they believe that the Constitution was drafted and approved by godly white brethren. President Lincoln's Emancipation Proclamation, which set black slaves free, was a satanic attack upon God's righteous laws and his righteous leaders. After all, didn't some of the founding fathers, such as Thomas Jefferson and George Washington, own slaves? Two of our nation's greatest patriots did not believe that blacks were equal, so why should the Freemen? Slave owners such as Jefferson and Washington knew their place in the world— on top. But now, after centuries of ungodly legislation that has tried to dethrone God's chosen people, it's time for holy war. As he did in the Old Testament, God will ensure victory.

"People like to think of the Freemen as stupid, with some far-off look in their eye," says Walters. "Skurdal is not stupid."[16] One study shows that many Freemen and other patriots have at least a high-school education. Some have completed two years of college. One left southern Oregon to earn a law degree so that he could defend his fellow Freemen.

Walters has received death threats from the Freemen of Justus Township, even though patriot leaders continually say that their anger is directed against the evil federal government, and Walters has no ties to the government. He simply disagrees with the Freemen and has publicly criticized their bizarre interpretation of Scripture. He is further proof that some patriots have a far-reaching definition of *an enemy*. The federal government is simply on the top of the list—they'll get to the others later.

The Freemen, says Walters and others, must be understood primarily in light of their religious convictions. *Soldier of Fortune* writer Jim Page, who spent time with the Freemen, says that their fanaticism is like a holy war, since their political philosophy is based on their religious philosophy. Page suggests that in the depth of their convictions the Freemen are similar to the convicted murderer of the prime minister of Israel.

Some Freemen believers are second generation. They were taught this theological perspective by their fathers during group Bible studies. In spite of all Walters maintains a loving, biblical perspective:

> These are people who are deeply loved by God. There is a danger of demonizing them. I hope for healing for the community and the friends and family of loved ones. . . . It isn't race, but forgiveness and adoption that sets us right with God. . . . What we must do, instead, is return again and again to what is central: the love and mercy of God for all people revealed in the crucified one who lives, Jesus Christ.[17]

The Weavers' End-Times Theology

America has been incubating a unique and dangerous strain of religious virus: an unhealthy obsession with evil due to the marriage of end-times prophecy and extreme political views. This virus devoured the mind of Randy Weaver's late wife, Vicki, and continues to live in his mind. But the Weavers weren't always so extreme.

According to close friends, the Weavers once adhered to an orthodox view of Christianity. They attended a Baptist church in Cedar Falls, Iowa, and were fundamentalists who expressed a genuine love and compassion for some of their closest friends and also for strangers. The Weavers participated in a Bible study group that met at Sambo's. During one of their meetings, Mike Roethler, a Cedar Falls police officer, brought with him a homeless man. While others sat and stared, not offering to help, Randy pulled out a $20 bill and gave it to the man. Randy was known for giving homeless people a place to stay. Even after they stole from him, he brought more street people home anyway.[18]

Beginning in the early seventies, the Weavers submerged themselves in apocalyptic literature and extreme political philosophies. According to Vicki, it was Hal Lindsey's bestselling *Late Great Planet Earth* that sent them looking for a rural chunk of land somewhere in the hills of the sylvan Northwest. They landed in Idaho, on Ruby Ridge.[19]

Before his week of infamy, Randy Weaver was a thin, hollow-eyed woodcutter who decided to drive down from his cabin one summer to attend a meeting of Aryan Nations. The Aryan Nations is composed of people who believe that Jews are the children of Satan and that white America should have its own homeland. But by far the biggest factor influencing the Weavers' faith after 1978 was their belief that they were living in the end times. Their lifestyle became that of looking for the end. Their obsession with the end times, fueled by Christian conspiracy preaching, became a gateway to the world of fear and, eventually, supremacy.

Randy would purchase guns from the Bullet Hole, a store owned by Baughn Truman, to prepare for the coming invasion described by Lindsey. Lindsey's proclamation that theirs was the last generation was coupled with Vicki's belief that she was a prophet who was chosen to relay God-given visions to all who would listen. Vicki's visions fell in step with what she had read in Lindsey's bestseller. She dreamed while taking a series of baths that the Holy Spirit showed her an empty cabin that would need to be fully supplied before the coming tribulation.[20] She also believed, based on Revelation, that she knew how much time she had: "Thou must prophesy again before many peoples, and nations, and tongues, and kings . . . and the holy city shall they tread under foot forty and two months" (10:11; 11:2 KJV). Vicki believed this passage told her that she had three and a half years to prepare.

They wanted to bring others with them. They often warned family members about the coming disaster. Randy's arguments sounded as if they came straight out of Don McAlvany's newsletter. He would tell Vicki's family during Sunday dinner that a social breakdown was just around the corner, orchestrated by the government so that it could declare martial law. The government would then crush democracy and install a godless form of government that would not tolerate God-fearing Christians and would murder them en masse. There would be riots in the streets when the government turned against its own people. The only protection, Randy argued, was to store up survivalist rations, guns, and gold and other precious coins.

It was from this point on that the Weavers, like so many Christians today, added conspiracy theories to their faith. They began believing that a secret shadow group, the evil Masonic Illuminati Order, was behind the satanic conspiracy of controlling world events. A host of other theories soon followed, for in this religion of conspiracy—once a follower makes the leap of faith and believes that nothing is as it seems—all things become possible. It's like learning foreign languages—once one conspiracy theory is mastered, learning and accepting another becomes much easier.

In the fall of 1983 an earthquake hit northern Idaho. In a letter to her friend Carolee Flynn, Vicki wrote, "That's just one more of the birth pangs of Matthew 24." She also wrote that the invasion of Grenada was another clear sign that the end was coming. "I still think the Russians are going to invade the United States from Canada," she wrote. "We've heard they built a highway down from Alaska that's 10 lanes wide."[21] A person can open popular Christian conspiracy books and read similar charges.

After finishing the cabin on Ruby Ridge, the Weavers resumed their Bible study on Friday nights. They had a new group of friends who believed that Jesus was the savior of Israel, that is, Anglo Christians. Jews were satanic impostors who controlled the world through an international conspiracy via banking, politics and control of the media. Randy Weaver later realized that his supremacist theology did not align with Christ's teaching: "I have my own take on things. Hell, I'm really not even a Christian."[22]

According to Randy Weaver, the Jewish conspiracy is alive and well in America. A family picture taken in May 1989 shows Randy with his wife and three kids sitting on a high-backed couch in their cabin. His shirt reads, "Just say 'NO' to ZOG [Zionist Occupied Government]." During the siege, Sara Weaver prayed that the evil agents of ZOG would just get it over with. She prayed that they would firebomb the house, something her parents told her would happen as part of the fulfillment of Bible prophecy.[23]

Theology at Waco

Though Davidians should not be considered self-described patriots, their conspiracy theories created an odd kinship with patriot groups across the country, which is one reason militia cells were so quick to rush to the Davidians' defense. After failing to become a California rock star, David Koresh went to Waco in 1981 and joined the Branch Davidians, who had settled in the area in 1934. Founded by Bulgarian immigrant Victor Houteff, the movement had a center called Mt. Carmel.

Houteff's followers believed that Houteff was the "antitypical Elijah" chosen to announce the second coming of Christ. Though they never made the announcement, the sect had planned to move to Palestine to greet Christ. Followers also believed that their leaders' writings were divine. This included the writings of Houteff, his predecessor Benjamin Roden, and Roden's wife Lois Roden, who took over after her husband's death in 1978. Lois is best known for her assertion that the Holy Spirit is female. She was the prophet of the group when Koresh drifted into town. They traveled to Israel together and had an affair while Roden was in her late sixties.

The path to Koresh's complete control was paved well before his violent takeover in late 1987. The residents at Mt. Carmel adopted rules that essentially made the theological leader king. After Roden's death, a struggle for leadership drew Roden's son, George, and Koresh into a heated conflict. Koresh retreated to eastern Texas but returned with seven male followers, five .223-caliber semiautomatic assault rifles, two .22-caliber rifles, two 12-gauge shotguns and nearly four hundred rounds of ammunition. Roden escaped with injuries to his chest and hands.

Koresh and his men were tried for attempted murder. Koresh told the jury that they went to Mt. Carmel to find evidence of corpse abuse by

Roden and that their shots were aimed at trees. All seven were acquitted, and Koresh's trial ended in mistrial.

By 1990 Koresh was the unchallenged leader. According to disenchanted followers who left Mt. Carmel, Koresh's teaching became ever more intense and controlling and pointed to his belief that he was divine.

Davidians believe in the imminent confrontation between God's chosen and the forces of evil. According to the Davidians and a growing number of orthodox Christians, these evil forces include the federal government. According to Koresh's theology, this confrontation was likely to have begun in 1995 as part of the fulfillment of end-times prophecy. This is at least one reason that he and his followers bought guns and learned how to use them in late 1991. According to Kiri Jewell, it was also the reason she was taught to place a gun inside her mouth to commit suicide.

Jewell testified during the Waco hearings in the summer of 1995. She described how Koresh committed statutory rape with many young girls. Called on the opening day of the hearings, Jewell told how she had sex with Koresh when she was ten and recounted Koresh's graphic description of sex acts with other women and children. Jewell said that Davidians expected to be "killed by the feds. . . . There was never a time when we didn't expect to be killed by the feds" as part of an end-times conspiracy against true Christians. "It was accepted that the best way to shoot yourself . . . was to put the gun into your mouth back to the soft spot above your throat before pulling the trigger."

Koresh matched events in recent history with angelic references in the book of Revelation. Koresh's prophetic scenario was increasingly complex. As outlined in the book *Why Waco?*[24] Koresh equated parts of the Adventists' history with the three angelic messengers described in Revelation 14. The roles of the first two angels were performed by William Miller in the nineteenth century with his prediction that Christ was returning. Ellen White performed the third angel's role. Koresh insisted that these three angels were a subgroup of the seven angelic messengers in Revelation 15 and elsewhere. Miller and White represented the first three angels, and various Adventist offshoots represented the next four.

A group in the 1920s predicted the restoration of the Davidic theocracy in Palestine, which is how the Davidians derived their name. In the 1950s came the discovery that Old Testament feast days must be reinstituted. Then came Lois Roden's belief in the feminine character of the Holy Spirit. Last but most important was the seventh angel—Koresh. He insisted that he was the Lamb found in Revelation 5, the only one worthy of interpreting the meaning of the seals.

Among the chief complaints from the Christian conspiracy community is that the federal government never planned to listen to Koresh's apocalyptic religious beliefs, proving that they never intended to truly negotiate but instead wanted him and his followers dead. They argue that if the negotiators had spent more time trying to understand Davidian theology and eschatology, they would have encouraged Koresh to finish his manuscript that he believed would explain the meaning behind the seventh seal found in Revelation. If negotiators had done so, critics contend, Koresh and his followers would have prepared to leave for Palestine to witness Christ's return.

As usual, this conspiracy theory has some merit. Koresh told negotiators on April 14 that he would not surrender until the manuscript was complete. Conversations between Koresh and negotiators reveal that just sixteen days into the standoff negotiators refused to listen to any more of Koresh's "Bible babble."[25]

But contrary to the conspiracy community's charge, negotiators were not always closed to theological discussions. Former FBI chief hostage negotiator Clint Van Zandt was one of a team of negotiators who tried to end the failed standoff. One night Koresh asked if he could talk with a Christian. Federal agents contacted Van Zandt, who was born again in 1979. They debated Scripture for two hours. "He was trying to persuade me that the Bible allowed him to have sex with young girls. I said, 'Hey, David, you're taking everything out of context, buddy,' but he kept leaping all over the place for justifications. Finally, he said, 'Brother Clint, do you know who I am? I am the Christ.'"[26]

A close review of recorded conversations between Koresh and lead FBI negotiator Byron Sage reveals a discussion in which theology is debated but in which ending the standoff is Sage's top priority. The following is a conversation between Koresh and Sage on March 17.

Koresh: And you will find out in the judgment that you're fixin' to witness that it was a lie. You will find out very clearly every detail, every thought, every statement made, every, every, ah, manipulation done behind the scenes will be made apparent to you. You do not understand what you're dealing with. You do not understand what position of time you're in. This nation does not understand. I know you don't want to hear this.

Sage: No, I wanna hear it because I, I answer to the same God you do, pal, but you don't have a corner on the market.

Koresh: (interrupts) No, you do not. You do not know the seals, Mr. Byron. You do not understand the seals. There are scholars that would help you out. There are scholars who would understand the indepthness of what I stated over the radio.

Sage: David, can I ask you a question?

Koresh: Yes.

Sage: Okay. I've read the same book, okay? . . . I found my Savior in a, in a ah, situation in Vietnam where I realized that I wasn't in control of my life.

Koresh: Right.

Sage: Okay? I read the same book that you are, are founding your faith on. I respect that book. I respect your faith, but I read in the Scripture and . . . I'm not claiming to be a Bible . . . theologian, and I'm not claiming to be anywhere near as well versed in word and quotation as you are, and I respect that capability, but I find in that book that . . . the only person, . . . the only entity that can open those seven seals is the Lamb of God.

Koresh: Exactly.

Later in the same conversation:

Koresh: Well, we know the rock's in heaven. We know that, right, Mr. Byron? It sits on a throne, right?

Sage: That's right.

Koresh: And we also know it's gonna hit the image in the feet, right? Daniel 2:44.

Sage: I'm not gonna get into a religious debate with you—

Koresh: No, it's not debate—

Sage: I believe what you're sayin' and I—

Koresh: Statements of Christian fact, everyone who loves Christ knows.

Sage: David, I know what you're sayin' and I agree with it, but it's time for you to bring your feet out and to place them . . . in a . . . proper forum to get your word out if that's what you really want to do.

Koresh: That's what's going to be done—

Sage: If that's what you really want to do.

Koresh: That is what is going to be done, I swear by God unto you.

Sage: How's it gonna be done until you come out?

Koresh: What I, what I'm saying—

Sage: Come out.

Later in the same conversation:

Koresh: I understand that you are trying to make statements for us to comply to your ideals, but here's the thing—you just told me you feared God.

Sage: I do.

Koresh: Which God do you fear?

Sage: I fear . . . I'm not gonna get into this debate with you, but I'm gonna tell you that I am personally convinced and secure in my salvation. I don't have to represent that to you one iota. What I do have to represent to you is that this is not an unlimited situation. Time is, is passing. You have not—

Koresh: I know it is—it's very close.

Sage: Let me finish, please. David, let me finish. You have not lived up to your promises.

Koresh: And have you lived up to yours?[27]

The FBI's eventual decision to end theological discussions did not mean it found them unimportant. According to Justice Department reports and interviews with FBI negotiators, authorities continually complained about the lack of progress in the siege. They also said that Koresh could not be trusted, since he had broken key promises, such as ending the standoff on March 2 after the one-hour audiotape of his religious teachings was aired on the Christian Broadcasting Network.

The tape was broadcast at 1:30 p.m. White school buses were ready to take the Davidians away from the compound in order to end the volatile situation. People, mostly children, were lined up with teddy bears, lunch boxes, suitcases and backpacks ready to leave. According to survivor Clive Doyle, many were crying and praying. But at 5:58 p.m. negotiators were told that Koresh had received a message from God to halt the exodus. The conversation between the FBI and Koresh's right-hand man, Steve Schneider, was replete with tension, drama, anguish and the sound of shattered expectations, with grave consequences.

Schneider tells Byron Sage, "Okay, uh, I just talked to [Koresh]. He's going through a lot of anguish. . . . What the guy just went through I've never seen anything like it. He wanted me to remind you to read Psalms chapter 2, then he wanted me to read to you Revelation 18."

Sage, clearly pained by the proceeding, interrupts. "Steve, what is this?"

Schneider responds, "Have you ever read the story of Christ, where he hung on the cross, where he actually [perspires] drops of blood because of the anguish?" Sage says he has read it. Schneider asks, "Can I just read Revelation 18 to you?"

Sage tries to interject, to steer the conversation back toward a peaceful resolution, to steer the lined-up children away from the cliff's edge. But Schneider continues, "Everything's ready to go right now, but all of a sudden [his voice begins to crack] he started praying—"

Sage sternly says, "He gave us his word."

Schneider retorts, "I know that. But what if there's a higher power than you and I that speaks to an individual? What do you do? This is what he [uncertain whether he is quoting God or Koresh] said: 'Be aware of who you're dealing with.'"

The conversation quickly turned into a verbal boxing match with both sides desperately trying to explain the gravity of what was happening.

Sage later said that when he heard that Koresh was going to wait he was devastated and embarrassed. As he pointed out, the FBI fulfilled its half of the agreement; Koresh didn't.

Koresh later told Sage on March 17, "My, my, my commander, my commander . . . my commander and chief told me to wait."

Sage replied, "Well, that's a pretty easy excuse to hide behind."[28]

It is understandable that since Koresh hid behind theological justifications for breaking promises, negotiators would consider his God-talk hypocritical and spurious. Law enforcement officials tend to be men and women of action. According to Justice Department reports, Sage and others, tired from the lack of progress, simply lost hope for a nonconfrontational resolution.

The foreshadowing evident from the note pinned on nine-year-old Heather Jones was hauntingly accurate. She left the compound on March 5. That day her mother wrote that once the children were out, the adults would die. Those deaths were due in part to a complex theology found in the minds of people such as Koresh, who believe that the U.S. government is part of an evil conspiracy as described in contemporary and popular end-times preaching.

Conclusion

Many conspiracy theorists have declared war against the federal government. They believe that it is a guilty party in an end-times war that is outlined in numerous books sold in Christian bookstores, written about in popular Christian newsletters and discussed on Christian radio. Some of the books may also be purchased from the Militia of Montana's "1998 Preparedness Catalog." They include *En Route to Global Occupation,* written by bestselling Christian conspiracy theorist Gary Kah, as well as *Unholy Alliances* and *The Planned Destruction of America* by James Wardner, another bestselling Christian conspiracy theorist.[29]

Conspiracists such as Randy and Vicki Weaver, Christian militia leaders and followers, Christian conspiracy talk show hosts and thousands of churchgoers did not come to their belief in a grand conspiracy overnight. This belief is the product of decades of speculative end-times preaching and date setting. For them, such end-times preaching has proven to be a type of political gateway drug that has pushed them into a deeper and ever more dangerous opposition to a cast of end-times enemies.

The fruit of such belief was deadly for Vicki Weaver, her son and the law enforcement official who was killed on Ruby Ridge. It is unlikely that they will be the last. More Weavers are tucked into hillsides with a weathered copy of *The Late Great Planet Earth* in their makeshift cabins constructed of salvaged plywood. They have front-row seats for the coming apocalypse that they read about in numerous Christian newsletters and hear about on Christian radio. Perhaps the only notable difference is that they haven't broken the law—yet. Or maybe they have, but there are numerous cases ahead of theirs, so they'll have to wait before embarking on their very own confrontation with the whore of Babylon, the U.S. government.

Disciples of apocalyptic thinking have sacrificed much for their faith. Some have lost jobs, spouses of many years, dear children and close friends and have even been kicked out of the very churches that helped to create them. Many of them have run for the hills to protect their family. As one man of retirement age from the Militia of Michigan admitted on national television, he had "lost everything" because of his belief in a coming New World Order. He is alone, a casualty of exegetical zeal.

Dean Compton and those he represents are people of faith and great action. I have sat at restaurant tables and told Dean's story, and I am disturbed by the criticism thrown his way by other people of faith. Popular but speculative end-times preachers are the ones who helped create this apocalyptic worldview. To be critical of Compton without also questioning those who created his worldview is like blaming a burning building for the work of an arsonist.

Christians should deny Compton's conspiracy theories and his hopeless view of our government. But they should not deny that he is their brother. Those who examine the militia's rhetoric will find a theological umbilical cord connecting it to a religious foundation of end-times speculation.

Now is the time to create a conspiracy for good—because if or when

Compton and thousands like him finish their tour of duty in the jungles of Christian conspiracy theory, they will need a church to call home. They already feel estranged from churches that spent decades convincing them that they are living in the end times and that this must entail numerous conspiracies. More than ever before, Christian conspiracy disciples need ministers to minister, not speculate about the end of the world.

The peaceful resolution of the Freemen standoff in Jordan, Montana, is a clear example of how federal agencies have responded to the changing face of religious extremism in America. It is past time for contemporary end-times preachers to modify their conduct as well.

5

Old Lies on
Life Support
The Jewish Conspiracy

The concerted campaign connected with *Schindler's List* points to a conspiracy
directed against the psyche of the American masses! . . .
There is no way that an overlong black and white movie about an event (or non-event)
could generate such rave reviews and incredible free publicity,
were it not for the power and influence of the Jewish leadership,
especially in the media and culture.
Hans Schmidt, contributing editor, *Criminal Politics*

Jewish control of that [Hollywood] "industry" is known by all.
Why haven't you ministers even wondered about that?
Television, with Jewish control of the networks and productions,
follows the same line. The same corrupting influence can be traced in liquor,
pornography, prostitution, rock music, drugs, sex education, sensitivity training,
subtle and open promotion of youth rebellion, anti-Bible and anti-Christian laws
and court decisions and attitudes, and on and on and on.
You express sorrow, sometimes even anger, at the corruption,
BUT YOU NEVER EXPOSE ITS JEWISH SOURCE. WHY?
Sheldon Emry, "pastor"

Historically no group has been more maligned by conspiracy theories
than Jews. They have been accused of starting wars and revolutions for
their own sordid gain, of spreading the Black Death in Europe during the
1300s, of killing Christian children in order to drink their blood and of
conspiring to wreck the morals of the Western world through the corrupting influences of television and popular music. These supposed goals are
part of an overarching scheme of world domination that anti-Semites
believe has been in place for hundreds, if not thousands, of years.

Christian conspiracy theorists believe in many of the same conspiracies, though they do not intentionally blame Jews or other races. But as the history of these theories reveals, many Christian conspiracy theories are altered anti-Semitic conspiracy theories that have been cleansed, for now, of their original intent to blame Jews for the bulk of the world's problems.

Before we explore the history of these theories, two points need to be clarified: there has never been enough actual evidence to support conspiracy theories of Jewish domination; and true Christians are not racists. In fact, racists who call themselves Christians despise Christianity's embrace of all people, regardless of national origin or race. Racist conspiracy theorists view nonracist conspiracy theorists as part of the "Jewish problem," but the apostle Paul sets the record straight:

> You are all sons of God through faith in Christ Jesus. For all of you who were baptized into Christ have clothed yourselves with Christ. There is neither Jew nor Greek, there is neither slave nor free man, there is neither male nor female; for you are all one in Christ. (Galatians 3:28 NASB)

The Anti-Defamation League affirms that orthodox Christianity views racists such as white supremacists as "twisted and warped, a perversion— not a reflection—of the faith."[1] The New Testament abounds with narratives that show the irrelevance of race. One is the relationship forged between Cornelius of Caesarea, a centurion in the Italian Regiment, and Peter, the converted Jew. In Acts 10 Peter receives the same vision three times—God commands him to eat non-Jewish foods and mix with Gentiles. This puzzles Peter, but he obeys. An angel then tells Peter to go with the men whom Cornelius has sent.

The next day Peter goes to Cornelius's home and addresses the crowd: "You know, I'm sure that this is highly irregular. Jews just don't do this—visit and relax with people of another race. But God has just shown me that no race is better than any other" (Acts 10:28-29 The Message).

The Myth of a Jewish Supreme Council
Christian conspiracy theorist Robert Sessler believes that the French

Revolution is being revived today as part of Satan's One World Order plan. He speaks for numerous conspiracy theorists when he writes, "Just by comparing the history of the French Revolution with what is happening today, we will see that the whole world is becoming involved in the very same revolution!"[2] Yet much of what the Christian conspiracy community believes about the French Revolution comes from conspiracy theories created by French Jesuit Abbé Barruel in 1797.

At first Barruel blamed the revolution on the Order of the Knights Templar. His original conspiracy theory did not include Jews, largely because they had no political power prior to the revolution. But after the revolution they were awarded equal rights, which fueled anti-Semitic sentiments in France.

In 1806 Barruel supposedly received a letter from retired Italian army officer J. B. Simonini of Florence, which claimed that Jews were really the ones behind the French Revolution.[3] Despite the questionable nature of Simonini's note, Barruel circulated it and integrated its elements into his theory. Just before his death in 1820 at age seventy-nine, he "emerged as an enthusiastic believer not simply in the Masonic conspiracy but in the Jewish conspiracy as well." He promulgated the idea that the whole of Europe "was in the grip of a vast revolutionary organization, which extended downwards into every single village of France, Spain, Italy and Germany and which was rigidly controlled by a supreme council, which in turn was controlled by Jews."[4]

This belief in a Jewish supreme council gained popularity with the release of another work of fiction designed to turn the world against Jews: *The Protocols of the Learned Elders of Zion*. Callers to *The Paul Thomas Show* have quoted it as a true account of Jewish ambition.

The Protocols of the Learned Elders of Zion

In the summer of 1993, our radio station devoted back-to-back shows to a shameful fact in history: Christian anti-Semitism. After those shows KDOV received a letter from a listener telling about a secret meeting of "European Rabbis in Budapest, Hungary, January 12, 1952." The supposed meeting allegedly was organized to discuss how Jews caused both world wars and are planning a third. (Why Jews would create a war in which nearly six million Jews perished he did not explain.)

The letter also described another supposed meeting designed to control the world, which is outlined in *The Protocols of the Learned Elders of Zion,* first published in Russia at the turn of the century. Authorship of the pamphlet-sized diatribe is a subject of some debate. In 1921 *London Times* journalist Philip Graves showed it to be a work of fiction. *The Protocols* is supposedly a verbatim account of twenty-four secret meetings of Jewish leaders plotting the takeover of religious and political life the world over.

As a junior in college I tried to check out a copy of *The Protocols* for a class paper. Though the University of Oregon's library system was the largest in the state, the staff apparently had a difficult time locating it. The library aide dove deep into the archives of the library, a dark, mysterious and fascinating place. I was told I might have to wait for a week, since it could not easily be found. This wasn't entirely true.

Within a few days I received a phone call from a professor in the history department asking me to come to his office. When I arrived he had in his hand a copy of *The Protocols,* and he told me that I could have the work. But while I was looking through it, he asked why I wanted the publication and what I already knew about it. I told him that it was going to be the subject of a class assignment about statements that seemed too radical to be true. I left his office having been told in no uncertain terms that the publication had been used to justify grim acts of anti-Semitism. This professor knew that in the hands of some this pamphlet is pure racist dynamite.

During the Bolshevik Revolution of 1917, White Russians revived *The Protocols* to convince the Russian people that the revolution was the product of a Jewish conspiracy to dominate Russia. It was also used in Nazi propaganda. But what must surely come as a shock to Christian conspiracy theorists is that *The Protocols* attempts to link Jews to an international conspiracy through the Illuminati.

Today's Christian conspiracy preachers have quietly dropped Jews from the Illuminati conspiracy, but they have retained the rest—including Catholics, Masons, Marxists and Satanists—and have added the New

Age/New World Order. Why are Jews omitted? After all, either Jews are part of the Illuminati conspiracy, which has been written about by most Christian conspiracy authors as proof of the New World Order, or they are not. Surely the writers who added Jews to the list had their "exclusive" sources.

Such a discrepancy is easily explained. Most Christian conspiracy theorists are conservative fundamentalists who honor God's covenant with the Jews and who otherwise denounce anti-Semitism. Second, most Christian conspiracy theorists are not aware that many of their theories come from the older, anti-Semitic community.

Omitting Jews from the Illuminati conspiracy is yet more proof that the groups who appear on the list of conspirators are the ones most hated at any given time, not because there is clear evidence against them. It also demonstrates that even the conspiracy community is not aware of its own past. But what if societal winds change? What if anti-Semitic sentiments increase?

Many roads converged to create the Holocaust. Could Christian conspiracy theories be unknowingly repaving one of those roads? Michael Lind, who has analyzed at length Pat Robertson's conspiracy theories in his bestselling *New World Order,* "suggests that not since the days of Father Coughlin has the grass-roots right been as overtly anti-Semitic as it is now."[5]

Open-Line Discussions

During one open-line radio show, I asked listeners to discuss the theory that Jews control the world. A man in his seventies, whom I call Bill, told me that the Jews indeed do control the world as outlined in *The Protocols.* He told me about the book *World War III Declared,* which he said clearly outlines the secret Jewish plan to take over the world via computers and other technological innovations.

He also mentioned Henry Ford. Bill said that he and Ford were farm boys from Michigan, which is where they met. Ford had also read *The Protocols,* but Bill said that Ford was not willing to accept the book at face value. According to Bill, Ford spent up to $2 million having *The*

Protocols investigated. This became the groundwork for his anti-Semitic work *The International Jew.*

Though Henry Ford was a visionary in automobile mass production, historians warn that his ability to grasp world events was thin. He was basically uneducated and given to racist ideas about the world. For years he financed anti-Semitic propaganda in his newspaper *The Dearborn Independent.* Ford blamed wars, the Russian Revolution, the breakdown of society, problems with liquor, immoral movies, media bias, even jazz music on the Jews. Though jazz is deeply rooted in the African-American experience, Ford argued that this music of "morons" was part of a "Jewish monopoly":

> Jazz is a Jewish creation. The mush, slush, and sly suggestion, the abandoned sensuousness of sliding notes, are of Jewish origin. . . . Glamorous youths mutter dirges in low monotones, voluptuous females with grossly seductive gestures moan nasal notes no real musician can recognize. . . . The general directors of the whole downward trend have been Jews.[6]

Not surprisingly, Hitler regarded "Heinrich Ford as my inspiration."[7] In 1923 Hitler gave Ford his support as if he were running for president:

> I wish I could send some of my shock troops to Chicago and other big American cities to help in the elections. We look to Heinrich Ford as the leader of the growing fascist movement in America. . . . We have just had his anti-Jewish articles translated and published. *[The International Jew]* is being circulated in millions throughout Germany.[8]

Ford would later become the first American to receive the Grand Cross of the German Eagle, Germany's highest honor. It was presented to Ford in Detroit, along with a personal letter from Hitler himself.

In 1927, after a prominent Jewish attorney filed a libel suit against him, Henry Ford retracted the anti-Semitic statements made in his paper, claiming they were published without his knowledge. Following his apology the suit was dropped, but the image of the communist-capitalist-

Jewish conspirator had become firmly established in right-wing minds.[9]

My caller, Bill, fits an all-too-common profile of a pessimistic conspiracy disciple. He told our station that he was fed up with seeing America slide into what he described as a nebulous abyss. If men from his generation did not serve in World War II, they lost classmates who did. They sacrificed, reared children, paid taxes—and for what? To see crimes committed unabashedly in the streets? To see their daughters risk a one-in-three chance of being raped sometime in their lives? To see the Bible go from being a source of inspiration to being an object of ridicule? To see drugs capture the mind and soul of a cynical generation that seems to have grown up with a paper-thin conscience? Bill and his brothers-in-conspiracy conclude that this slide could not have come from natural, sinful causes—it must have been planned. Some blame the Jews.

Another Christian conspiracy theorist told me that secular Jews are behind the New World Order. This young man, who attends church regularly, claims that followers of Marx and Lenin received loans from American Jews to fuel the Bolshevik Revolution. He justifies his anti-Semitism by asserting, "They aren't real Jews," by which he means they aren't religious Jews who believe in the God of Abraham, Isaac and Jacob. They are evil, communist, *secular* Jews determined to overthrow democracy the world over and to set up the New World Order, thus fulfilling end-times prophecy.

The belief that international bankers create war for profit is very much alive in Christian conspiracy publishing. Ken Klein, author of *The False Prophet,* argues that "America's industrial might was harnessed by the creation of the Federal Reserve System." The resulting "mobilization of credit became available to finance a New World Order." According to Klein, all that needed to be done was to create a world war. "International bankers had everything to gain from a world war. . . . The gigantic cash flow off the interest of mega-loans to the nations would be used to create a New World Order. A world order fashioned after the pattern suggested by Engels and Karl Marx, whose principles were based upon Adam Weishaupt's Order of the Illuminati."[10]

During his two-day seminar in southern Oregon, Klein repeated the long-standing accusation that international Jewish bankers control the world. Klein, a former pro football player who says that he is an ethnic Jew, told the crowd of about 250 people that Jews, his own people, are also behind the grand conspiracy. Judging by the passive reaction from the crowd, this group of evangelicals and fundamentalists, who are usually supportive of Jews and Israel, didn't seem to notice that Klein was unintentionally keeping this age-old lie on life support—a lie that has been used to persecute Jews for centuries.

International Blood Sport

The belief that Jews are evil international schemers has an international following. Some of the bestselling books in Japan during the early 1990s included *Jewish Plan for Conquest of the World, Japan with Understanding of Jewish Power* and *Scenario for Annihilation.* One of these books argues that Jews are accountable for trade disputes, Japan-bashing, the Chernobyl disaster—even AIDS. In his book *Jewish Business Methods,* a former McDonald's president in Japan, Den Fujita, claims that Japan "is being ravaged by a pack of Jews." He then advises his fellow businessmen to emulate the Jewish way of business.[11]

Japan hasn't always been so hostile toward Jews. In 1940 it issued five thousand visas to Lithuanian Jews fleeing approaching Nazi troops. But during the early 1990s Japan searched for a scapegoat for its ailing economy. A self-professed Christian minister had three bestselling books that found such a scapegoat. Masami Uno claimed that an international Jewish conspiracy was secretly plotting the destruction of Japan's economy. He believes that the Mellons, Rockefellers, Du Ponts and Morgans are at the center of this conspiracy. One of his books has sold more than 1.5 million copies.

Masaaki Nakayama, then Japan's posts and telecommunications minister, said in September 1991, "The Jews . . . control agriculture in America, and the international precious metals market. Both George Bush and Michael Dukakis are related to Jews."[12] Japan's infamous Shoko Asahara, the blind, self-professed Buddhist prophet who stood trial in April 1996 for the murder of twenty-five people in the sarin nerve-gas attack in Tokyo, also preached anti-Semitism. He predicted that Armageddon, in the form of a final nuclear battle and high-tech man-made earthquakes, would begin in late 1995 and that behind this coming third world war was a conspiracy of Jews.

When Saddam Hussein invaded Kuwait, he quickly blamed Israel. He said that Iraq's problems were caused by an evil "Zionist conspiracy," which was ruining his country's economy. In an attempt to deflect Arab outrage for the attack on his neighbor, he vowed to never pull out of Kuwait until Israel released the West Bank and Gaza to the Palestinians.

Holocaust Denial

Some racists, and racist publications such as *Spotlight,* deny the truth of the Holocaust. These racists believe that the Jews are behind the "Jew World Order," a fact that is hidden by the evil Jews who run the press. Yet Christian conspiracy theorist James Wardner recommends *Spotlight* to his readers who search for "greater truth in news."[13]

These anti-Semitists believe that Hitler never ordered Jews to be murdered but had them placed in labor camps where they could not subvert the war effort as they had in World War I. During war horrible conditions brought widespread disease and malnutrition in these labor camps. The benevolent authorities were left with no choice but to build crematoriums to dispose of the few thousand who died. Cyanide was used to fight the widespread typhus. Besides, their argument goes, by this time most Jews had left Europe for North America or the Middle East.

According to Richard V. Pierard, professor of history at Indiana State University, Holocaust denial should concern Christians greatly:

We must never forget that anti-Semitism has its roots in the theology and practice of the Christian church, from the writings of the church fathers, through the Inquisition, even in the comments of Martin Luther. Moreover, the U.S. government and people did little to help Jews in the years 1933 through 1945. Opinion polls in our "Christian nation" in 1942 found that people disliked Jews more than the German and Japanese enemies. . . . The bottom line is that to deny the Holocaust is to set the preconditions for yet another one. It behooves evangelicals to stand up and utter a forthright no to the "revisionists" and their fellow travelers. The very credibility of our faith is at stake.[14]

After World War II, when evidence of Nazi atrocity had been broadcast throughout the world, thousands of potential war criminals were put on trial to document their duplicity in the systematic genocide. Not one of the thousands who stood trial, who spoke of how they were simply following the orders of superiors and were not aware that their work was part of a larger plan of destruction, ever said that the Nazi-produced Holocaust never happened.

Not one took the stand at Nuremberg and said, as some do now, that the atrocities were actually the fabrication of a "Jew-controlled" media and judicial system. Not one invoked this conspiracy theory in an attempt to avoid jail or save his life. It is a conspiracy theory that was too extreme even for some of history's most notorious racists, who rose to power by trafficking in the tantalizing pornography of conspiracy theories.

The Nation of Islam

Christian conspiracy theorists believe in many of the same conspiracies as radical black supremacist and noted anti-Semite Louis Farrakhan, leader of the Nation of Islam (NOI). When asked, "Do you think that there's a cabal—that there's a central planning group within the Jewish community?" Farrakhan replied, "I do believe that. I believe that there are very, very wise Jews who plan good and there are very wise Jews who plan evil." The one who asked Farrakhan this question wrote, "Within his own lifetime, one of every three Jews on the face of the earth died at the hands of a regime suffused by the same language about nefarious Jewish influence."[15]

This minister of racial politics is not the originator of his faith in black superiority or Jewish conspiracies. Before Farrakhan came fellow black supremacist and conspiracy theorist Malcolm X, who on February 21, 1965, was murdered in the Audubon Ballroom in Harlem. Many, such as

Qubilah Shabazz, who witnessed her father's murder when she was only four, believe that Louis Farrakhan masterminded the assassination after her father publicly criticized Nation of Islam founder Elijah Poole.

Malcolm X, like some who called in to *The Paul Thomas Show,* said Jews own the news media. They "bought Atlantic City and Miami Beach and anything else they wanted. Who owns Hollywood? . . . When there's something worth owning, the Jew's got it."[16] Shortly before his assassination, Malcolm X recanted his racist beliefs, which is also sometimes offered as an explanation for his assassination.

Farrakhan said on *This Week with David Brinkley* (ten days before his Million Man March on Washington, D.C., in October 1995) that Jews were responsible for paying Hitler to turn "poor Jews into soap."[17] While speaking at Harvard, one NOI speaker said that Jews were even responsible for creating a hole in the ozone layer.[18]

Crossover

Why put anti-Semitic conspiracy theorists in the same category as popular, nonracist Christian conspiracy theorists? This was the sentiment of one listener who wrote a letter to KDOV: "I'm sorry to have to write you this letter. Usually, I would much rather be the encourager than the critic. However, I just have to let you know how disappointed I was with the 'News Talk Hour' show this morning with Paul Thomas."

During this show I systematically laid out for my listeners how popular end-times preachers had quoted anti-Semitic authors and sources as proof of a New World Order. I then went on to air my distress that such occurrences did not rally much concern on the part of many Christians who would normally be quick to denounce such acts. But the listener just didn't "see what anti-Semetic [sic] conspiracy theories . . . have to do with people like Don McAlvaney [sic]." The listener then delivered a threat that other listeners would make—that she would not listen to KDOV ever again if I continued to air my concerns about Christian conspiracy theories.

Another listener wrote, "You have just succeeded in airing one of the most disgusting talk shows I have ever heard (secular or non-secular). It was so sickening to me, I can't even comment. I am both embarrassed and ashamed for KDOV airing such a misleading program."

These listeners were reacting to a shocking fact: Christian conspiracy theorists have forged a clear connection between themselves and racist organizations. Unfortunately there are plenty of examples.

It is not surprising that the Nation of Islam's official publication, *Final Call,* recommends two of the Christian conspiracy community's favorite authors: Texe Marrs, whose *Circle of Intrigue* says that the Jewish Rothschild family runs the global Illuminati conspiracy, and A. Ralph Epperson, who wrote *The Unseen Hand* and *The New World Order.* These books are "highly recommended" by Farrakhan.

Pat Robertson's *New World Order* has sold more than half a million copies and supposedly exposes many of the same conspiracies that racist theorists believe. Though Robertson is staunchly pro-Israel, his book demonstrates that racist conspiracy theorists are influencing nonracist Christians. Robertson's bibliography lists a book by racist and anti-Semite Eustace Mullins *(Secrets of the Federal Reserve)* as a reliable source.[19] Mullins is also the author of *Proof of Negro Inferiority,* which "compares Negroes to gorillas," *Who Brought the Slaves to America,* a study "proving" that the Jews "were mainly responsible for the slave trade and bringing the blacks to America," and *The Hitler We Loved and Why,* a pictorial exposé on why Germans loved Der Führer.[20]

Robertson isn't the only Christian author quoting Mullins. James Wardner in his bestselling *The Planned Destruction of America* refers extensively to Mullins as proof that the New World Order is real. For Christians to profess to be pro-Israel and yet recommend Mullins as a reliable source is puzzling. It is even more enigmatic that Mullins thinks that Robertson is a pawn of Jewish control over the media, part of the "Jew World Order."

Chuck Missler has been a guest on KDOV more than once. One time he was brought on the station in an attempt by another talk show host to prove to me that the New World Order conspiracy was the fulfillment of Bible prophecy. Missler gave KDOV listeners sound advice about how to get out of debt and live better, simpler lives. Much of what he said was valuable. Unfortunately he has also served as yet another bridge between the fundamentalist Christian community and the anti-Semitic community.

In the November 1995 issue of his newsletter *Personal UPDATE,* Missler quotes from and expresses thanks to the American Patriot Fax Network and *The Spotlight.* According to a 1995 *Los Angeles Times* investigation, the American Patriot Fax Network supplies and receives information from the following: the "Arizona Patriots, a militant, white supremacist Christian Identity group; Guardians of American Liberty (GOAL), led by Stewart Webb, who from the mid-1980s and into the 1990s 'made a series of threatening anti-Semitic phone calls'; and James Wickstrom, a vehemently anti-Semitic Posse Comitatus leader."[21]

Soldier of Fortune magazine has stated that *Spotlight* habitually prints "misinformation writings, convoluted reasoning and outright fabrications of fact. Any crackpot sighting, no matter how insignificant, *Spotlight* will print it, misidentified photo and all." *Soldier of Fortune* also states that "*Spotlight* slithers around obvious, irrefutable facts to present a lie based on skewed half-truths."[22]

By recommending *Spotlight,* however inadvertently, Missler shows how close today's Christian conspiracy theorists have become with other conspiracy theorists and how important it is for people to reevaluate their devotion to such self-described experts. Without ever asking for it, I received my copy of the anti-Semitic weekly newspaper from a listener who delivered it to our radio station with a kind of religious devotion. Conspiracy theory expert Richard Abanes studied *Spotlight* articles from January 1994 through June 1995. He discovered fifty anti-Israel articles, forty international Jewish banker stories and thirteen stories that denied that the Holocaust occurred.[23]

Abanes asserts that it would be nearly impossible for Missler not to notice such articles. Then he comments, "It is odd that Missler, who professes to be pro-Israel would read *Spotlight,* a publication of a quasi-Nazi Liberty Lobby founded by Willis Carto, whose history of anti-Semitism dates back as far as 1960 when he edited a publication 'calling for voter support for the American Nazi Party.'"[24]

Carto described integration as "'race mongrelization' and the 'niggerfication of America,' while continually decrying 'the power of organized Jewry.'"[25] Carto also started his own publishing company, Noontide Press, to distribute *"The Protocols, Mein Kampf,* and such works as *Anne Frank's Diary—A Hoax."*[26] One of the Carto's goals is to gain support from nonracists such as Missler as a way of fortifying antigovernment forces.

Louis T. Beyers, who used to be an associate of Carto, said, "Willis has talked to me about playing the role of a respectable conservative when his true feelings are those of a racist nationalist." He also says that Carto's ultimate goal is to "form a new power base ready to act when the country turned hard right."[27] To prepare for such a turn, Carto has set up an interesting plan: "To draw the support of those whose political beliefs might not include hatred of Jews, [the Liberty Lobby] has established an array of front groups, surrogates, and publications. These enterprises have not so much expanded the Lobby's influence as made it seem to represent a vast constituency."[28]

Part of this covert jigsaw puzzle is *Spotlight.* In one fundraising letter the Liberty Lobby lists some of the most hated government incidents and agencies to draw support from more than racist conspiracy theorists:

> GATT & NAFTA . . . Waco & . . . Randy Weaver. . . . Foreign troops on American soil . . . the truth about the JFK assassination . . . the drive to abolish the Federal Reserve. . . . Who's out to wreck the Constitution . . . the POW cover-up. . . . The news you need to know appears only in The SPOTLIGHT.

These are the same incidents and concerns that Christian conspiracy theorists are sworn to fight as well.

Missler does not deny quoting *Spotlight.* During a sermon delivered at Calvary Chapel Costa Mesa, California, on February 14, 1997, Missler said that he mistook the publication for another one called *Media Spotlight,* which claims to provide a "Biblical analysis of religious and secular media." He admitted during the sermon that *Spotlight* is an anti-Semitic publication, but he blamed the error on his being in a rush to meet deadline pressure.

Spotlight, a tabloid-sized, black-and-white publication with large photos, is printed on standard newsprint. *Media Spotlight* is also a black-and-white publication, but it is magazine-sized and contains few photos. In addition it is printed on a brighter bookstock paper, providing a cleaner and much whiter appearance. *Spotlight* carries numerous advertisements spread throughout the publication, but *Media Spotlight* has no advertising other than a catalog of books, videos and music located in the center of the publication.

Missler and Robertson are not the only bridges into the racist conspiracy community. Don McAlvany has also quoted *Spotlight* and Eustace Mullins. He recommended Mullins's book *Murder by Injection: The Story of the Medical Conspiracy Against America,* which claims to "bare the bloody secrets of the monopoly sources, drug trusts and insurance scams." *Murder by Injection* is also advertised in the neo-Nazi Sons of Liberty resource catalog as well as in *Criminal Politics,* the vehemently anti-Semitic magazine published by renowned racist Lawrence Patterson.

Christian conspiracy theorist Robert Sessler quotes extensively from Nesta Webster, who in the 1920s wrote a series of bestselling books supposedly exposing the Jewish plan to control the world, which included the French Revolution. She believed that she was the reincarnation of a countess who was executed during the revolution. In 1923 she further revealed her political views by joining the British Fascist Party. Webster cited *The Protocols* in her 1924 book *Secret Societies and Subversive Movements,* ensuring that occultism would continue to be seen as a force in the Jewish plot.[29]

Sessler isn't alone in quoting fascists and anti-Semites. Christian conspiracy theorist and bestselling author Gary Kah quotes Webster extensively in *En Route to Global Occupation.* Fellow Christian conspiracist William Still does the same and includes her in his selected bibliography in *New World Order: The Ancient Plan of Secret Societies.*

Pastor and evangelical author Tim LaHaye learned about the alleged Illuminati conspiracy from the book *Pawns in the Game* by William Guy Carr. This Canadian conspiracy theorist advanced a nonbiblical view of Christ's crucifixion. He wrote that Christ, being omniscient, chose to be born in a stable so that he could mingle with the workers and the sinners and preach to the multitudes. He knew that it was useless to appeal to the ruling classes and those who controlled the teaching of education, politics and religion. He knew that they were controlled by the 'Illuminati,' as they still are today.[30]

According to Carr, "Christ exposed and denounced the Illuminati," and because of this "they plotted his crucifixion and death."[31] Carr was not beyond revising Scripture to give his points some glue. He claimed that when Christ was asked "Who are the Illuminati?" he replied, "By their fruits ye shall know them."[32]

Such a plot must be news to countless evangelicals and fundamentalists who believe that Christ's death showed, among other truths, the sinfulness of all people, not just of an elite and powerful group of fabricated conspirators. Carr represented Christ's life and teachings in purely political terms and made it appear as if God's only Son had the power to overcome sin and death but not enough power to topple the Illuminati. By putting the crucifixion in the political realm, Carr's theory undermined nearly two thousand years of orthodox theology, which evangelicals and fundamentalists claim to defend—except, it seems, when it comes to pet conspiracy theories.

The implications of Carr's conspiracy theories for orthodox theology are disturbing enough to the evangelical and fundamentalist—or at least should be. Even more troubling is Carr's identification of Jews as the leaders of the Illuminati. He wrote that Jewish plotters control history and argued that these Zionists are from the synagogue of Satan.[33] In *Pawns in the Game* Carr argued that Hitler was an innocent victim of the Illuminati-controlled press:

> The anti-German Press speeded up its torrents of abuse against Hitler because he had dared to defy the power of the international Money-Barons. Hitler had earned their hatred by his independent financial policy and monetary reforms. The public was made to believe, *and at that time I was also made to believe,* that Hitler's word couldn't be trusted.[34]

Carr also supported the reliability of *The Protocols*.[35]

During the early 1990s Christian journalists Jon Trott and Mike Hertenstein courageously exposed the fraudulent claims of popular speaker and Christian conspiracy theorist Mike Warnke: "That Christians [such as Warnke] could read Carr and not pick up the decidedly unorthodox plus unfactual flavor of his offering surprised [us]."[36]

Sympathy for Freemen and Other Racists

The Freemen believe that whites are true Israelites, God's chosen people. Since, however, they believe that Eve had intercourse with the serpent in the Garden of Eden, which produced Cain, they see Jews as the seed of Satan. All other races are the "beasts of the fields" as described in Genesis (see chapter four). This is Scripture twisting in the extreme. Yet when the self-described sovereign people in Jordan, Montana, began their standoff with federal officials in the spring of 1996, Christians within the militia movement rushed to their defense in spite of the Freemen's anti-Semitic theology.

Two self-described patriots from southern Oregon took a road trip to Jordan to support their brothers-in-arms. Their decision to go, they said, was made for them: "I think the Lord decided. We were just following our hearts," one said.[37] Former Baptist preacher and militia leader Norman Olson also went to Jordan to lend his support to his fellow conspiracy disciples. There is no report that Olson ever publicly denounced the Freemen's racist theology. But Olson had plenty to say about the federal government, which he claimed was carrying out the same New World Order tactics found at Ruby Ridge and Waco. Olson warned of probable bloodshed if his friends in Jordan were harmed.

One sympathizer, turning a blind eye to the age-old anti-Semitism of the Freemen, argued in a letter to *U.S. News & World Report* that "one of the items the Freemen are accused of doing is really no different than what the Federal Reserve has been doing since 1913. It amazes me that so many people never look beyond the information the main stream media force-feeds us. I very much hope that in time this changes." Another wrote,

The Freemen are no more radical [than] this famous American that had this to say: "This country, with its institutions, belongs to the people who inhabit it. Wherever they shall grow weary of the existing government, they can exercise their constitutional right of amending it, or their revolutionary right to dismember or overthrow it." Abraham Lincoln.

During my interview with Dean Compton, cofounder of the Alliance of Christian Militia, Compton admitted that within the militia movement are devout racists who have used the movement to further their own separate agenda. Yet Compton referred to Bob Fletcher and John Trochmann, founders of the Militia of Montana (MOM), as "decent folks." Trochmann was a featured speaker at an Aryan Nations gathering in 1990. Since then he has tried to distance himself from this community, saying his visits to Aryan Nations were limited. But Aryan Nations founder Richard Butler says that Trochmann visited his compound many times and even helped "us write out a set of rules for our code of conduct on church property." Butler insists that Trochmann even made six or seven trips to the compound for Bible study.[38]

Another Christian conspiracy theorist, Don McAlvany, seeming not to view racism as a grave concern, referred to supremacist Randy Weaver as "a born-again Christian." He admitted, however, that Weaver is "kinda part of the Identity movement and they've got some kind of weirdo ideas about who is Israel and who are the Jews and so forth."[39]

Identity doctrine includes the belief that Jews are the seed of Satan. As a follower of such theology, Randy Weaver believes that a person becomes a "Christian" by means of his or her identity, which is determined by skin color (white) and place of origin (northern Europe or North America). As mentioned in chapter four, Weaver, knowing that his supremacist beliefs do not align with orthodox Christianity, has admitted that he is "not even a Christian."

Over the Edge

Though many aspects of Christian conspiracy theories are troublesome, it was the anti-Semitic portion that pulled me into active opposition one bitter winter morning. As I settled to my desk at the radio station, I noticed atop my stack of mail an interesting publication: *Criminal Politics: The Magazine of Conspiracy Politics Exploring the World's Secret Power Structure*. A long-time listener had left it with a note that said, "If you really want to know what is going on, read it."

Criminal Politics boasts about the same claims to "exclusive" information found in leading Christian conspiracy publications. It professes to expose the same conspiracies—only the names of the alleged conspirators change. In the February 1994 issue, a headline read "Schindler's List—is ZIONIST PROPAGANDA!" Written by *Criminal Politics* contributing editor Hans Schmidt, the article questions Germany's plan to build a Holocaust memorial in Berlin:

> [The] hullabaloo about the Spielberg-Propaganda film "Schindler's List," [has] proven better than anything else why I—we—have to continue to hark on the "Holocaust" tale, and counter (as best we can) the never-ending Jewish lies and allegations against the Germans and the world. . . . What bothers the Holocaustians most is the fact that many or most Americans seem to have lost that certain awe that was always connected with the reminiscences of the "Holocaust survivors." Now, almost suddenly people just don't care less, and a tattoo on the forearm of a former Auschwitz inmate elicits nothing but a yawn. No doubt the Jews have finally overplayed their hand. The concerted campaign connected with "Schindler's List" points to a conspiracy directed against the psyche of the American masses! . . . There is no way that an overlong black and white movie about an event (or non-event) could generate such rave reviews and incredible free publicity, were it not for the power and influence of the Jewish leadership, especially in the media and culture.[40]

This publication blames the New World Order on an international Jewish conspiracy of banking, media and politics. It also claims to be Christian. It refers to Easter as a holiday "honoring the suffering, death and resurrection of our Lord Jesus Christ." It warns, "Let us keep in mind that the war between Christians and Jews started at the persecution and murder of Jesus [which] continues to this very day."[41] That someone would even consider bringing such a publication into a Christian radio station in hopes that it would receive a sympathetic review baffles me.

Conclusion

Ironically, the work of one noted Jewish physician has kept many anti-Semites alive and well. The research of Jonas Edward Salk (1914-1995) on an influenza vaccine led him and his colleagues to develop an inactive vaccine against polio in 1952. After successful wide-scale testing in 1954, the vaccine was distributed nationally, helping to reduce the incidence of the crippling disease.

This Jewish physician has helped anti-Semites the world over live better lives. Perhaps Eustace Mullins, Willis Carto, Louis Farrakhan and others of infamous repute would not have lived to keep anti-Semitism on life support if it weren't for the work of this one Jew. Though Salk helped the children of anti-Semites dodge one of the most debilitating diseases, many anti-Semites believe that Jewish children should not be allowed to live.

Chuck Missler says that his mistake in quoting anti-Semitic sources was just that—a mistake. And even those who have called this error to Missler's attention do not accuse him of being anti-Semitic. They do, however, explore the significance of this mistake.

When Missler and so many other self-professed experts in world affairs and Bible prophecy receive some of their information from ardent anti-Semites, it should cause evangelicals and fundamentalists to question the accuracy of their increasingly conspiratorial world-view. It shows how dangerously similar Christian conspiracy theories are to those harbored by racist conspiracists. The only real difference is that these theorists do not intentionally blame Jews for the world's problems. But they do blame international bankers, which for most of the twentieth century has been an argument designed to incriminate Jews. This fact has been brought to the attention of numerous Christian conspiracy theorists who amass a strong following, but they have yet to amend their message.

Spotlight, the publication Missler has quoted, is the same publication that sold a prepaid phone card to Timothy McVeigh and Terry Nichols. They used this phone card to make calls across the country to various establishments that sold fertilizer, chemicals, explosives, racing fuel, remote-control switches and large plastic drums. These were the components that when mixed by the hands of racist conspiracy theorists—who believe in a New World Order nearly identical to that described in Christian newsletters—created the greatest act of domestic terrorism in U.S. history.

True to the corrosive nature of conspiracy thinking, some anti-Semitism, as well as sympathy for known anti-Semites, has seeped into the Christian conspiracy community. If these self-described experts in world affairs and Bible prophecy so generously quote from anti-Semitic sources, doesn't it stand to reason that the rest of their message should also fall under increased scrutiny? Yet it has been my experience that to even ask such a question within fundamentalist/evangelical end-times circles is to create even more controversy. Some Christians within the end-times conspiracy community seem willing to tolerate some degree of racism in their attempt to fight the larger enemy—the federal government.

But seasoned Christian conspiracy theorists are not likely to believe reports that they have grievously erred. They believe that people associate them with anti-Semitism primarily because of the New World Order's misinformation campaign. This campaign, they argue, is waged through the invective and evil of the "secular press."

6

Big, Monolithic & Anti-Christian

The Media Conspiracy

We the people have had about all we can stand of the twisted, slanted, biased media in America who take their signals from a few private, covert interest groups bent on destroying what's left of the American way. We request that you rely upon your own investigations, steering clear of the media and their rumor-gossip mills of dis-information.
Bob Fletcher, Militia of Montana

After finding out about the establishment's control of mass communication, I was even more appalled, but now, at least, I understand why I hadn't learned about the conspiracy any earlier. The Rockefellers controlled every facet of the information industry.
Christian conspiracy theorist Gary Kah

People need to question and analyze what they hear, and ponder the motivations of those spreading the propaganda. The truth lies deeper.
Timothy McVeigh's letter to the editor

The Christian conspiracy community believes that more people would heed their concerns were it not for the deceptive control of the information industry. The media, they argue, will not reveal the true nature of domestic or international affairs, which are designed to usher in the New World Order. They do not believe that the media occasionally get a story wrong. Even the reports written by Christian journalists are intentionally deceptive, they say, so people must look to the conspiracy community alone to know what is *really* happening in the world. It is this belief that has led to the rise in the number of militia-produced newsletters and catalogs, antigovernment Web sites and patriot talk shows.

Media Blackout

Christian conspiracy theorist James W. Wardner has a name for this alleged refusal to report the real story behind international affairs: "media blackout." The Council on Foreign Relations (CFR), he says, "owns Congress and the media."[1] (Christian conspiracy theorists believe that the CFR is part of an anti-Christian socialist conspiracy to usher in Satan's New World Order.) As proof Wardner includes in his book a list of publishers who are supposedly part of the conspiracy. The list includes Macmillan, Simon & Schuster, Random House, and Harper & Row. But this is an impossible accusation to support, given the content of some of these publishers' books.

Macmillan publishes many of the works of C. S. Lewis. Harper & Row, which was part of what is now HarperCollins, published Paul Johnson's *Intellectuals,* a scathing critique of liberal or socialistic thinkers, including Karl Marx (one of the supposed conspirators), Jean-Jacques Rousseau, Bertrand Russell, Bertold Brecht, Norman Mailer and Lillian Hellman. HarperCollins published *Hollywood vs. America,* an incriminating review of Hollywood by movie critic Michael Medved. This Jewish conservative fills in for Rush Limbaugh on his radio show from time to time and is critical of the liberal views expressed in Hollywood. Simon & Schuster published *The Book of Jesus: A Treasury of the Greatest Stories and Writings About Christ.* Edited by Calvin Miller, professor at Southwest Baptist Theological Seminary, the work includes the writings of Max Lucado, Billy Graham, Martin Luther, Elisabeth Elliot and T. S. Eliot.

Wardner says that textbooks from these publishers sew the CFR's secret "philosophies into the fabric of our nation's children and college students as well." He receives this information from fellow conspiracy theorist Gary Kah: "After finding out about the establishment's control of mass communication, I was even more appalled, but now, at least, I understand why I hadn't learned about the conspiracy any earlier. The Rockefellers controlled every facet of the information industry."[2] Yet as chapter four demonstrated, Kah quotes extensively from anti-Semitic sources. Also, if the Rockefellers have so much control, why would they allow for the explosive growth of the World Wide Web, the medium to which the militia owes so much?

Media Cover-ups

Don McAlvany often accuses the press of aiding the New World Order conspiracy, yet he quotes major news magazines as proof of the New World Order's increased government surveillance. For example, he writes that dozens "of different government agencies maintain millions of records on the America public. Articles about these records have been published in *Newsweek* and *Time.*" McAlvany, like many Christian conspiracy theorists, wants it both ways. On the one hand he dismisses the mainstream press as propagandists of the New World Order. On the other hand, when the press prints information that supposedly proves the existence of a widespread conspiracy, he is quick to accept the information without question. The troubling inconsistency is this: if the press were conspiring against Americans, why would it print proof of the conspiracy?

Christian conspiracy disciples who called in to *The Paul Thomas Show* also revealed similar inconsistencies. Some read the *Wall Street Journal* religiously every business day, yet the *Wall Street Journal* has editors on the Council on Foreign Relations. These disciples were aware of that membership, but for some reason they did not find the discrepancy worthy of their concern.

McAlvany's sweeping claims have been challenged by some within the Christian community. One is Richard Abanes, who has written a compelling book about rebellion, racism and religion within American militias that are saturated with conspiracy theories. While obtaining information for his book, he decided to research one of the numerous claims made by this leader within the church.

McAlvany claims in his newsletters that "SWAT teams from several Idaho police departments participated in a practice raid on the Community Presbyterian Church in Post Falls. Captain Travis Chaney of the Kootenai County sheriff's department said the SWAT teams' goal is 'to provide a controlled, measured response to critical incidents . . . to successfully resolve threats to public safety.'" McAlvany then asks, "Why would a SWAT team practice a forced armed entry of a *church?* Are Bible believers a 'threat to public safety'?"[3]

Abanes called the church to verify the report. According to Jennifer

Chapman, the church had donated its old building to the police. "It had become vacant and condemned" after the congregation moved into a new house of worship. Chapman said, "There was nothing anti-Christian about it, or anything at all bad. . . . They were just going to tear the building down, so we let [the police] have it to practice raids in and train their dogs to search for drugs. There's *nothing* to it."[4]

Given their loyalty to McAlvany, it is doubtful that Christian conspiracy theorists took the time to check out this or any other assertion. As one former conspiracy disciple said on *The Paul Thomas Show,* "These people claim to be Christian. I didn't think they could be wrong."

If the media have for decades been part of a one-world global conspiracy, then Christian conspiracy theorists must find it difficult to explain away William Randolph Hearst (1863-1951). Perhaps the most powerful member of the media of his time, he built the nation's largest chain of newspapers. Born in San Francisco, he took over his father's newspaper, the *San Francisco Examiner.* By 1927 he controlled a chain of twenty-five newspapers published in major cities across the United States. He also produced newsreels and feature films.

He exerted so much influence on America's public opinion that reports in his newspapers of Spanish atrocities in Cuba helped lead to the Spanish-American War in 1898. Yet Hearst was a staunch isolationist, especially during World War I. He despised Newton Baker, Woodrow Wilson's secretary of war, who wanted America to join the League of Nations.[5] Yet the Christian conspiracy community argues that the League of Nations was one of many New World Order organizations controlled by satanic forces to pave the way to a world government—all with the help of the "evil secular media," led for many decades by Hearst.

U.N.-Media Connection

Callers to *The Paul Thomas Show* have often repeated the belief that the press has done the bidding of the United Nations in an ever-expanding attempt to usher in the New World Order. It was only a matter of time before politicians prone to conspiracy thinking joined in. Talk of a media/United Nations conspiracy entered the political mainstream with the help of beleaguered Republican Representative Wes Cooley from Oregon.

Representing the Second Congressional District, Cooley found himself embroiled in controversy about false statements he made in the *Oregon Voters Pamphlet,* as well as on the campaign trail. The press, especially the *Oregonian* newspaper, ran a series of articles that helped cause many true-blue Republicans to call for his resignation, but Cooley dug in. In a speech given in La Grande, Oregon, in July 1996, Cooley went on the offensive, saying that the real reason the press criticized him was because it was part of a one-world conspiracy: "There's a movement to make this a UN country, and the press is part of that."[6]

Chris Williamson, political reporter for KTVL television in Medford, heard Cooley's accusation. "Cooley was in attack mode, railing off a list of attacks against the media. He stunned me. How does he know what I think about the New World Order and American sovereignty?" Williamson admits that most people in the media fall on the liberal end of the political spectrum, but he does not believe this necessarily means that their stories are slanted. He speaks for many in the media who are accused of aiding nefarious conspiracies: "When I go to Rotary, I put my hand over my heart and pledge allegiance to the flag. We have the best political system in the world. I do not want to destroy it."[7]

Cooley pled no contest and was convicted in March 1997 for his false statements in the *Voters Pamphlet.* Yet conspiracy theorists believe that this conviction and the pressure against Cooley to step down were part of a greater conspiracy on the part of the media, Newt Gingrich and Republican Representative Bob Smith, who replaced Cooley. Writes conspiracy theorist Gary Wean, "The newspapers and TV programs throughout the state of Oregon constantly were full of lies and innuendoes against Cooley every minute of the day, every day of the week for months."[8]

Conspiracy theorist and self-professed militia leader Linda Thompson also believes that the media are government controlled. She came to such a conclusion after realizing that most progovernment articles, especially from the Associated Press, have no byline. "Every time there's a piece of government propaganda, it comes across the wire services with no author on it."[9]

I have sold stories to the Associated Press, and contrary to Thompson's accusation, my name has appeared on most of them. But the name is often irrelevant to many of the stories that come across the "wire." Editors will often drop the name of the writer if the story is small, if the name is irrelevant to the overall story or if the information is of common knowledge and does not justify attribution.

David Aikman

If the press is part of a global conspiracy, what does the Christian conspiracy community do with a man such as David Aikman, a senior correspondent for *Time?* Aikman has formed a fellowship for Christian journalists nationwide and is a member of a charismatic Episcopal church in Fairfax, Virginia. He has reported from Vietnam, China's Tiananmen Square, the Persian Gulf and hot spots throughout the Middle East. He has also provided extensive coverage of the Soviet Union.

Aikman was once a guest on *The Paul Thomas Show* for two days. Topics included his book *When the Almond Tree Blossoms,* his work with Prison Fellowship and the belief among Christian conspiracy theorists that the Soviet Union never fell. Aikman, who is not a member of the Council on Foreign Relations, says that most Russians would be astounded at the news that the Soviet Union never fell. "A lot of people long for the 'law-and-order' days of the old Soviet Union. But they're gone for good," he said.

In fact, the Russians propagated conspiracy theories about the West, which made it extremely difficult for Russian spin-doctors to explain the fall of a U.S. president. They had a great deal of trouble explaining how President Nixon was driven out of office: "Here was the man who supported détente, he was anti-Communist, and all of a sudden he was under pressure to resign." The Soviets then created an improved conspiracy theory. "They said twenty-three major American corporations that were anti-Nixon ganged up and kicked [out] Nixon" by means of their control of Congress and the media.

Conspiracy theorists argue that as part of the media conspiracy against them, officials at bureau headquarters alter fair and honest stories submitted by reporters who may not be part of the conspiracy. They say that the evil New World Order editors change the story in order to keep the conspiracy hidden. I asked Aikman if any of his stories were ever dramatically changed by *Time* editors. He said no journalist would tolerate such abuse of his or her stories. If such a thing did happen, a reporter would be furious and blow the whistle. "I have found some Christian leaders making absolutely outrageous statements about the media. . . . It's inconceivable that any conspiracy can be so superbly organized that hundreds, perhaps thousands of [journalists] are sworn to secrecy and wouldn't even tell their neighbors. It is as lunatic as the paranoia of the left," as seen in Oliver Stone's movie *JFK*.

Aikman has interviewed CIA officers in the United States and overseas, as well as people in the State Department. "Believe me, it's almost impossible for people to keep secrets. There are very, very few secrets that ever last for more than a few years. The only secrets I know that have been well kept are military ones because military people are better disciplined."

Aikman says that a journalist would skyrocket to stardom if he or she could prove even part of the alleged conspiracy. "I know a lot of people in news organizations who are profit-minded. They couldn't care less who was behind a conspiracy"; they would expose it.

Aikman knows Christians who believe that the CFR controls world events. "I've met members of the Council on Foreign Relations. They can't even control their neighborhood watch committee, much less another country. The real world is a very complicated place. Things happen that even the most brilliant people can't predict. Who would have predicted the fall of the shah of Iran or the sudden collapse of the Soviet Union?"

People who oppose end-times conspiracy theories find themselves accused of being part of the conspiracy. Aikman calls this "ecclesiastical McCarthyism." Sigmund Freud used a similar line of attack: when people adamantly disagreed with his psychoanalysis, Freud shot back that those who disagreed with him were in most need of help. Likewise, when those in the press refute Christian conspiracy theories, they are quickly labeled as coconspirators. After my interview with Aikman, a conspiracy disciple called him a "quack" and said that Aikman was indeed part of the media conspiracy.

Media Bias Against Christians?

Christians have varying viewpoints regarding how the press treats the church and issues of faith. Many evangelicals and fundamentalists believe that the press often maligns them, so they are somewhat sympathetic to rhetoric about a media conspiracy. Yet Christian journalists such as Aikman and others disagree.

Freelance writer Carey Kinsolving graduated from divinity school in 1989, then went straight into journalism. "Most Christians see the media as big, monolithic and anti-Christian—and that's not true," he says.[10] Peggy Wehmeyer, religion reporter at ABC, was handpicked by news anchor Peter Jennings. Wehmeyer has portrayed Christian faith in America as it is: strong, complex, imperfect, real. Wehmeyer says that Jennings has "been pushing the networks to take religion more seriously and cover it as news."[11]

Granted, the popular press has clearly shown ignorance of Christianity. *Bridging the Gap: Religion and the Media,* a report sponsored by Vanderbilt University, reveals that both the media and religion foster unhealthy distrust and even fear of each other. It concludes, however, that there is "more ignorance than bias" in the average newsroom.[12]

Charisma magazine talked with Christian journalists across America who work in mainstream media:

> From CNN correspondent Craig Heaps, who's also a San Francisco TV-anchor, to Hal Wingo, a Southern Baptist in New York who is an assistant managing editor at *People* magazine, nearly all the Christian journalists interviewed agreed there is no organized "conspiracy" against Christianity within the industry.[13]

I am a graduate from a school of journalism. I was the editor of my school's only conservative publication, the *Oregon Commentator.* During my senior year at the University of Oregon, the committee that controlled our funding, led by members of the Gay and Lesbian Alliance (GALA), took away my publication's funding because of its conservative editorial content. There was a storm of protest among the student body and in the school's daily paper, *The Oregon Daily Emerald.* The committee that took our funding away reversed their decision two days later, failing to give an adequate explanation for their reversal. The committee's original decision was a clear incident of political correctness, a problem that has plagued other university campuses.

I know that my experience of prejudice was not as profound as that of racial minorities who have experienced the deep and humiliating pains that come from discrimination. But for those two days and the following months, I did feel a particular pain, anger and humiliation that makes a person either stronger or bitter. You cannot remain indifferent toward something so powerful.

While all this controversy was swirling in my head, the dean of the journalism school called me into his office. Fresh in my mind were the death threats I had received from anonymous, angry and sometimes hysterical men. I had been compared to a Nazi in the school's paper. A roommate of mine was criticized for sharing the same roof. One fellow journalism student, once she recognized me, got up and moved across the room for fear of being seen with me. Staff members would later quit the publication.

Needless to say, I was not at my best. I was in great turmoil, though I tried not to show it. The wind was knocked out of me. Though I never told anyone, I was making plans to forget it all and move back home. If he had wanted to, the dean of this liberal school of journalism could have dealt me the final blow, but he didn't. This man, who I later learned supported the ACLU, told me to keep up the fight. He said that I was talented and encouraged me to persevere. It was a defining moment for me. Though we were worlds apart politically, he did his job of nurturing another student of journalism, even one of the most conservative students in the program.

It is bewildering to me how such an experience fits into the CFR's secret philosophy for our nation's "college students." If the dean of my school of journalism, as Wardner argues, was part of this anticonservative conspiracy, he did exactly the opposite of what he should have done. When I hear people say that journalists are liberal and that sometimes this bias shows in their reporting, I agree with that criticism. I have even heard liberal journalists admit as much. But it is another issue when one contends that leaders in the world of information dissemination are part of a century-old satanic conspiracy designed to murder those who disagree with them.

As a former editor of a weekly newspaper and a freelance writer for a daily newspaper, I am familiar with the secular perspective in newsrooms. They are one of the most sober places in which to work. As in a library, laughter is uncommon. Many journalists think deeply about life and do not settle for simplistic, easy answers. They work long hours and receive little thanks either from their bosses or from their community. Large egos are common, especially among those who contribute to the editorial page. Many have received their degrees from universities that, as Henry David Thoreau observed, laugh at the old but follow religiously the new. These universities have infused in them major tenets of liberalism, which include a potent distrust of traditional religions and "heartless" conservatism in general.

These universities have also taught students to put their faith in relativism—that moral decisions should be based not on absolute truth but on what is considered appropriate at a particular time and place. Thus many embraced a relativistic philosophy, though later, as adults or parents, they have experienced mental turmoil.

Journalists also attend meetings and join groups that give the impression of bias, which is also a legitimate beef among their critics. That is why some newsrooms have both written and unwritten policies that reporters and editors should not give money to political organizations. Smart editors do not join politically charged organizations, whether they be on the left or right. When journalists attend secretive retreats, such as the Renaissance Weekend attended by President Clinton, and take an oath that they will not report what they see and hear, it does smack of special interest and perhaps even conspiracy. It gives the strong impression of being in President Clinton's camp. Journalists should avoid such associations. In light of rising conspiracy paranoia in America, responsible journalists should reject such invitations.

There is a secular perspective within journalism, and a conservative journalist, especially one whose conservatism comes from religious conviction, is in the minority. According to Yale law professor Stephen Carter, this secular perspective saturates much of society. America's "culture of disbelief," a term coined by Carter and chosen for the title of his book, assumes that "no one of learning or sophistication could possibly be a religious believer."[14] Worse, the media, among others, hand out social penalties to those who express religious beliefs in a secular setting.[15]

When I told one news editor that I would be reporting for a conservative radio station, he told me, "That's good. Your ideas would fit in better there." One of these ideas was my opposition to abortion on demand in most cases. Opposition to abortion on demand is slightly tolerated when derived from ethical, practical, sociological or medical considerations. "But should someone stand up and oppose abortion for reasons of faith, he is accused of trying to impose his religious beliefs on others. Call on Timothy Leary or Chairman Mao, fine. Call on St. Paul, and all hell breaks loose."[16] Writes Charles Krauthammer in an essay for *Time:*

> Oddly, though, in our thoroughly secularized culture, there is one form of religious intolerance that does survive. And that is the disdain bordering on contempt of the culture makers for the deeply religious, i.e., those for whom religion is not a preference but a conviction.[17]

An example of the media's skepticism (which some might label disdain) for religious conviction comes from its response, or more accurately its lack of response, when presidential aide Sidney Blumenthal labeled Whitewater prosecutor Hickman Ewing a "religious fanatic." Ewing's "fanaticism" included daily prayer, membership in a fundamentalist church, and a sincere belief in God. The media's response to this brazen religious bigotry? "The question of Ewing's alleged fanaticism so pricked the interest of *The New York Times,* zeitgeist arbiter of the Establishment, that it dispatched a reporter to investigate. The result was hilarious: a classic of condescension posing as judiciousness."[18]

As part of its investigation into Ewing's religious convictions, the *Times* pointed out that Ewing's 1980 law-review article "Combatting Official Corruption by All Available Means" began with an Old Testament quotation. Writes Krauthammer, "The horror! By that standard Martin Luther King was not just a fanatic but a raving zealot."[19] Ewing's peers defend him, saying that when he enters his office, he leaves his Christian faith at the door. To which Krauthammer warns:

We've come a long way in America. After two centuries, it seems we finally do have a religious test for office. True religiosity is disqualifying. Well, not quite. Believers may serve—but only if they check their belief at the office door.

Believe in something, and beware. You may not warrant presidential-level attack, but you'll make yourself suspect should you dare enter the naked public square.

For a profession that prides itself on objectivity, journalism has a long way to go. Some yell that this is a conspiracy, but as the dictionary defines it, there is a world of difference between perspective and conspiracy.

Filling in the Media's Gaps

Dick Reavis, an investigative journalist from Texas who quit his job with the *Dallas Observer,* wrote perhaps the most important book about the tragedy at Waco. Reavis testified during the congressional hearings, leveling significant and damaging charges against some federal agencies. He also testified in the trial against Timothy McVeigh, helping to expose McVeigh's antigovernment conspiracy theories.

In *The Ashes of Waco: An Investigation,* Reavis complained about the lack of interest among journalists in the Waco tragedy. "It was incredible. The most amazing thing about this was I had no competition. Everyone said, 'Reavis is crazy. He's off pursuing a dead subject.' Nobody cared about it anymore."[20] Reavis carried on, unearthing many important facts about Waco, facts that would later put the FBI and ATF on the hot seat. Yet according to Christian conspiracy theorists, the press is part of the New World Order. If so, it should have hidden the mistakes made at Waco.

Data, information or news? Because information that disagrees with theirs is labeled part of the conspiracy, the Christian conspiracy community has formed its own media, primarily through the Internet. But as Clifford Stoll asks, are they getting information or data?

This information highway is actually delivering a fountain of data. We're drowning in data—which is different from information. Information has context, content, utility, timeliness, accuracy. It has a pedigree—you know who wrote it. Information has value. Data doesn't. Classically, we've had people who filtered information—reporters and editors. That's what the Internet is missing. People who will filter out the chaff.[21]

Conspiracy theories disguised as news have floated in cyberspace for years. It was only a matter of time before some seasoned newsman got taken for a ride on the information highway. As mentioned earlier, this is what happened with long-time ABC news correspondent Pierre Salinger, who said that he had evidence that friendly fire, a U.S. missile, destroyed TWA flight 800.

Another disturbing example of an Internet conspiracy theory that made its way into the popular press was a story run by the *San Jose Mercury News* in October 1996. The paper released information gleaned from the Web that the CIA had sanctioned cocaine sales and launched a crack epidemic by supporting Nicaraguan drug dealers whose profits went to the Contras. Though the paper later admitted that the story "Dark Alliance" was "significantly flawed,"[22] Rep. Maxine Waters convened a town meeting in south-central Los Angeles. She and her fellow African-Americans were outraged by the news and grilled CIA representatives, such as director John Deutch, on live television.

This further fueled African-American conspiracy theories. Jewelle Taylor Gibbs, a University of California Berkeley professor, said, "Black-oriented talk-radio shows are rife with conspiracy stuff."[23] (For more about African-American conspiracy theories, see chapter seven.) The Web allowed the story to bypass the mainstream media and enter the national debate, a unique position that many African-Americans and their supporters utilized. For example, *Final Call Online,* the journal of Louis Farrakhan's Nation of Islam, created an Internet link between the article and a short commentary entitled "The CIA Drug Pipeline: How the U.S. Government Spread Cocaine in the Black Ghetto."[24] *Slate* magazine's Karenna Gore wrote, "Not only has it allowed the series to leapfrog the mainstream press, but it has also made the mainstream press as much the enemy as the CIA."[25]

The question of footnotes. Christian conspiracy theorists often begin with verifiable facts. It's the life-after-the-fact that causes many problems. For example, with the secrecy of the Masonic brotherhood comes the possibility, if not probability, that insider deals will be cut. Writes Richard Hofstadter, "There *was* something to be said for the anti-Masons. After all, a secret society composed of influential men bound by special obligations could conceivably pose some kind of threat to the civil order in which they were suspended."[26] The typical procedure of those who attempt to exhaustively document a conspiracy is to start with "defensible assumptions and with a careful accumulation of facts, or at least of what appear to be facts, and to marshal these facts toward an overwhelming 'proof' of that particular conspiracy that is to be established."[27]

It is an aggressive effort that leaves little room for mistakes, failures or ambiguities. For example, *The Politician,* written by Robert H. Welch Jr., founder of the John Birch Society, includes a hundred pages of bibliography and notes that purport that President Eisenhower was a treasonous communist. (Many ardent Christian conspiracy theorists receive a substantial number of their theories from the John Birch Society. They would be shocked if they knew Welch's liberal religious beliefs—so shocked they might accuse him of being part of a New Age conspiracy.)

Welch, a retired candy manufacturer, attended a Unitarian church and believed in evolution: "In *The Blue Book of the John Birch Society,* he described his beliefs in a way that sounded very much like deism."[28] The "Divine Being," he wrote, created laws and purposes that "caused planets like our Earth to develop; and by creating evolutionary forces." He wrote that communism was a threat to those who adhere to the "great religions of the world," which includes Catholics, Jews, Muslims and Buddhists.[29] (But some Christian conspiracy theorists believe that Catholics are part of the communist/Marxist/New World Order conspiracy.)

Careful documentation is a virtue, not a vice. But what distinguishes the documentation of conspiracy theorists from others is the "curious leap in imagination that is always made at some critical point in the recital of events."[30] For example, Robison's writing about the Illuminati more than a century and a half ago is filled with pages of details about the history of the Illuminati. "Then, suddenly, the French Revolution has taken place, and the Illuminati have brought it about. What is missing is not veracious information about the organization, but sensible judgment about what can cause a revolution."[31]

Consumer beware. Often during *The Paul Thomas Show* I have warned listeners that with the "liberation" of information from established news entities comes the responsibility of every news gatherer to become a more sophisticated consumer of information, as well as a disseminator of important news. Who provides the information is as important as the information itself. With the popularity of the Internet also comes the problem of instant experts—people who write with charismatic certainty but without credentials or any formal training in information gathering or in-depth knowledge about the topic they expound upon.

A person does not need to be a graduate of a school of journalism to disseminate information, but some formal training is in order. A responsible journalist is better off learning the basics in the classroom than after his or her faulty story appears on page one. Reporting the facts as they appear at the time is serious business. There is a pecking order within journalism, and it is an important one that helps ensure quality and content documentation:

> The Net is a means of communication, not a news service. Everybody who's spent five minutes there knows it's full of self-indulgent rantings, junior-high school feuding—and porno. Just because something's on the Net doesn't give it gravitas. . . . With so much information out there today, people have to know whom to trust. For better or worse, this trust still resides in some TV news organizations and a handful of newspapers and magazines.[32]

High-tech attorney Michael Godwin concludes: "You have to be your own editor. That's called being an adult in an information society."[33]

Conclusion
Contrary to what the Christian conspiracy community believes, the reason

people do not accept their theories is not an "evil secular media" conspiracy. Even Christian journalists find their arguments unbelievable and alarming.

With the explosion of cable television has come a diversity of opinions from news and talk programs that further weakens the "media conspiracy" argument. I have been accused many times of aiding and abetting some sort of cover-up because of a story or editorial I had written. Some of these accusations have come from the Christian community. But an end-times media conspiracy theory creates troubling consequences.

Because conspiracy disciples believe that the established press is part of an overall plan designed to brainwash them into the New World Order, they wade deeper and deeper into a world thick with paranoia and fear, two of the most potent byproducts of conspiracy thinking. Since sources of information that disagree with their view of the world are part of the conspiracy, stopping such a slide becomes increasingly difficult. Given such a powerful belief, people who attempt to pull loved ones from the Christian conspiracy community find themselves in an uphill and seemingly never-ending battle. Those who try to extract loved ones from extreme religious groups express the very same complaint (see chapter nine for a detailed explanation).

As a school of journalism graduate, a former editor of a weekly newspaper and a former news and program director of a Christian radio station, I have seen how a secular perspective influences the thinking of many within journalism. This secular perspective, which relegates most things religious to the bottom of the newsroom totem poll, is hypocritical and disturbing. But such a perspective does not equal a masterful conspiracy among the nation's elite. It is not a signpost of the end times, no matter how many times Christian conspiracy theorists say it is. As journalists such as Peter Jennings realize, it is simply one more area within our culture in need of reform.

7

Conspiracies from Both Right & Left

The only conspiracy I'm part of is getting Bill Clinton out of the White House.
**Republican presidential candidate Robert Dole,
Medford, Oregon, 1996**

The Truth Is Out There.
Ending credits of *The X-Files*

Some Christian conspiracy theorists might be shocked to find that many of their beliefs, such as a media conspiracy, are shared by others across the political spectrum—even among the groups that they believe are part of the conspiracy, such as radical environmentalists and others on the far left. Americans of all stripes are intrigued and sympathetic toward conspiracy theories.

Hollywood and television have mass-marketed these theories in blockbuster movies such as *Independence Day,* the seventh highest grossing movie ever, and Chris Carter's foreboding *The X-Files.* One ambitious *X-Files* episode claims that a government cell was responsible for the assassinations of John F. Kennedy and Martin Luther King Jr., among others. In the movie aptly titled *Conspiracy Theory,* Mel Gibson plays a cabdriver who finds out that one of his conspiracy theories is actually true.

Oliver Stone need not be sitting in the director's chair, for others in Hollywood have tapped into America's chic fascination with these multifaceted and politically divergent theories. Journalist Jeffrey Toobin lambastes the motive for this: "For Hollywood (and not just Oliver Stone), few story ideas are as unsexy as a single criminal acting alone. Conspiracies provide zingier plot points and splashier action sequences."[1]

In 1996 America Online (AOL) launched ParaScope, a Web site for conspiracy theorists. A poll taken in 1994—the twenty-fifth anniversary of the Apollo moon landing—revealed that twenty million Americans believe it possible that the moon walk was a Hollywood-style, special-effects hoax held in an Arizona desert to benefit NASA contractors. According to a 1997 CNN/Time poll, 80 percent of Americans believe that the federal government is hiding knowledge of the existence of extraterrestrial life.[2]

When Princess Diana's death made headlines around the world, some journalists and other writers argued that British and other Western intelligence agencies conspired to murder her and boyfriend Dodi Fayed. According to conspiracy theorists from Egypt, the home of Fayed, the British "Palace would never allow Diana to marry a Muslim, convert to Islam and bear Muslim children who would be brothers to the future King of England."[3] They believe that the queen of England gave "orders to terminate their relationship."[4]

As these examples reveal, conspiracy theories are not the sole property of conservative Christians or the far right. They are shared by numerous people across the political and racial spectrum, including some African-American leaders who believe that their opponents are plotting their demise. This rise in conspiracy thinking was predicted in the 1960s with the release of *The Paranoid Style in American Politics* by the late Columbia University historian Richard Hofstadter.

Hofstadter wrote that the conspiratorial mind "is manifest on the extreme right wing, who believe that we have lived for a generation in the grip of a vast conspiracy. But this is not a style of mind confined to the right wing. With modulations and differences, it exists today, as it has in the past, on the left."[5] This rise in conspiracy thinking may have been foreseen as early as the late-nineteenth century. Ironically, groups that traditionally held each other in contempt have formed peculiar allegiances born from their fellowship in conspiracy.

The Political Right

Though most Christian conspiracy theorists are from the right and beyond, some believe that the Grand Old Party and its political victories are also part of the grand conspiracy. Political pundits, voters and even President Clinton were stunned by the extent of the "Republican Earthquake" on November 8, 1994. Republicans won a majority of seats in both houses of Congress for the first time in more than forty years.

But just one day after the landslide, KDOV received passionate phone calls during its morning talk show claiming that Republican Representative Newt Gingrich, who became Speaker of the House, was a member of the CFR and that this change in political power was just another step toward the New World Order. Christian conspiracy theorist Ken Klein put it this way in his *Storm Warning* newsletter:

> Many throughout the land are hailing the most recent turn of events with the unprecedented vote for a new Republican Congress as a political Christmas present. The euphoria that has swept many sectors of the country has been embraced as though this Congress is the answer to our country's greatest dilemmas. . . . Not wanting to be a political scrooge, I am reluctant to say this—but, NOT SO FAST! The fundamentals have not changed. Let's not get deceived.[6]

Fueling the Christian conspiracy community's anger toward the GOP was the storm that brewed with the continued discussion of the General Agreement on Tariffs and Trade (GATT) during the special session of Congress called by President Clinton before the general election. The U.S. reached the GATT trade settlement in Geneva through the European Community. Such a decision became a kind of end-times catnip to the Christian conspiracy community. Some said it would be the beginning of the Great Tribulation because the European Community is supposed to be the revived Roman Empire—launching pad of the antichrist.

But conspiracy theorists weren't the only people opposed to GATT and its cousin, the North American Free Trade Agreement (NAFTA). Democrats, including Montana Senator Max Baucus and Oregon Representative Peter DeFazio, denounced them as well. Opponents argued that America would trade its independence for lower tariffs. Only America's CEOs, they said, would benefit. They believed that the agreements would hurt an already hemorrhaging American job market, reducing America's status to the level of nations that employ child labor.

Majority Leader Robert Dole held his tongue on the issue for weeks. He later came out in support of GATT after reportedly cutting a deal with President Clinton. Dole pushed for an independent council to monitor American economic interests in the World Trade Organization if GATT passed. If Americans suffered, he said, America could withdraw its support for the 123-country treaty.

I asked Bob Dole when he was running for president in 1996 if he was aware of the claim that he was part of the New World Order conspiracy, given his support for GATT and NAFTA. Dole was taken aback by the question and wasn't quite sure how to handle it. He said he received the same accusation during the 1988 campaign. "I'm not a member of the Council on Foreign Relations," he said. Dole described GATT as a necessary risk in order to sustain America's standard of living, saying that he wasn't fully supportive of GATT, but America must be aggressive toward international trade if it is to retain a strong economy. He said if GATT did not foster our interests, then America could "get out of the agreement." He concluded, "The only conspiracy I'm part of is getting Bill Clinton out of the White House."

To Klein and many other doomsayers, the GOP's willingness to support international trade agreements is proof enough that party leaders are part of an evil international conspiracy. But what if member nations, such as the U.S. and Japan, who have continually voiced their concerns about the agreement, pull out? It is not as if trade agreements were etched in stone, handed down from God on Mount Sinai. They have been broken in the past, and there is no assurance that they will not be broken in the future. What will the Christian conspiracy community say? It's unlikely that they will recant their accusations. Instead, they will probably say that such a reversal is yet another ploy designed by the one-worlders to divert their critics.

Rush Limbaugh. Klein, like many conspiracy preachers, believes that the die has been cast in favor of the evil conspirators, just as the Bible predicts. He and other staunch Christian conspiracists believe that it is fruitless, even ridiculous, to try to improve our culture through civic activity and other political involvement. So it is not surprising that during one of his seminars in southern Oregon Klein often criticized Rush Limbaugh. He said that the Christian community should not listen to this man, for Limbaugh does not see the world spiritually—which is to say, the same way Klein sees it.

Fellow conspiracist Texe Marrs asserts that Limbaugh is a "draft dodger who has sold out to political big wigs."[7] John McManus of the John Birch Society also believes that Limbaugh, as well as William Bennett, is part of the New World Order conspiracy.

Perhaps another (if not the main) reason Klein and his colleagues attack Limbaugh is that the popular conservative talk-show host denounces damaging and irresponsible conspiracy theories. He even received threatening e-mail when he voiced his concerns about Pat Buchanan, the Christian conspiracy community's choice for president in 1996. Limbaugh is perhaps one of America's most influential and passionate opponents of irresponsible conspiracy theories, and the Christian conspiracy community knows that Limbaugh has the ear of numerous conservative evangelicals who might otherwise believe their end-times conspiracy theories and buy them in tape, newsletter or book form. Limbaugh's opposition to these theories includes a humorous "kook test," which he uses to discover if a person's opposition to various government decisions stems from commonsense concern or from overblown conspiracy theories.

Richard Nixon. Conspiracist William T. Still also believes that Republicans, as much as any other political party, are behind the conspiracy. He claims that he received a secret memo that outlines the conspiracy devised by Richard Nixon, called the "October 1973 Nixon Coup":

> On about October 15, 1973, I was given a memorandum by my father, Lt. Col. William T. Still, a retired Air Force Officer. . . . On October 3, 1973, he was approached by an acquaintance, Joe Josephson, who claimed he had connections with the White House of President Richard M. Nixon. This acquaintance asked my father how he and his military friends would feel about a military takeover of the U.S. government.[8]

Though the actual "secret memo" never appears in the book as proof, Still says that it reads as follows:

A committee exists which is dedicated to the repeal of the 22nd Amendment to the Constitution. Its goal is to place Mr. Nixon in the White House for a third term. . . . [A] second committee is dedicated to keeping Mr. Nixon in office by any means: —INCLUDING A MILITARY COUP BY HIGH RANKING OFFICERS![9]

Still ponders why the president would consider such a "drastic action, if, indeed he did." He concludes:

The only logical alternative is very complex and requires an entire book to explain. In a nutshell, President Nixon was probably used and when proven no longer useful, discarded by the same group who brought us the American, French, and Russian revolutions in the eighteenth and twentieth centuries, and the World Wars, the United Nations, the Korean War, and Vietnam in the twentieth century.[10]

The accusation that Nixon is part of the New World Order conspiracy is baffling. As explained in the previous chapter, the press is supposed to be part of the New World Order as well. Yet it was the press that released such damaging information about Nixon and his involvement in Watergate that he was forced to resign. It defies logic and common sense that one conspirator would actively destroy another in their attempt to control the world, for according to Christian conspiracy theorists, they are on the same evil team.

Arguing that a supposed conspirator was used "until he was no longer useful," as Still contends, is a favorite answer among conspiracists. But their sweeping charges do not add up.

The Catholic conspiracy. Today's more conservative Protestant and Catholic leaders and laypeople are often political allies. They line up on the same side of an issue, such as abortion on demand. Yet all is not what it seems. Since colonial times Protestants have feared a Catholic conspiracy: "a grand plan to take control of America and integrate it into a world empire run by the Pope."[11] One reason for this belief came from the Catholic Church itself, which proclaimed through the Council of Trent that Protestantism was a Christian heresy. But during the Second Vatican Council in the early 1960s, "the Catholic Church liberalized its attitude toward other churches and expressed hopes of forming a spiritual union with all forms of Christianity. The result was the current ecumenical movement."[12]

It is this ecumenical movement (of which Promise Keepers also stands accused) that has some Christian conspiracy theorists up in arms. They would have been less alarmed if Catholicism continued its attack on Protestants, for they believe that today's ecumenical movements are the fulfillment of end-times prophecy. In the last days, they contend, a world religion will try to unite all nations. But behind this move is Satan himself. The Protestant church, they claim, is cutting deals with the devil when it accepts the Vatican's invitations, further proof that in the last days even God's true church will commit acts of apostasy.

As the son of immigrants from Dublin, Ireland, I know the resentment Catholics have felt toward Protestants in general, especially those denominations that keep the theories alive. When young Irish women immigrated to America during the 1800s, many sought work as nannies and maids. With increasing Irish immigration came pamphlets that spoke of how "Catholic domestics" were dispatched to America on behalf of the pope to spy on Protestants. These tracts, called "The Female Jesuit" or "The Spy in the Family," promoted a fear that Irish Catholic girls would report any wrongdoing in the homes of Protestants to their priest or parish as part of a papal conspiracy to undermine Protestant society and Christianity specifically.[13]

Lyman Beecher, father of Harriet Beecher Stowe, author of *Uncle Tom's Cabin,* wrote that Protestantism was engaged in a life-and-death struggle with Catholicism, which was "multiplying tumult and violence, filling jails, crowding poorhouses, quadrupling taxation, and sending increasing thousands of voters to 'lay their inexperienced hand upon the helm of our power.'" Beecher wrote these accusations because of the increased immigration of Catholics (mostly Irish) to America. These Catholics, "condensed and wielded by the Catholic powers of Europe, might decide our elections, perplex our policy, inflame and divide the nation, break the bond of our union, and throw down our free institutions."[14]

There was some merit to Beecher's argument. Irish Catholic immigrants did tax the social structure. Wherever they landed, the Irish brought with them fatal communicable diseases and little skilled labor. Those Irish who became successful would send money back home so that their young children would be able to reunite with their parents. But often the parents did not know on which ship their children would arrive. Emergency social programs were exhausted as Irish children became needy street urchins who desperately needed Protestant help, not their conspiracy theories. One such theory appeared in a newspaper in 1855:

> It is a notorious fact that the Monarchs of Europe and the Pope of Rome are at this very moment plotting our destruction and threatening the extinction of our political, civil, and religious institutions. We have the best reasons for believing that corruption has found its way into our Executive Chamber, and that our Executive head is tainted with the infectious venom of Catholicism.[15]

In his *Foreign Conspiracy Against the Liberties of the United States,* S. F. B. Morse, the inventor of the telegraph and son of anti-Illuminatist Jedidiah Morse, wrote in 1835 that a Catholic conspiracy had attacked America "in a vulnerable quarter which cannot be defended by our ships, our forts, or our armies."[16] After three incendiary sermons by Beecher, "whose 1835 *Plea for the West* likened the immigrant threat . . . to an invasion of Egyptian locusts," a mob burned a convent at Charlestown, Massachusetts, on August 11, 1834. Other anti-Catholic disturbances, some fatal, followed in New York, Philadelphia and Louisville.[17]

Irish immigrants were seen as satanic spies when discrimination based on religious beliefs came without recourse. These men and women were shut out and spat on economically. Men were destined to dig ditches and women to change the soiled diapers of other people's children. Allowing an Irish Catholic to hold a job with influence was seen as partaking in treason and even heresy. The rural Midwestern American Protective Association during the late 1800s had members who "pledged never to vote for a Catholic, hire one if Protestants were available or join Catholics in a strike."[18] This is one reason Irish Catholic immigrants rushed to form or join labor unions, the bane of conservatives, some of whom forced them in that direction by promoting their damaging conspiracy theories.

Various and more contemporary anti-Catholic conspiracy theories circulate today in Protestant circles. They are taken from books such as *A Woman Rides the Beast,* written by Christian conspiracy theorist Dave Hunt. The title originates from Revelation 17:7, where an angel tells the apostle John, "I will explain to you the mystery of the woman and of the beast she rides."

Hunt believes that he has cracked this mystery: "The woman represents a world-wide religious system which is based in Rome and claims to be Christian but which has its roots in Babel and Babylon."[19] Unlike other Protestant end-times conspiracy theorists, Hunt, an accomplished synthesizer of past and present conspiracy theories, does not believe that a pope could be or is the coming antichrist: "A pope will not be the Antichrist, but will be his right-hand man, the false prophet of Revelation 13:11-17; 19:20; 20:10."[20]

End-times conspiracy theories often have more to do with a group's standards for good society than with actual Bible prophecy. In regard to anti-Catholicism, this view is called nativism, an "intense opposition to an internal minority on the ground of its foreign (i.e., 'un-American') connections."[21] No other group in America's history has had it used more powerfully against them than Catholics.

Chick Publications creates compact tracts jammed with end-times conspiracy theories that in 1980 grossed $1 million.[22] "The endurance of phenomena such as Jack Chick Publications suggests that, given sufficient stimuli, anti-Catholic nationalism might resurface."[23] Similar to Hunt's writing, a Chick character claims in *Sabotage?* that Catholicism descended from pagan, occult religions and was invented by Lucifer. The pope is accused of using the ecumenical movement to pave the way for the antichrist's one-world religion and government. Freemasons are also part of this papal conspiracy.[24]

"Throughout the comics, cartoons of the contorted faces of priests, nuns and victims of the Inquisition capture the fear and hatred [that] is the essence of the Catholic church. The illustrations include pictures of a nun who has been whipped so severely that her back is encrusted with blood."[25] Two Chick Publications were banned in Canada as "immoral and indecent."[26]

The Political Left

Though many are aware of the Left's political views, they may not be cognizant of the community's affinity with conspiracy theories, which today, given the rise in militia activity, has been mistaken as the exclusive property of the far Right. One reason is that they don't grab headlines the same way. The conspiracy theories of the Left are more subtle and sophisticated. While the Right yells the word *conspiracy,* the Left prefers to avoid the word itself in favor of words that carry only the implication or connotation of conspiracy.

Another reason is how the media treat them. Because most journalistic analysts sympathize with the Left, they are less likely to be as condemning of it. For example, when Hillary Rodham Clinton blamed a "vast right-wing conspiracy . . . a media frenzy based on innuendo, rumor and gossip" for reports of her husband's sexual misconduct with Monica Lewinsky among others, analysts were not quick to condemn the first lady's trafficking in conspiracy theories. Analysts are much more likely to attribute trips into conspiracy and paranoia to an individual on the far Left rather than to the movement itself. The Left has a sizable list of evil conspirators, such as the "conservative" press, the CIA, the FBI, Ronald Reagan and greedy multinational corporations run by Republicans.

The loss of a father, especially one who was gunned down by a madman, can leave a son groping for answers and resolution. Unfortunately for Sean Lennon, son of the late Beatle John Lennon, this answer comes in the form of an evil government-sponsored conspiracy against liberal counterculture "revolutionaries." "[My father] was a counter-cultural revolutionary, and the government takes that kind of shit really seriously historically. He was dangerous to the government. If he had said, 'Bomb the White House tomorrow,' there would have been ten thousand people who would have done it. These pacifist revolutionaries are historically killed by the government, and anybody who thinks that Mark Chapman was just some crazy guy who killed my dad for his personal interests is insane, I think, or very naïve, or hasn't thought about it clearly. It was in the best interests of the United States to have my dad killed, definitely."[27]

Prevailing Winds. A person who wants to research the far-Right conspiracy community is usually forced to resort to exploring alternative sources of information, such as patriot Web sites. But some of these deny access to those who are not part of their inner circle. That is not so with the far-Left conspiracy community. *Prevailing Winds* magazine is sold next to *Time* and *Newsweek* at Barnes & Noble. It is packed with the same claims of "exclusive information" that can be found in leading Christian conspiracy newsletters. It has the same voluminous list of materials to enable the reader to sink ever deeper into the behind-the-scenes world of sinister international affairs.

Those accused of conspiring against the American people are usually flip-flopped, but the marketing is surprisingly similar. Just as Christian conspiracy theorists are fond of blaming socialism and liberalism, *Prevailing Winds* blames conservatism and Republicans, who supposedly own the world's multinational corporations.

Its extensive list of resources includes a wide range of conspiracy books. *Orders to Kill* "contains," the magazine claims, "proof of James Earl Ray's innocence and startling revelations about the powerful forces in government and organized crime that banded together to murder one of America's greatest visionaries [Martin Luther King Jr.]." There are books on the Kennedy assassination: *Acts of Treason: The Role of J. Edgar Hoover in the Assassination of President Kennedy; JFK Murder Solved: Killing Coordinated by CIA.* Other books include *CLASS WAR: The Attack on the Working People; Reagan, Bitburg & the Nazi SS; Old Nazis & the New Right; All the Congressmen's Men: How Capitol Hill*

Controls the Press; The Media Silence; Hemp: The Plant That Can Save Mother Earth.[28]

Prevailing Winds contends that Christian fundamentalists are conspiring against the public good. In *Fundamentalism and the New Right,* Joan Bokear supposedly exposes "how fundamentalist cults have affected America's foreign and domestic policy. Today, with the religious-right vying for ever-greater power, you *must* understand this important piece of social history."[29]

The far Left does not believe that America is what it is due to natural forces, so it employs conspiracy theories to explain away America's rejection of its views. These theories have a dual purpose: they help explain away their opposition, and they fuel increasing anger and paranoia against the government they claim must be overthrown.

The far Left cannot believe that most Americans will not embrace socialism, so the editors of *Prevailing Winds* include the article "Operation Mockingbird: The CIA and the Media, Takeover of the Corporate Press and the Programming of Public Opinion."[30] This article claims to expose how Americans would embrace socialism if it weren't for the CIA's control of the media.

Christian conspiracy preachers believe in similar nefarious acts, but in their minds it isn't the CIA that controls the media—pagan New Age editors control it. But the Christian conspiracy community isn't the only group trying to corner the market on this growth industry. The sale of each conspiracy book, video and audiocassette by both the Left and the Right increases anger and fear toward the U.S. government.

Environmentalists against GATT. Some environmentalists believe that GATT is a scheme designed by conservative international corporate leaders to circumvent environmental regulations. They believe that the treaty will lead to the depletion and destruction of the world's natural resources by those in pursuit of personal wealth.

In *The Case Against the Global Economy and for a Turn Toward the Local* the world's leading environmentalists square off against international corporations and others they believe to be enemies of ecological stewardship:

Each of the forty-three chapters in *The Case Against the Global Economy* takes one part of the story and delves into it, to show both the root assumptions of globalism and its multiple failures. In the end, it is clear that we need to reverse course; away from the global toward a revitalization of local political and economic control, self-sufficiency, and ecological health. . . . The world's political and corporate leaders have begun a radical restructuring of the planet's economics and politics that will affect human life and the natural world as profoundly as anything since the Industrial Revolution. Expressed in such new institutions as GATT, NAFTA, and World Trade Organization, and Maastricht, as well as by the development schemes of the World Bank and the International Monetary Fund, economic globalization has been bulldozed through legislative bodies throughout the world, with scant public debate or discourse.[31]

Left-wing presidential candidate Ralph Nader argues that GATT and NAFTA were at their core a subversion of the democratic process.[32]

That environmentalists are opposed to GATT must be shocking news to Christian conspiracy theorists such as Larry Abraham and Franklin Sanders. In their book *The Greening of America* they argue that environmentalists are among the major players ushering in the New World Order:

In the building of the great one-world plan, the future holds the corporate state: fascism. And fascism, as any careful reader knows, is nothing but corporate socialism. . . . Greenies worldwide are preparing the way for a new, improved, and more potent version under the guise of "environmental consciousness."[33]

They argue that environmentalism, or what they call "Greening," was "created and controlled by the Insiders of the Establishment."[34] They propound, "If John Muir is the patron saint of the environmental movement, Ralph Nader is the Ignatius Loyola."[35] That Nader and other environmentalists can be against the conspiracy through their opposition to GATT and NAFTA and yet still be part of the alleged conspiracy is a puzzling inconsistency.

The African-American community. As mentioned in chapter one, some blacks did suffer at the hands of a government-sponsored conspiracy when the U.S. Public Health Service allowed four hundred African-Americans with syphilis to go untreated for forty years. African-Americans have been targeted for destruction by groups such as the Ku Klux Klan. Sadly, these real plots designed for destruction and injustice have predisposed the African-American community to believe in unfounded conspiracy theories. Some polls reveal that 30 percent of African-Americans believe that the AIDS epidemic may come from an antiblack conspiracy, and up to 60 percent said the same thing about the crack epidemic.[36]

Incredible urban legends abound: AZT was created to help white, but damage black, AIDS patients; chicken sold at Church's Fried Chicken includes a sterilizing agent aimed at black men; something called "The Plan" exists to "ruin or even kill black politicians such as D.C. Mayor Marion Barry and late Commerce Secretary Ron Brown."[37] Fortifying this belief in a widespread conspiracy against African-Americans was an accusation made by Dexter King, the son of slain civil rights leader Martin Luther King Jr. He said on ABC's *Turning Point* that his father's murder was part of a conspiracy that involved several government officials, including the late president Lyndon B. Johnson.[38]

As is often the case with conspiracy theories, this one is fed by nagging ambiguity and is fortified by sealed government documents. The U.S. House Select Committee on Assassinations concluded in 1978 that James Earl Ray was the killer but that a group of bigots in St. Louis, reportedly with a fifty-thousand-dollar bounty on King's head, might have been involved too. The House committee released a report on the killing, but its investigative files are sealed until the year 2029. Civil rights groups have lobbied for those records to be opened. On the surface, closed files lend some credibility to Dexter King's accusation and encourage related conspiracy theories to spread.[39]

Dexter King's influence, however, on conspiracy-minded African-

Americans pales compared to that of Nation of Islam (NOI) leader Louis Farrakhan. Farrakhan has been caught numerous times repeating anti-white and anti-Semitic conspiracy theories.

Elijah Muhammad, Nation of Islam's Messenger of Allah, injected into the minds of Malcolm X and Louis Farrakhan that the black man is endowed by God with superior traits—morally, intellectually and spiritually. (Malcolm X later rejected this notion of black superiority shortly before his assassination.) Like today's end-times preachers, Muhammad derived highly subjective interpretations of Bible prophecy. One was that "America is the only white government out of the European Race that answers the description of the symbolic 'Fourth Beast'" in Revelation 19:20 and Daniel 7:19.[40] The white man, whom Poole called a "devil," will die as part of Armageddon for his injustice toward blacks and others.

Malcolm X agreed: "I don't know when Armageddon is supposed to be. But I know that the time is near when the white man will be finished. The signs are all around us." These signs, he said, included Southern blacks defying local customs during the 1950s, black Africa's revolt against the British, Indonesia booting out "such would-be imperialists as the Dutch" and the French exodus from Algeria.[41]

Farrakhan also believes in a Masonic conspiracy theory similar to the one propounded by Christian conspiracy theorists, except that he believes that the Great Seal, which incorporates Masonic imagery, is a "whites only" seal. The Nation of Islam's newspaper, *Final Call,* even makes the argument that the blockbuster movie *Independence Day* was a multiple plot against the NOI in general and Farrakhan in particular.

According to *Final Call* the movie's acronym, *ID4,* is really a reference to a genetic inhibitor that halts certain processes in evolution and life, identified by researchers at MIT, the alma mater of the "Jewish genius" played by Jeff Goldblum.[42] The huge alien ship that appears in the movie is really a rip off of NOI's own Mother Plane, a "human-built planet, a half mile by a half a mile" carrying "1500 smaller baby planes" with bombs "designed for the destruction of the world," a ship that Louis Farrakhan supposedly visited on September 17, 1985. According to *Final Call* this Mother Plane will be used in the apocalyptic future as part of

Allah's judgment against the white man.[43]

In his first public speech since the Million Man March and his tour through eighteen African and Middle East nations, which included visits with fellow conspiracists Saddam Hussein and Muammar al-Qaddafi, Farrakhan repeated a claim that is found within the Christian conspiracy community: the U.S. government is the modern-day equivalent of Sodom and Gomorrah, and U.S. government agencies are agents of deception, aided largely by the media.

But the reproofs Farrakhan receives for his conspiracy theories, says black writer Roger Wilkins, don't

> hurt him in his base; they enhance him, because he has told his people that though he is not anti-Semitic, there's this free-floating Zionist plot that is directed at him. So when the Anti-Defamation League attacks him all he has to do is turn to his people and say "See?" Then, of course, one of the messages is "They are attacking me because I am supporting you and your interests."[44]

When Richard Abanes challenged Christian conspiracy theorist Chuck Missler for quoting anti-Semitic authors as proof of a New World Order, Missler used a response similar to Farrakhan's. He claimed that he was being unfairly attacked by an individual who was "posing as a Christian [and] . . . doing a smear attack on people like me."[45] Missler painted himself as the persecuted truth-teller and, like Farrakhan, pointed to the messenger as the real culprit.

Farrakhan, like many Christian conspiracy theorists, talks about an age-old conspiracy of international bankers. He throws around names such as Rothschild and Warburg. "The Federal Reserve, the IRS, and FBI, and the Anti-Defamation League were all founded in 1913," says Farrakhan. Actually, writes Henry Louis Gates Jr., "the IRS was founded in 1862 and the FBI in 1908, but never mind." Then in an interview conducted by Gates, Farrakhan "poses the favorite rhetorical question of all paranoid historians: 'Is that a coincidence?'"[46]

Saddam Hussein. Though Farrakhan is a master at the conspiracy shell game, he has an equal halfway around the world. Throughout his ruthless regime Saddam Hussein has used conspiracy theories to justify the execution of potential rivals. When Hussein became ruler of Iraq in 1979, he orchestrated a political event calculated to fortify his role as supreme ruler. After just five days in office Hussein called for a special session among his country's political leaders. Then, as he had throughout his sordid career, Hussein shocked the crowd by saying that he had discovered yet another conspiracy to ruin his country. Quoting exclusive sources and information, he described the alleged conspiracy and how it would have succeeded were it not for his quick and drastic response.

Hussein had his "informant" read the names of the people who were part of the alleged plan as the event was recorded on film for posterity. The attending politicians knew that if their names were read, they would die. Grown men were captured on camera fanning themselves, sweating and fidgeting in their seats. They would not have attended this meeting had they known that Hussein was going to deal from the bottom of the deck and play yet another game of conspiracy theory. It took hours to finish the list of more than two hundred people, all of whom were escorted out of the building and never seen again.

Left-wing conspiracy theories in the near future. Given its fondness for using words that carry the implication of conspiracy without really using the word itself, it is likely that the feminist community will enter the conspiracy publishing game within the next few years. Authors such as Naomi Wolf in *Beauty Myth: How Images of Beauty Are Used Against Women* and Susan Faludi in *Backlash* already play footsy with such notions.

Backlash argues "that the gains of the Women's Movement were systematically undermined during the Reagan years—by 'a kind of pop-culture version of the Big Lie,'" comments Sanford Pinsker. Faludi "seems to back off from calling the equation that 'freedom equals unhappiness' a full-blown conspiracy, but it's hard to turn her 550 pages without feeling that feminists have been *had.* Indeed her forays into history suggest that *Backlash* owes as large a debt to Richard Hofstadter as to Betty Friedan."[47] Conspiracy critic Daniel Pipes adds further criticism:

Faludi finds women to be the victims of a "largely insidious" and "powerful counter-assault on women's rights" that has "moved through the culture's secret chambers" and been perpetrated by the government, lawyers, scholars, the media, fashion designers, and Hollywood. The media, for example, "have circulated make-believe data," and high-profile men in trouble use women, especially feminists, as their "all-purpose scapegoats." Faludi presents her argument with polish and elegance; she even states that "The backlash is not a conspiracy." But her basic thesis is no less conspiracist— "the culture's secret chambers"?—than those of the unwashed Right.[48]

Beauty Myth contends that an organized male ruling class intentionally "uses images of female beauty as a political weapon against women's advances" and that "the beauty myth is not about women at all. It is about men's institutions and institutional power."[49] But even moderate and conservative men and women admit that in the past women have been "had" by being denied the right to vote, the right to equal compensation for equal work and the right to own property in their own name. The current debate seems to focus on the extent of this discrimination now and in the past.

Women, much like members of the African-American community, *have* been victimized. Deplorably men sometimes discriminate against women on the sole basis of their gender. However, a difficulty arises when complex societal issues are distilled into a conspiracy or systematic plan. In light of theories that dodge the C-word, Pinsker writes, "I intend to stay tuned as the feminists slug it out in much the same way that I figure we have not heard the last from those tonguing a sore tooth about the Kennedy assassination."[50]

It is likely that a bright but little-known feminist will take off the gloves and pen a story of a sinister conspiracy that will include the names of specific organizations (besides the standard conservative culprits), if not specific people. Perhaps it will become a bestseller as more and more shiny conspiracy tomes roll off the publishing line. Given the fusion and intermarrying among conspiracy theorists, don't be surprised if conservative evangelicals and fundamentalists, who historically have laughed at feminists, use the work as yet more proof of a New World Order.

If feminists do cross the line into conspiracy theory (if they haven't already), it will illustrate once again how conspiracy theories discredit the movement from which they originate, reducing it to one-liners on late-night talk shows.

It is also likely that the conspiracy theories that circulate within the African-American community may be influenced by generational distinctions. As the current generation becomes more eager to accept conspiracy theories, it becomes small wonder

> that Malcolm X has been rediscovered by a generation proud to wear an X baseball cap or a T-shirt with Malcolm brandishing a firearm over the words "by all means necessary." As Spike Lee's *Do the Right Thing* stridently insists, Martin Luther King, Jr. pales when compared to Malcolm X in much the same way that "We Shall Overcome" is no match for Public Enemy's "Fight the Power." . . . Given these realities—and the realization that militant posturing is a special prerogative of the young—what can one who happens to be white and of a certain age say? . . . Conspiracy hawkers are in the saddle, and they ride us, blacks as well as whites.[51]

One of these hawkers is *X-Files* creator Chris Carter. His influence on middle America has surpassed that of fellow Hollywood conspiracist Oliver Stone because of Carter's ability to tap into a larger universe of material. Carter has gone where few conspiracy theorists have gone before—at least with a weekly television show. Like Stone, who with his movie *JFK* intentionally fused his footage with actual assassination footage (an exercise that intends to sow doubt and distrust), Carter blurs the line between the normal and the paranormal, yet all with an antigovernment story line that reflects his own antigovernment beliefs.

Stone's movie is an exercise in manipulation. How many young adults, the moviegoing age group, could defend themselves against his onslaught of alternate history? His conspiracy theories encompassed nearly the entire federal government, but he kept his theories firmly planted on earth. By doing so Stone opened the door for talented storytellers and fellow conspiracists such as Carter to pull in Roswellian alien beings, even if such beings were actually crash-test dummies with "bluish skin coloration and no ears, hair, eyebrows or eyelashes" that fell from the government's high-altitude weather balloons fifty-some years ago into the dusty New Mexico desert so that their impact could be studied.[52]

Twenty-odd years ago, Carter's weekly invasion of conspiracy theories would have been primarily entertainment. Today, in a conspiracy nation where 80 percent believe that the federal government is involved in an extraterrestrial cover-up and where church leaders such as Chuck Missler preach a kind of *X-Files* antichrist, Carter's cosmic conspiracy theories are as destructive as the conspiracy theories of the far Right—if not more so.

The far Right may command the conspiracy theories of the Internet, but their numbers cannot rival Carter's cash crop. However, even cash crops come with a price. For America this price tag has been, and will continue to be, the loss of faith in government competence and other bonds that tie a culture together. This is ironic, since today's baby boomers have asked government to take an increasingly intrusive role in their lives.

Years from now, once Americans taste the mature but injurious fruit of these cosmic conspiracy theories, many will likely look back on their kinship to such theories with amazement and, hopefully, disgust. By that time, if he invests wisely, Carter should be able to afford his own island, his own conspiracy nation if you will, on which to sun himself and enjoy the fruits of his labor.

Conclusion

Many long for the age when public policy, to paraphrase Emerson, will lead to public poetry. But this longing will be hope deferred in America, a country that snuggles warmly under the wings of conspiracy and that is inhabited by a Christian community that believes the country is going to be destroyed soon anyway. The United States is home to ideas

that are diametrically opposed, and this natural opposition is something
that the extremists will not accept as part of real life.

As a result genuine public opinion, necessary dialogue and profound
differences are pushed to the sidelines by these self-appointed guardians
of a better society. Calling those who disagree with them criminals and
conspirators, they drink from the cup of strong-arm politics, straw-man
arguments and destructive propaganda. When repeated often enough in
books, magazines, videotapes and hit television shows and movies, this
propaganda embeds itself as imitation truth in the church, as well as in
America's collective soul.

Conspiracy theorists are enemies of democracy. They will not concede
that reasonable people disagree with their vision of a good society. So
they embark on an explanation that includes a conspiracy among those
who wield the most power and influence. Violence is done to truth in the
process, but either truth doesn't matter to the theorists or it is seen as a
necessary casualty—similar to the children in the Oklahoma City bombing—in their ideological war against the establishment.

The popularity of conspiracy theories is due in part to end-times
speculation. This speculation has become a two-edged sword. For some
the belief that Christ will return in their lifetime has been a blessing, to
others a curse.

8

A Healthy View of End-Times Prophecy

There's something captivating with the prophetic message
that seems to consume a person's mind,
and often very bright people get into this subject
and it's like drilling a well deep into their lives
and they can't get out of the well they dig.
Chuck Swindoll

I'm convinced that the Lord is coming for His Church before the end of 1981.
I could be wrong, but it's a deep conviction in my heart,
and all my plans are predicated upon that belief.
Chuck Smith, in *Future Survival*, 1978[1]

In my earlier years, I really was convinced
that I would live to see the Rapture of the church. I was *convinced* of that.
Now I'm beginning to realize that just may not be the case for me.
The Lord may come for me before He comes for his whole church.
Now, I'm still *hoping* that I'll live to see the Rapture.
I used to be *convinced* I was going to.
I'm no longer certain that I'm going to.
**Chuck Smith, preaching at Calvary Chapel Costa Mesa,
May 22, 1997**

I was in a conference in New York with Dave Hunt recently
and he said something very provocative about the lack of interest in prophecy.
He went back a few years
especially in the early days when Calvary Chapel was beginning.
How excited we were.
Oh, some of the prophecy preachers got a little out of hand . . .
and we were even told that a generation is forty years,
and when Israel became a nation in 1948 it would be forty years
and then the Lord would come. So we back it up seven.
So the rapture is coming in 1981.
I've met people all over this country who believed that, followed that, anticipated that.
It did not come and as a result many of them bombed out, dropped out, copped out;
they're not around anymore.
**David Hocking, preaching at Calvary Chapel Costa Mesa,
June 22, 1997**

Many people have been blessed by contemporary end-times prophecy. Friends and numerous radio callers have told me how these predictions, made popular by Hal Lindsey, Chuck Smith and others, have caused them to think more seriously about life. They say that being exposed to the belief that theirs is the last generation became a kind of battering ram, causing them to change their ways for the better.

Yet for other people popular end-times prophecy, especially when fused to conspiracy theories, has become a type of gateway drug, sometimes leading them to tragic ends. These theories can produce bitter fruit, such as consuming fear and paranoia, character assassination, apathy and paralysis and a disbelief in the validity of the Scriptures.

As millennial fervor increases, some scholars and religious leaders are concerned that apocalyptic thinking will become as destructive as it is inspiring. C. Marvin Pate, a professor at Moody Bible Institute, says that mistakenly linking current events with Bible prophecy is "an obsession" that has "undoubtedly caused more harm than good."[2] Such an error is remedied by a healthy view of prophecy free of the conspiracy theories that are so popular and powerful within today's evangelical/fundamentalist church.

There and Back Again

Most who believe in end-times conspiracy theories will not head for the hills, denounce their citizenship or try to spy black helicopters flying overhead. They are laypeople who attend normal, Bible-believing churches, but their theories wear and grate on their mind, creating a war of attrition in their soul.

John was a fairly frequent listener of *The Paul Thomas Show*. He had a "romance" with Christian conspiracy theories but admits that he never got into them as much as some people he knew. He was "sucked into" the conspiracy community's worldview one convincing message at a time, starting with some of the programs on the Trinity Broadcasting Network. There he heard Jack Van Impe say that these theories were indeed the fulfillment of Bible prophecy. Pat Robertson's view of the New World Order was also a "huge" influence on him. "I placed all of my belief into what he was saying. How could he be wrong?"

During the Persian Gulf War, preacher John Hagee also convinced John that all the information he received from the press was not true. "I remember that night he was on TBN. He said it was going to be one of the bloodiest baths for American soldiers and how it was the beginning of World War III. He said things that were totally untrue. But he just keeps saying them, and people hear those things and they forget . . . the very next day" that it doesn't happen.

When John moved to southern Oregon he began listening to the Christian Research Institute's radio program *The Bible Answer Man* and to *The Paul Thomas Show.* He started looking at the community represented by these shows from a different angle. "I began reading the Bible more and started checking things out for myself. I don't buy into these theories anymore. They are a bunch of garbage. I used to listen to these people and think to myself, *They are Christians, they can't be wrong and they certainly wouldn't be doing it for the money.* They pump you up about the return of Christ, but it's a false pumping up. Their message leads you into bondage and fear."

When his faith in these theories was almost dead, John was introduced to the late James McKeever, a Christian economist and geopolitical analyst with a strong following and worldwide reputation. "He told me over lunch that the Oklahoma City bombing was an all-out conspiracy. That did it for me. I slammed the door on that kind of information."

John has felt the return of joy into his life. "I still believe we are living in the end times, and I am excited about Christ's return, but I'm more balanced. I don't put so much energy in that direction." That "energy" came in part from conspiracy newsletters crammed with pages of that ever-present "exclusive information" that assigns the most evil of intentions to the highest levels of government.

John admits that conspiracy authors often try to end their newsletters on a high note. They claim that although nearly every institution in America is permeated by evil and that evil leaders are searching for and destroying those with traditional values, their readers should not worry. God, they affirm in a short paragraph or two at the end of the newsletter, is in control. These footnotes of comfort, says John, are designed to put the issue in perspective, but it is like putting a Band-Aid on a gaping wound. "It doesn't help."

The Prophecies of Hal Lindsey

How do people such as John come to believe in these theories? Most Christian conspiracy theorists, whether or not they belong to a militia, adhere to the contemporary interpretation of end-times prophecy made popular by Hal Lindsey, the "father of the modern-day prophecy movement." His *Late Great Planet Earth,* first published in 1970, has sold at least twenty million copies. It was made into a film, narrated by Orson Welles, in 1978. Lindsey taught that the rapture, the event that will physically remove Christians from the earth, would enable true believers to escape the coming great tribulation, which would take place within "forty years or so of 1948,"[3] that is, sometime in the 1980s.

Lindsey and others arrived at this conclusion by means of a speculative interpretation of Matthew 24:32-33: "Now learn this lesson from the fig tree: As soon as its twigs get tender and its leaves come out, you know that summer is near. Even so, when you see all these things, you know that [he] is near, right at the door."

This is interpreted by Lindsey and others to prophesy the rebirth of the nation Israel, fulfilling a number of Old Testament prophecies. It has become a cornerstone of this community's eschatology. But nowhere in this chapter of Matthew, or in the entire Bible, does the Bible conclusively reveal that Israel is symbolized by a fig tree.

This interpretation is even more difficult to support when the parallel passage, Luke 21:29-30, is examined: "Look at the fig tree and all the trees. When they sprout leaves, you can see for yourselves and know that summer is near. Even so, when you see these things happening, you know that the kingdom of God is near." If Lindsey's interpretation is correct, that the budding of the fig tree represents the rebirth of the nation Israel, then it follows that all nations ("all the trees") must also become nations once again. Though countries restructure themselves, usually as a result of some economic collapse or civil war, it is nearly impossible for all nations to become nations again in the time frame Lindsey endorses.

The belief that the fig tree symbolizes Israel is even harder to support when read in light of Matthew 21:19: Jesus said to a fig tree, "May you never bear fruit again!" He was speaking to a fig tree he found at the side of the road that had nothing on it but leaves. "Immediately the tree withered." Israel may indeed play an important role in the fulfillment of Bible prophecies, but people will need to look to other Bible passages to support this position.

Since the eighties have come and gone, Lindsey changed the beginning of his timetable to 1967, the year the Israelis occupied Jerusalem. The erroneous prediction that Jesus would return toward the end of the twentieth century is troubling to Christians who believe Lindsey's prophetic timetable but who do not believe that Christians will be spared from a coming tribulation. People have joined militia cells across the country to escape the misery that Lindsey and many others say is about to escalate.

Lindsey's predictions grew bolder when in 1981 he wrote, "The decade of the 1980s could very well be the last decade of history as we know it."[4] There are other interpretations of end-times prophecy, but judging from the tremendous book sales even after his false predictions, Lindsey's is the most compelling and influential. But Lindsey is no longer merely the "father of the modern-day prophecy movement." He is the prolific grandfather, with a huge flock of grandchildren, many of whom are found in Calvary Chapel churches.

I have seen just how much influence he has on his listeners. Once, due to equipment limitations, KDOV was unable to air Lindsey's daily twenty-minute program. This continued for weeks as we tried with limited success to install additional equipment. During this time, I received urgent and sometimes angry phone calls insisting that our station put Lindsey's program back on the air immediately. Some asked whether I was intentionally "censoring" Lindsey. These callers said that by suspending Lindsey's daily show, our station severed them from information that they could receive nowhere else. The media, they said, was part of the conspiracy and so could not be trusted. Only from Lindsey's program could they discover what was really going on in the world and if Jesus' return was at hand.

The Weaver family's flight to Ruby Ridge was greatly influenced by

The Late Great Planet Earth. Though Vicki Weaver, the family's spiritual leader, was also influenced by H. G. Wells and Ayn Rand, it was Lindsey's prophetic work, coupled with her home-spun visions, that convinced her to pack up her family and move to Ruby Ridge. She believed that the enemies of God predicted by Lindsey were prepared to strike at any moment.

Calvary Chapel's Chuck Smith

Pastor Chuck Smith, founder of the Calvary Chapel movement, has made similar predictions. In 1978 he wrote:

> We're the generation that saw the fig tree bud forth, as Israel became a nation in 1948. As a rule, a generation in the Bible lasts 40 years. The children of Israel journeyed in the wilderness for 40 years until that generation died. Forty years after 1948 would bring us to 1988. . . .
>
> From my understanding of biblical prophecies, I'm convinced that the Lord is coming for His Church before the end of 1981. I could be wrong, but it's a deep conviction in my heart, and all my plans are predicated upon that belief.[5]

Smith made similar predictions in other books, such as *End Times* and *Snatched Away.*[6]

Those who defend predictions made by Smith and other Calvary Chapel preachers say that Smith never actually set a specific date. They were simply predicting the "season" of his return. Such an argument contends that predicting the year of his return is not the same as predicting a specific date, such as August 13, 1981. But this argument relies on a flawed assumption regarding time.

Lindsey, Smith and a legion of fellow end-times preachers believe that current events fulfill specific Old and New Testament prophecies, though some contend that this sort of matchmaking is thrust upon the Scriptures as opposed to coming from them. Even in light of their failed predictions, which began during the early 1980s and have since become more frequent, these end-times preachers still attempt with dogmatic certainty to match current events to as yet unfulfilled Bible prophecies. What is surprising is that others such as Louis Farrakhan have incorporated this unique newspaper exegesis into their worldview as well, and they adhere to similar conspiracy theories.

Bitter Fruit

Looking back at past predictions about the end of the world and how they supposedly fulfill Bible prophecy is perhaps the clearest way to understand the fallacy of these predictions. Yet many end-times preachers within the Christian church have not learned from their own past. They simply revise their predictions without acknowledging or apologizing for their past mistakes. What is even more troubling is that, though unintentional, speculation from these popular and self-described end-times experts has helped produce a bumper crop of bitter fruit.

Fear and paranoia. Christian conspiracy theories often riddle lives with fear and paranoia. They produce what has been called "3-G Christians": people who buy *gold* to avoid economic collapse, stockpile *guns* because the New World Order is after them and stock up on *groceries* because daily life as we know it will end under the rule of the antichrist.

Ken Klein, apocalyptic author of *The False Prophet: Evil Architect of the New World Order,* was a guest on KDOV in December 1994. He said that the New World Order with its global domination was right around the corner and that both major political parties were part of the conspiracy. America, he said, was about to sink into a cesspool of unstoppable tribulation.

Klein's apocalyptic vision had the ring of sincerity. He spoke with confidence and seemed to quote Scripture accurately. Soon after the hour-long interview, a woman who was broken and weeping called into KDOV. Taking Klein's message to its logical conclusion, she feared for herself, her children and other children.

Another example of fear and paranoia was given in an interview with B. J. Oropeza, a researcher with the Christian Research Institute (CRI). He related a troubling story of how a group of Christian conspiracy theorists were threatening the life of a conspiracy defector. In November 1994 a Florida woman decided to leave the group, but soon her life was threatened because she knew "information, addresses and names of [the] members." These members were afraid that the government would find out where they are hiding, put them in concentration camps and place on them the mark of the beast.[7]

These alleged concentration camps are described in the book *Black Helicopters over America,* which was given to KDOV by a Christian conspiracy theorist. This work claims that these camps, run by the United Nations, will detain Christians who do not bow to the one-world antichrist. The book details twenty-three "known" U.N. concentration camps throughout the United States, as well as ten other "suspected" detention camps.[8] Oropeza said that some people who call CRI will not give their name or address because they believe that the government might tap into CRI's phone line, discovering where they live, and exterminate them. The paranoia that these conspiracy theories breed becomes even more bizarre.

During one New World Order seminar in southern Oregon, attendees stared straight ahead like deer caught in headlights. Says one observer, "People just sat there with their eyes glued on the information they were given. They were stuck in their seats"—stuck there by fear. The information included how various cancers are the result of the medical industry's goal of reducing the world's population. Partly because of this theory, conspiracy radio programs are peppered with ads promoting alternative medicine and dietary supplements.

It was revealed during the seminar that common household appliances are designed to take away a person's ability to think. Speakers were not talking about rotten television fare but about the television itself. One conspiracy theorist said that televisions are designed to emit mind-altering rays. This theory contains a grain of truth, for more than six hundred Japanese children were hospitalized in December 1997 after watching the popular TV show *Pokemon.* On the show Nintendo-based characters flashed a yellow light so many times per second that it made the children susceptible to "photosensitive epilepsy," a rare but documented condition.[9] According to the conspiracy speakers, not all shows are part of the particle-beam conspiracy, just some—such as the 1996 Summer Olympics. After all, the world was watching. What better time to contact it?

This same seminar, which projected articles from the *National En-*

quirer on a screen as evidence of the New World Order, presented the argument that alien forces, controlled by the Trilateral Commission, will drain the world's fresh water lakes and transport the precious commodity to the moon so that the evil conspirators will have something to drink after they destroy the world and flee to the nearest orb. Such outer-space conspiracy theories take on a Christian veneer when Christian leaders such as Chuck Missler claim that the antichrist may either be an extraterrestrial or have an extraterrestrial connection.[10]

The attendees of this seminar are reluctant to buy bulk food from places such as Price Costco, which requires a membership. They believe that from this membership the authorities will monitor bulk orders of rice, beans and other food items of survival. Attendees are told to make such orders through co-ops and to pay cash.

After one show devoted to Christian conspiracy theories, KDOV received a letter from a respected member of the community: "Thanks for having the courage to take on conspiracy theorists. There is just enough truth in anything they say to make their arguments seem plausible to those with paranoia." He said later that his late father, who had been an ordained minister, showed classic symptoms of clinical depression and paranoia. His father was convinced that certain alleged conspiracies were the fulfillment of Bible prophecy. The son confessed with candor that this fearful worldview robbed his father of Christian joy and that his father's belief in these Christian conspiracy theories led to moments of domestic tyranny for him, his mother and his siblings.

Hurting congregations. These theories not only tear apart families; they also divide congregations. Gayle Replinger, with the help of Texe Marrs, argues that *all* versions of the Bible except the King James are untrustworthy and the product of a hidden alliance between Bible translators and the New Age Movement's one-world religion.[11] Replinger says that the new versions prepare the apostate church of the last days to accept the antichrist, his mark, image and religion. In short, it prepares the apostate church to worship Lucifer.

This message has a following. A church member wrote Zondervan Publishing House (now part of HarperCollins) to tell them that the elders and pastors of his church confessed their "sin" in leading the congregation astray by placing New International Version (NIV) Bibles in the pews. The elders announced that they would use only the King James translation from then on. The church member wrote that he worries that children in Sunday school won't understand God's Word if his church uses only the King James Version.

These theories are also likely to damage congregations financially. Conspiracists believe that a worldwide conspiracy will quickly bring about economic disasters such as staggering inflation and unemployment. It will also collapse such basic industries as food and power delivery. Consequently it is likely that Christians who adhere to end-times conspiracy theories will give less or stop giving altogether, since they believe that they must stock up on resources to prepare for the coming tribulation. When doomsday conspiracy theories are followed, giving to local churches and ministries does decrease, hampering the church's ability to support missionaries and minister to the needy.

Apathy and paralysis. In his book *Fit Bodies, Fat Minds,* Os Guinness diagnoses eight major plagues unleashed on the evangelical mind. Guinness says that a person in whom these plagues are combined has a "mindset that has often been openly hostile to thinking Christianly about life and culture."[12] The aspect of this mindset that is relevant to Christian conspiracy theory is dispensational premillennialism. This teaching is based on Revelation 20:1-10, which says that there will be a one-thousand-year reign of Christ on earth at the end of the present age.

Premillennialism by itself is not the problem, Guinness says. But problems do arise when it is married to dispensationalism, the belief that history can be divided into economies or dispensations according to God's progressive revelation.

> Most agree that dispensationalism has adversely impacted the . . . Christian mind in a number of ways. . . . If once-powerful churches and denominations are rotting from apostasy, if in these "End Times" decadence is spreading through civilization and secularism through its leaders, if both the church and the world are beyond reform and beyond hope this side of the millennium, then the only answer is

simple, basic, biblical truth taught by simple, basic, biblical believers. . . . What is always prized, by contrast, is charismatic certainty. For when biblical infallibility blends into personal infallibility and becomes dogmatic certitude, the way is open for self-styled and self-assured populism of the worst sort.[13]

A letter from a radio listener, Nancy, reinforces Guinness's point:

The fear within the body of Christ over some of these conspiracy theories is most unbecoming. . . . I used to listen to a man named Harold Camping on Family Radio out of Oakland, California. He was *certain* he had cracked the code of the books of Daniel, Revelation, etc., and the world was almost certain to end in 1996. . . . *He was very convincing.* There seemed to be no joy in his ministry, just condemnation for believers. (italics added)

Guinness concludes:

When the End Times are on the slipway, such cultural pursuits as art and music are frivolous. Where earlier Christians fell into dualism and placing the spiritual above the secular, contemplation above action, "full-time Christian service" above ordinary life, and "soul saving" above study, many dispensationalists have followed the course of "End Times" events with the consuming fascination of a betting man at a race track. In doing so they have virtually turned their backs on the world in which they live.[14]

Friends as well as foes of President Ronald Reagan became alarmed when he embraced the dispensationalist view of the fast-approaching Armageddon propagated by Lindsey.[15] They feared that this thinking would influence his foreign policy. As an example they refer to when James Watt, secretary of the interior (1981-1983) under Reagan, remarked that there may not be much purpose in protecting our natural resources since it is all going to be destroyed soon anyway.

Because disciples of dispensational premillennialism believe that the current age is hopelessly doomed, they usually avoid long-term programs for social betterment and encourage others to do the same. I have been told by numerous evangelicals that it is a waste of time to engage our culture. Some argue that this self-imposed boycott of our culture has led to a large imbalance, for Christians have allowed a secular humanist worldview, not balanced by the virtues of religious belief, to gain control of institutes of public and higher education and news and entertainment media. No wonder Christian airwaves are filled with evangelicals bemoaning the current cultural condition and lack of involvement. As more and more evangelicals are realizing, the cultural wound is partly self-inflicted.

Stumbling block. When events in the Persian Gulf escalated to armed conflict in 1992, end-times preachers worked overtime, seeing it as the doorstep to the final days. One popular evangelical preacher focused many of his sermons on the events in the Middle East. As a student of Hal Lindsey and Chuck Smith, he tailored his sermons around the event, suggesting that the war could well mark the time of Christ's return. He grew increasingly certain that the end was likely at hand, just the way the Bible predicted.

Some elders and deacons in the church caught the spirit of the message and repeated it often. One asked his father to attend church. With the uncertainty of war circling the globe, this self-made man gave pew sitting a chance. His attendance was regular. Fruits of the Spirit seemed to manifest themselves. Wealth and its corroding influence seemed to be falling under healthy control. The heat of the Gulf War appeared to be creating spiritual heat as well.

Yet this man has rarely attended church since the Gulf War. He has reverted to a garden-variety pagan, renewing old sins and a love for money. He came to church out of fear of the future and heard a convincing pulpit message that his global fears were real, a prelude to the beginning of the end. But international waters, though never tranquil, calmed. What was hailed by so many self-professed end-times experts as Armageddon was just one of many battles in a troubled part of the globe. It is said that there are no atheists in foxholes, but their minds revert once they crawl out in one piece.

There is another if not more troubling result when rash connections are made between current events and prophecy. When non-Christians are told that current events "prove" they are living in the last days, some show a genuine interest. But as the last few decades have shown, it is charismatic certainty, not biblical truth, that has led many to give church a try. These non-Christians hear a convincing message—that the Bible predicted today's headlines and that these headlines prove that we are in the end times—but when current events do not support such predictions, why should non-Christians listen? Once the reliability of Scripture has been weakened, why should they believe when told about salvation?

Fueling lawlessness. According to Christian conspiracy theorists, no established political party can be trusted. That is why conspiracy radio is often promoting a third political party and the candidacy of men such as patriot and survivalist James "Bo" Gritz—that is, until his attempted suicide.

As a result conspiracy disciples wander the wilderness, looking for a political stretch of land to call home. But since third parties traditionally hold little power in America, attempts to change the system from within are continually thwarted. What results is a political no man's land where anarchy and violence often become the only avenues of influence. As Christian conspiracy theorists delve deeper into these theories, the Bible is only relevant in as much as it exposes the conspiracy. Scripture takes on new meaning, justifying armed confrontation with God's end-times enemies and creating a hearty self-centeredness in the process.

Born-again Ken Medenback in Klamath Falls, Oregon, claims that God told him to take ten acres of federal land in central Oregon. The federal government heard no such message and ordered him to get off. "If they want the land, they can take my life. Our forefathers died for these rights 200 years ago. I'll die for them now," he said.[16] The forty-year-old laid claim on April 18, 1995, to 640 acres belonging to the U.S. Bureau of Land Management next to his own 2.5-acre parcel. He began cutting down trees and hauling them in an old beer truck.

After a federal judge ordered him off the land, Medenback reconsidered and reduced his hefty claim to ten acres. He felt that was a fair share of the thirty million acres of federal land in Oregon, since the state has three million residents. As a member of the Central Oregon Regional Militia, he thinks the federal government has no constitutional right to own the land for purposes other than military installations and post offices. He also refused to get a driver's license or building permits.

This sort of lawlessness is certainly not what Christian conspiracy theorists intended to fuel. But militia leaders have referred to Pat Robertson's book *New World Order* as proof that their conspiracy beliefs are true and that they may need to use violence in resisting the federal government. Robertson and other conservative Christian leaders are in a unique position to inject balance into this community that grows larger and more troubled with every law-enforcement maneuver gone bad.

The psychological shortcuts that conspiracy theories provide give Americans plenty of reason to worry about additional acts of domestic terrorism, says investigative reporter Daniel Junas:

> A person who believes in conspiracy theories tends to believe that the problems of the world are caused by a fairly, relatively, small number of people. And if you really believe that the problem is the people who are in charge, or the people who are secretly orchestrating the conspiracy, sooner or later you are likely to come to the conclusion that the solution is to kill those people, to eliminate those people, and that will somehow eliminate our problems. And that won't work. Eliminating scapegoats is not a solution to our problem, it just leads to a continued search for scapegoats.[17]

Proof of such a dehumanizing attitude is found in the rhetoric of self-described patriot Mark Koernke. People are no longer people, they are "internationalists." Militia leader Koernke warns,

> What is the true motive and nature of the beast, of this creature? I will not give them the honor of calling them human beings, for I think that many of them are very alien to what we would consider human now. I look at their eyes . . . the eyes of any butchers the like of which this planet has not seen in the past.[18]

This dehumanizing rhetoric has an established history in the world of conspiracy theorists. Des Griffin, in a speech delivered in 1983, referred to Illuminati founder Adam Weishaupt as a "Human Devil."[19] Two militia members in Livonia, Michigan, were charged with killing a comrade they suspected had infiltrated the militia cell and was spying on them. The body of William Gleason was found buried in the woods. *The Hillsdale Daily News,* quoting court documents, said that he was shot in the head.

In Fort Davis, Texas, militia separatists who believe that Texas should be an independent nation took two neighbors hostage in April 1997 in retaliation for the arrest of two of its members. The group, called the Republic of Texas, contends that the annexation of Texas as a state in 1845 was illegal. Therefore the group's leaders say they constitute a legitimate government. The two people held hostage were average citizens with no connection to the federal or state government. They were simply neighbors who lived within fifteen miles of the group's headquarters.

More and more people are being victimized by the conspiracy mindset, not because they are connected to the alleged conspiracy but because their neighbors resort to drastic measures. The militia movement in America has at its foundation a complex religious component that includes the belief that the New World Order is the fulfillment of Bible prophecy. If these conspirators are the same evil conspirators described in end-times prophecy, why shouldn't the militia violently resist them? Doesn't the Bible say that these agents of evil are God's enemies too?

The taking of life in the name of God has already happened in the shooting of abortionists. Oregon's born-again Rachelle Shelley Shannon of Grants Pass, a prolife activist, shot Kansas abortionist George Tiller in August 1993. Other shootings have followed and have included the shooting of people who worked in the same office as abortionists. In their misguided desire to fight evil, conspiracy disciples are likely to follow suit and take matters into their own hands—some in God's name because of their interpretation of end-times prophecy.

Michael Fortier, who had Timothy McVeigh serve as his best man, revealed how chilling such a view can become, especially when justifying the murder of innocent people. During the Oklahoma City bombing trial he said that government workers who died in the blast "may be individually innocent, but because they were part of the evil empire [in the mind of Timothy McVeigh] they were guilty by association."[20]

Christian conspiracy disciples are neither crazy nor deranged. For instance, conviction and Scripture roar from former Baptist preacher and Christian militia leader Norman Olson's mouth, and his eyes blaze like an Old Testament prophet's when he speaks about his love for family, God and country. But in the Christian conspiracy community, the road between fact and fiction is washed away because of speculation—not revelation—committed in the name of end-times prophecy. So when Olson sweats and muscles his way through the woods, practicing for the end-times war he believes is coming upon the land, he is living out a worldview that has been pumped into Christian churches for the last few decades.

The next time you see Norman Olson on television, try not to look at him. Look behind him, and you'll see that he is not alone. You'll see a paper trail created by McAlvany, Robertson, Missler, Kah, Wardner and a host of other writers. They are pushing him along the forest maze, telling him that with every current event comes the need to run even harder. Olson and his brothers in conspiracy are to some degree the creation of Christian leaders who do not restrain themselves from predicting Christ's return and who do not see the frail and frayed line separating prophetic revelation from human speculation.

Christ warned against such speculation, and you need look no further than Olson to figure out why. Pray for Olson, a true believer on a diet of bitter fruit. What Olson and his brethren need is an infusion of end-times balance.

A Healthy View of Prophecy
Robert Lightner, professor of systematic theology at Dallas Theological Seminary in Dallas, Texas, emphasizes how important balance is when considering the last days:

> Evangelicals believe the whole Bible. They believe everything it teaches to be true. And, yet having said that, in all honesty we must add that there are some things in Scripture that we hold with more

certainty than other things. For example, we can be altogether certain the Bible teaches that Jesus Christ will come again to this earth, but we might not be nearly as certain about the identity of the twenty-four elders of Revelation 4:4 or of the man of sin in 2 Thessalonians 2:3. . . . Let's not suspect people of being less than orthodox just because they don't subscribe to the viewpoint on prophecy that we have been taught and believe and that may, or may not, be the true view. . . . Scripture does tell us to fight but not over prophecy. Paul told Timothy to fight the good fight of the faith (1 Tim. 6:12), and it is a responsibility that every believer has. However, the specifics of unfulfilled prophecy can hardly be called essentials of the faith once delivered to the saints. We, like Timothy, are all to keep the faith (2 Tim. 4:7), but "the faith" surely cannot be construed to mean a particular order of future events.[21]

Among Christian conspiracy disciples, Lightner's words are almost unforgivable. But as Lightner points out, "All the positions that evangelicals hold on unfulfilled prophecy have strengths and weaknesses. No one view is all right and all the others all wrong."[22]

Don't be so dogmatic. As a former program director of a Christian radio station, I have heard numerous messages concerning end-times prophecy. One of these, a message delivered by Chuck Swindoll, achieves the healthy balance so desperately needed today regarding premillennialism—the belief that Christ will return before the millennium (a thousand-year period defined by earthly bliss) and in fact will establish it when he returns to the earth.

During his *Insight for Living* radio program, Swindoll devoted one show to a healthy view of prophecy and how it should help Christians live better lives today. His talk, "Let's Be Realistic About the Present,"[23] laid out a beautiful balance that is able to restore joy into the lives of Christian conspiracy theorists. "For some reason there is a sense of fascination that is planted in everyone's mind, and when a preacher hopes to increase the crowd or at least add a little spark to his church, he often turns to a prophetic theme," he said. "There is something within all of us that makes us long for knowing something about the future."

When he was a young minister, Swindoll was acquainted with a man who was known for his work within prophecy and his ability to decipher future events. "He used to say to me in private moments that he regretted some of the fascination connected to [prophecy]." People, he said, often came only to "have their ears tickled." He told Swindoll that he would do an experiment to prove his point. During a week-long speaking engagement he spoke about prophecy for five days, and the place was packed. The other two days he spoke about something nonprophetic, and the crowd dwindled.

Swindoll says there is nothing wrong with studying prophecy. Scripture has much to say about future events, though not as much as some people believe. "We are to be informed of the future, and as we are [informed], that will help calm our fears and help us to remember that what is happening today is running its course exactly the way God planned it."

Swindoll is concerned about the negative response to prophecy, which he calls extremism and fanaticism. "Some people see a great deal revealed in Scripture that really does lack evidence. But they are so bent and determined . . . that they hoist upon the Scriptures."

The pastor admits that he has been uneasy at times about people setting dates for Christ's return. In the 1970s some preachers said that communism would rule the world, thereby fulfilling the one-world government described in Revelation. "Be very careful on the subject of prophecy," which, he says, has a unique ability to control and captivate a mind. Also be on guard against dogmatism.

Isn't it interesting that we can be open and teachable and willing to talk back and forth about interpretations on every other subject, but not when it comes to prophecy? It seems as though we set our jaws, we make our statement, we come to our conclusion, and there is no slack given. No room provided for a difference of opinion. Great church fights, great religious fights, down through history have revolved around the theme of prophecy.

He said that preachers need to choose their words carefully, lest they eat them later. As an example, Swindoll told about a certain preacher who was active when John Kennedy was running for president. "The pastor . . . was so concerned about a Roman Catholic occupying the White House that he decided he would do a series ahead of time, and he entitled the series 'What Will Happen If a Roman Catholic Occupies the White House.' The church was packed as you can imagine." Swindoll admits that he too was caught up in the series, taking copious notes, writing down the Scriptures that backed up the claims. Words were chosen that were startling, dramatic and that sounded so plausible at the time. "Then John Kennedy became president and none of those things happened. I always look back and wonder how that man handled that rather embarrassing moment."

Often, he says, future events addressed in Scripture are covered in symbolic language. Swindoll believes that people need to recognize this and allow for greater flexibility within their interpretation of these symbolic passages.

Knowledge of future events should lead to godly living here and now. Swindoll finishes his list of inappropriate responses to prophecy with the tendency to make prophecy an end in itself:

> Have you noticed how that can happen? Virtually every time a prophetic note is sounded in the Scriptures—now hear this well— the writer of that passage of Scripture takes the time to bring you back to the present and to say, "Now in light of this, what godly people we are to be today." It's funny, from one prophetic conference to another there is just an increasing number of statements made about the future, but not a whole lot said about living as we should today, when in fact that's a major reason prophecy is addressed in Scripture.

He uses 2 Peter 3:3-7 as an example of how knowledge of the future is meant to prepare people to live better lives today:

> First of all, you must understand that in the last days scoffers will come, scoffing and following their own evil desires. They will say, "Where is this 'coming' he promised? Ever since our fathers died, everything goes on as it has since the beginning of creation." But

they deliberately forget that long ago by God's word the heavens existed and the earth was formed out of water and by water. By these waters also the world of that time was deluged and destroyed. By the same word the present heavens and earth are reserved for fire, being kept for the day of judgment and destruction of ungodly men.

Later in the chapter Peter reveals how the world will be destroyed. But as usual he swings the focus back to how people are to live in the present: "So then, dear friends, since you are looking forward to this, make every effort to be found spotless, blameless and at peace with him" (3:14).

Swindoll's next example is 1 Thessalonians 4:13: "Brothers, we do not want you to be ignorant about those who fall asleep, or to grieve like the rest of men, who have no hope." Swindoll said, "You see, there is nothing to be gained of ignorance of prophecy. We are to know, of a general matter, that which lies ahead of us. He does not want us to be uninformed about those who have fallen asleep. That is a reference [to] those who have died." Believers need to know that when a Christian dies it isn't the end but a passing through time into eternity. That means that Christians will never be away from the Lord, for when they die the spirit goes instantly to him.

Those Christians who are alive to see his coming, Swindoll said, will be "caught up together with [those who died before his return but who now have glorified bodies] in the clouds to meet the Lord in the air. And so we will be with the Lord forever" (1 Thessalonians 4:17). This general knowledge of things to come is brought back to the present in the very next verse: "Therefore encourage each other with these words" (4:18).

Knowledge of future events should be tempered by other biblical knowledge. An appropriate response to prophecy, he says, is a balanced knowledge:

God would have us to know his Word, and if we are ignorant of prophecy, then our knowledge of his Word is limited. . . . There is no virtue in remaining ignorant of God's prophetic program. . . . God is honored as we equip our minds with the truth concerning the future. So don't shun it simply because there are arguments over it and fanaticism about it.

The second appropriate reaction, he says, is to use these truths as a continual reminder that God has everything under control:

> If you read the day's newspaper as it arrives through the eyes of biblical prophecy, you won't panic. I'm not saying you won't be concerned, but you won't panic. It brings peace in the midst of today's chaos, brings confidence in the midst of today's insecurity and confusion. The warnings to stay ready will be brought back to you time and again as you read the news of the hour. And always there is the encouragement for holy living.

Swindoll ends his message about a healthy view of prophecy with a sobering example of what happens when someone lives on the extremes:

> When people say such things as "Let's live our lives only in light of his coming," and do so to the extreme, they are in peril. When they say, "The earth is going to burn up, there isn't going to be any peace, trying to live in harmony is a waste of time because Jesus brings a sword," that individual is heading for deep emotional and mental troubles.

The "Rainbow Man" is a disturbing example:

> In the Wednesday, July 14 edition of the Orange County Register, the headline reads, "Religious Zealot, Rainbow Man Gets Three Life Terms." The Rainbow Man was the man who wore rainbow-colored hair at sporting events who displayed Scriptures, such as John 3:16 big enough for everyone to read. His name is Rollin Stewart. He held a maid hostage and made terrorist threats during an airport hotel standoff. The article describes him as a "David Koresh waiting to happen." A deputy attorney said, "He has the same beliefs, and he stands by them so strongly that he is willing to die or kill for them."

Swindoll concludes:

> That's an extreme example of a man who has lost contact with reality. And I have seen it happen with prophecy more than any other subject. That's why I warn all of us. . . . There's something

captivating with the prophetic message that seems to consume a person's mind, and often very bright people get into this subject and it's like drilling a well deep into their lives and they can't get out of the well they dig.

The focus should be the person of Christ. Writer Wendy Murray Zoba believes that much of what people focus on when it comes to end-times prophecy, such as date setting, misses the real point of Christ's return:

> When it comes to living under the shadow of the end, we find ourselves suspended between two seemingly contradictory realities. On the one hand, we need the faith to let go of worldly attachments. . . . On the other hand, we need to live fully, here and now, with assurance and abandon, like the weeping prophet (Jeremiah) who invested in smoldering real estate. Paul captures the essence of this tension when he suggests that "to live is Christ" (this life is worthy of the best that we can give it . . .) but "to die is gain" (. . . joyfully relinquished for the better portion). Both dispositions depend upon unremitting faith in the promises of God. As Paul Erb wrote, "We live in a tension between that which we already have received and that which we look forward to with hope."[24]

Erb also wrote, "Eschatology is . . . concerned, not so much with the 'last things,' as with Him who is 'the first and the last.'"[25]

End-times speculation is dangerous business. Theologian Reinhold Niebuhr wrote, "It is unwise for Christians to claim any knowledge of the furniture of heaven or the temperature of hell."[26] In terse fashion, George Eckman warns, "Revelation is enough. Speculation is more than enough."[27] When a believer adheres to a healthy view of prophecy, that believer lives with the knowledge that this world is not his or her home and hence lives with a misfit abandon, which provides a unique type of power. When Christians think about the Lord's return, wrote J. I. Packer, they should be "packed up and ready to go, and packed up and ready to wait."[28]

The writing of the late C. S. Lewis also injects much-needed balance into the increasing end-times hysteria. He wrote that we do not know and cannot know when the world will end. In the grand scheme of things we do not know if we are in act one or act five:

> We do not know who are the major and the minor characters. The Author knows. The audience, if there is an audience (if angels and archangels and all the company of Heaven fill the pit and the stalls), may have an inkling. But we, never seeing the play from outside, never meeting any characters except the tiny minority who are "on" in the same scenes as ourselves, wholly ignorant of the future and very imperfectly informed about the past, cannot tell at what moment the end ought to come. That it will come when it ought, we may be sure; but we waste our time in guessing when that will be. That it has a meaning we may be sure, but we cannot see it.... We are led to expect that the Author will have something to say to each of us on the part that each of us has played. The playing it well is what matters infinitely.[29]

Conclusion

"Playing it well"—that is what Scripture tells Christians to do. It is what God desires. How Christians live today indicates to some degree whether their understanding of the end is right and good or flawed and sometimes dangerous. Given all the anger, fear, false teaching and groundless anti-government sentiment in the Christian conspiracy community, there is good reason to conclude that this community does not have it right and is not playing it well.

It is sobering and ironic that a follower of David Koresh encourages those who harbor conspiracy theories to behave in a Christian fashion. Clive Doyle, who still follows Davidian theology, prays that nothing tragic like the Oklahoma City bombing will happen on another anniversary of the Waco inferno. Though he believes that the government carried out an evil plan that hot summer day, he says that he is not angry about the affair: "We're not asking people to take revenge or action on our behalf. The Bible says vengeance belongs to God, so we leave it in His hands. He'll sort this all out one of these days."[30]

It is of great consequence that it takes the words of a follower of David

Koresh's troubled theology to speak wisdom to numerous deluded Christians who have decided to fight a cast of end-times enemies. It is not the responsibility of the Christian to end evil. The Christian's task is to be light in a dark world.

By deciding to fight the horsemen of the apocalypse, some Christian conspiracy disciples have become more like the enemy and less like Christ. Such people should take Doyle's words to heart. After all, if today's evil is indeed the beginning of the end, how could they possibly stop it? God, in his good judgment, will sort the bodies.

I have debated the Calvary Chapel/end-times conspiracy theory connection with close friends. Since I am a deacon at a Calvary Chapel-style fellowship, it is difficult not to get into such debates. When I am critical of how Christian conspiracy theorists such as Chuck Missler have used these theories as a "witnessing tool" to save souls, I am criticized in turn. I have been told that his intentions are good, so who am I to question him?

Good intentions alone, however, are never good enough in the real world. Some Christians during the Crusades held weapons to the throats of non-Christians and told them to accept Christ as their Savior or die. Christ never meant for people to come to him by way of the sword, nor does he say to bring people to him by way of unfounded conspiracy theories, regardless of the intentions of those who promote them.

Christians during the Crusades slaughtered in the name of Christ. Today Christian conspiracy theorists are perpetrating a kind of bloodshed of the soul. They are unintentionally stealing people's joy, fueling their fears and spreading apathy and cultural paralysis. With every failed prediction concerning the end of the world, they diminish people's perception of the Bible as the ultimate source of truth.

Whether end-times Bible prophecy produces bitter fruit or blessings is in the hands of today's prophecy preachers. If balanced and forthright, end-times prophecy helps to produce a fruitful life. But when mixed with speculative and dangerous conspiracy theories, the result is often tragic. No longer can the church remain indifferent.

9

Why Conspiracy
Theories Are So
Prevalent & Attractive

That's the struggle of humanity,
to recruit others to your version of what's real.
Saul Bellow's Augie March

[Conspiracy theories provide] the double advantage of
exclusive information about the present as well as the ability to anticipate the future. . . .
A self-chosen elite is thus created.
When the leaders of any movement proclaim the qualities of absolute knowledge,
courage, and . . . persistence, one can expect the followers of such a movement
to have little chance to ask questions
except those concerning what they themselves must do.
William Chandler Baum

Part of shunning indifference toward damaging conspiracy theories
includes understanding why they are so popular and what advantages,
such as political and financial gain, they bring to those who promote them.
Christian conspiracy theorists share many of the same concerns as other
Christians: American sovereignty, the return of family-wage jobs, the
dangers of an increasingly secular society not balanced by the virtues of
religion, and foreign trade policies that hurt American industry. Christian
conspiracy theorists are within the realm of genuine political discussion
when they question growing dependence on world organizations and
complain that a small handful of wealthy and powerful bankers have too
much say in the political realm.

But the purpose of this chapter is to look at their mindset from both a secular and a religious viewpoint, since today's conspiracism is often a swirling combination of both. Conspiracy theories offer the allure of exclusive information, a world that appeals to those who fear ambiguity and long for a clearly delineated world, who look for scapegoats when times change or get hard, and who crave other tantalizing placebos. These theories are also plump with Machiavellian utility, which is being extracted for both political and financial gain.

These qualities and more have been described by the late historian Richard Hofstadter in his prophetic writing *The Paranoid Style in American Politics*. Originally a speech delivered at Oxford in November 1963 but later revised and expanded, *The Paranoid Style in American Politics* is more of an essay than a book. But it is an extraordinary prediction about the mindset of the kind of people I would talk to during my show more than thirty years later.

Hofstadter's work is still regarded as the most terse and scholarly explanation of the mindset behind today's conspiracy theories. It is targeted primarily at a group that he describes as "pseudo-conservatives, who believe that we have lived for a generation in the grip of a vast conspiracy." But it is not a style of thinking that is confined solely to the right wing. "With modulations and differences, it exists today, as it has in the past, on the left, and it has recurred at times in democratic movements from anti-Masonry to populism."[1]

Hofstadter explains why this mindset is so attractive and where it can lead:

> The model on which the world is interpreted contains . . . the same sense that all our ills can be traced to a single center and hence can be eliminated by some kind of final act of victory over the evil source. If the warnings of those who diagnose the central treachery are not heeded soon enough, it is argued, we are finished: the world confronts an apocalypse of a sort prefigured in the Book of Revelation.[2]

Some argue that those who adhere to apocalyptic and antigovernment conspiracy theories are purely delusional. But as Hofstadter points out, those who suffer from clinical paranoia usually believe that the conspiracy is focused only against *them*. With the conspiracy spokesperson, however, the conspiracy is focused against a nation, a culture, a way of life.[3] "His sense that his political passions are unselfish and patriotic, in fact, goes far to intensify his feelings of righteousness and his moral indignation."[4]

No Shades of Gray

Christians believe that they live in a world where good and evil war. Taking this war to extreme levels by believing that most if not *all* actions are either good or evil, allowing for no middle ground, was first considered to be a heresy called Manichaeism in the fourth century. Manichaeism is regarded as a complex dualistic religion that is largely associated with cults. Christians, even influential church leaders such as Augustine of Hippo, author of the fifth-century classic *Confessions,* have been diverted by this seductive worldview for centuries. But as Thomas Cahill, former director of religious publishing at Doubleday, writes, Augustine discarded this worldview that seduced him then as it does now with its simplistic answers and its ability to help one believe that one is smarter than the rest. Manichaeism "can only strike us as a California cult—a little Christian symbolism, a large dose of . . . dualism, and some of the quiet refinements of Buddhism. . . . For a while, it let Augustine off the hook. For one thing, it absolved him from any responsibility for his raging lusts." Within Manichaeism, good is passive, "unable to battle the gross and fleshly evils that raged against it." It's an ideal religious view that allows people such as Augustine to explore their dark lusts while believing themselves to be "above the herd." But Cahill writes that it cannot satisfy a robust mind. "Like Jehovah's Witnesses or Mormonism, it was full of assertions, but could yield no intellectual system to nourish a great intellect."[5] Roger Olson, professor of theology at Bethel College, believes that Manichaeism thrives in America's militias. Olson describes Christian militia leaders as people who see "everything in the cosmos in terms of stark good and evil. There is no gray."[6]

Such an extreme religious view has led to an extreme view of all human activity. Hofstadter says that to a conspiracy theorist history *is* a conspiracy, set in motion by demonic forces of almost transcendent power, and what is felt to be needed to defeat it is not the usual methods of political give-and-take, but an all-out crusade. . . . He constantly lives at a turning point: it is now or never in organizing resistance to conspiracy. Time is forever just running out. Like religious millenarians, he expresses the anxiety of those who are living through the last days and he is sometimes disposed to set a date for the apocalypse.[7]

When all is viewed as either of God or of Satan, battle lines become crystal clear as the earth and its people race precariously toward the apocalypse:

The enemy is clearly delineated: he is a perfect model of malice, a kind of amoral superman: sinister . . . powerful, cruel, sensual, luxury-loving. Unlike the rest of us, the enemy is not caught in the toils of the vast mechanism of history, himself a victim of the past, his desires, his limitations. He is a free, active, demonic agent.[8]

Through his study of the millennial sects of Europe from the eleventh to the sixteenth century, Norman Cohn came to believe that millennialists are preoccupied with

the megalomanic view of oneself as the Elect, wholly good, . . . persecuted yet assured of ultimate triumph; the attribution of gigantic and demonic powers to the adversary; the refusal to accept the ineluctable limitations and imperfections of human existence . . . ; the obsession with inerrable prophecies . . . systematized misinterpretations, always gross and often grotesque . . . ruthlessness directed towards an end which by its very nature cannot be realized—towards a total and final solution such as cannot be attained.[9]

As program director of KDOV I was approached either in person or by mail by individuals who were convinced they were prophets. They would tell me that they had a special message that must be shared with

God's people during these "last days." This message included the warning that America was on the verge of receiving God's holy wrath as as a result of its moral depravity, which they pointed out, has never been worse. At any other radio station, such people would be labeled crackpots. But in evangelical and fundamentalist circles this rhetoric is not as rare as it should be.

One person in particular saw herself as a kind of modern-day John the Baptist. She told me that she was not the one who received the message of America's coming judgment, but she knew the person who did, and it was *my* responsibility to let this person share his vision over the airwaves. She was a plain-faced, makeup-free woman who wore plain, unadorned dresses. But what she lacked in style she made up for with the blazing intensity of her hazel eyes.

I agreed to meet with this man. He was accompanied by plain and gaunt-faced women whose expressions held a mixture of military obedience and sober excitement, for they were spreading God's final message to all who had ears to hear. In 1992 I recorded his message and told the visitors I would have to think about it long and hard before playing it over the radio. I related how I had been told many times, with only subtle changes in the story line, that America would be destroyed at any moment. Yet these predictions had, over time, all turned out to be false.

At this point they exhibited many of the characteristics described by Cohn and Hofstadter. They, the elect, were transmitters. They were not accepting any criticisms from me. Only blind allegiance to the message, which at this point was put in the same category as inspired Scripture, would be tolerated.

The women, who held their tongues during the interview, came on like God's holy soldiers. By doubting the credibility of their message I was standing in the way of God's holy work. Thus the decision to play this message was a determination of either good or evil. They declared with utmost clarity that there would be blood on my hands. This was Christian love, end-times style, revealed by those who mistake the holiness of God as their own.

The warning issued from this prophet-in-our-time ran out of time.

God's deadline came and went, and dens of iniquity such as New York City and Las Vegas were still ringing with the sound of gunshots and humming from coins slipping smoothly into slot machines. I have wondered what happened to their faith once God's alleged prophetic message came up short. I have also wondered what damage I would have done to the church and my community if I had aired the message.

The Outside Enemy Now Is Inside

Influential Christian conspiracy theorists of the eighteenth and nineteenth centuries, such as Boston preacher Jedidiah Morse, his son S. F. B. Morse, and Yale president Timothy Dwight, promoted with apocalyptic imagery a coming war against America the Righteous by satanic *outside* forces. For Morse and his son, this satanic force was Masonry. Dwight argued in his 1798 Fourth of July discourse that anti-Christian thinkers and the Illuminati were set to destroy America:

> The sins of these enemies of Christ, and Christians, are of numbers and degrees which mock account and description. All that the malice and atheism of the Dragon, the cruelty and rapacity of the Beast, and the fraud and deceit of the false Prophet, can generate, or accomplish, swell the list. . . . Shall we introduce them into our government, our schools, our families? Shall our sons become the disciples of Voltaire, and the dragoons of Marat; or our daughters the concubines of the Illuminati?[10]

But one essential difference distinguishes Christian conspiracy theories of centuries past from contemporary Christian conspiracy theories: conspiracy theorists of past centuries believed that the forces of Satan were trying to attack America from *outside;* today's conspiracy theorists believe that the conspirators are working from *within* America's most powerful institutions. This dissimilarity helps explain why today's conspiracy theorists, such as Timothy McVeigh and Christian militia leaders Norman Olson and Dean Compton, are so determined to fight federal and state agencies.

Hofstadter warned, "Since what is at stake is always a conflict between absolute good and absolute evil, the quality needed is not a willingness to compromise but to fight things out to a finish. Nothing but complete victory will do."[11] Such a mindset brings about predictable frustrations. Because conspiracists foster unrealistic goals, especially in a pluralistic society, "failure constantly heightens [their] frustration. Even partial success leaves [them] with the same sense of powerlessness."[12]

It has been my observation that this sense of powerlessness is offset by an odd strain of pride. Leaders and disciples within the Christian conspiracy community elevate themselves to the enviable position of an elect group that is "in the know." Being part of an elite group that is constantly on the "inside" provides these members

> the double advantage of *exclusive information* about the present as well as the ability to anticipate the future. . . . A self-chosen elite is thus created. When the leaders of any movement proclaim the qualities of absolute knowledge, courage, and . . . persistence, one can expect the followers of such a movement to have little chance to ask questions except those concerning what they themselves must do.[13]

Fundamentalist Fellowship

These theories are so prevalent within the church partly because of their accord with a contemporary religious movement. Christian conspiracy theories and the militia it has helped produce have their roots anchored in a contemporary religious movement and philosophy broadly termed *fundamentalism.*

Christian journalist Stefan Ulstein interviewed more than twenty people who grew up with this rich and complicated worldview, which is influenced as much by culture and preference as it is by Scripture. All the conspiracy disciples I have interviewed adhere to one or more of the planks within fundamentalist doctrine. Ulstein outlines these planks:

> Fundamentalism is more than a theological movement. It is a subculture with a complete value system that encompasses aesthetics, education and *politics.* The fundamentalism that white baby boomers grew up with during the fifties and sixties was concerned

with biblical inerrancy, personal piety and the *imminent, physical return of Christ,* but it was also on the right end of the political continuum. It was distrustful of *government,* yet it was strongly, almost unquestioningly, patriotic. It equated America with the kingdom of God, yet preached the wickedness of society. Communism and "creeping socialism" were aligned with the forces of darkness. . . . Fundamentalist churches preached the good news of Jesus Christ, along with *anticommunism* and a fear of intellectualism, modernism and humanism.[14]

Ulstein traces the origins of fundamentalism and concludes that it is really a twentieth-century American movement "rather than an unbroken line of thinking that began with the apostles. Fundamentalism, like all 'isms,' originated in a specific place as a reaction against other isms, most notably the German higher criticism that led to various forms of theological relativism and modernism."[15]

Since the beginning of Christianity many religious leaders have preached that the world will be judged and destroyed. But the current practice of inventing complex end-times scenarios, complete with subjective interpretations, dates back to the roots of fundamentalism as well. That was when evangelicals "were disturbed by the rising interest in biblical criticism and Charles Darwin's theory of evolution, which contradicted the account of creation in Genesis."[16]

A rift occurred between liberals and conservatives that split American Christendom. "Liberal theologians favored modernizing Protestantism by discarding the notion of the infallibility of the Bible. . . . While the liberals reacted to modernism by adapting, the conservatives dug further into the foundation of their faith, the literal truth of the Bible."[17]

Shortly before World War I the conservative movement gained momentum with the appearance of twelve paperback books called *The Fundamentals.* This series opposed modernist theology with, among other positions, premillennialism.[18] More and more conservative evangelicals took on the name *fundamentalist* to describe their opposition to liberal theology and modernism. Fundamentalists even adopted their own version of the Bible—the Scofield Reference Bible, first published in 1909. This reference Bible was the King James Version heavily footnoted by fundamentalist scholar C. I. Scofield. On some pages the footnotes take up as much space as Scripture itself. It is this version of the Bible that helped give birth to today's end-times scenario of wars, famines, one-world government, rapture, tribulation and other apocalyptic events.

"The Scofield Bible has become so widely accepted among fundamentalists that many pastors and laymen take its commentaries as literally as the text."[19] As sure as atheists attempt to use fossils to prove evolution from one species to another, fundamentalists attempt to use history to prove that the Bible does not err. Premillennialists are so dogmatic in part because they are trying to show that their end-times scenarios prove that the Bible contains in minute detail all the important events of history (past and future).

This helps explain why today's Christian conspiracy theories are so popular. Aspects unique to fundamentalism—its anticommunism, skepticism about government, fear of New Age/humanism and politically conservative views—fused to the certain belief that we are living in the end times, have produced a contemporary Christian worldview predisposed to conspiracy thinking. Fundamentalists can easily identify the sources of the evil unleashed during the last generation. These are the same evil forces that fundamentalists have hated and feared for decades: communism (former Soviet Union), advancing socialism (the United Nations), government (especially the FBI, CIA, Federal Reserve and IRS) and anything outside fundamentalism (the mainstream press, Hollywood, academia, psychology, Catholicism, Promise Keepers and so on).

Fundamentalism provided a long list of enemies who fit easily into simplistic end-times equations. So fundamentalists attack James Dobson, not because his work or his organization fulfills end-times Bible prophecy but because counseling and psychology are seen as the work of the devil. Billy Graham is attacked because he once golfed with John Kennedy, who was seen as part of a papal conspiracy. Graham also shared the pulpit with Martin Luther King Jr., who was despised by some fundamentalists, not because of his race but because they said he was a covert communist agitator. They attack Promise Keepers because of its charismatic overtones, found especially in its praise style of music and in the sermons preached by some of its speakers, who espouse the organization's ecumenical mission.

Identification of someone as part of the conspiracy has more to do with whether that person or group disagrees with fundamentalism's view of good culture and politics than it does with actual Bible prophecy. Yet Christian conspiracy theories have also produced serious side effects that were not intended three decades ago. They have managed to change the structure of the fundamentalism that bestowed it with so much power.

For example, where fundamentalism once preached undying support for America the Righteous (especially in international military missions), conspiracy disciples have eroded the notion of America's national goodness. By doing so they are completing what the radical Left never dreamed it could accomplish: encouraging mass numbers within the church, especially conservatives, to denounce their government.

An Explanation for Everything

Another tendency within fundamentalism is the desire to explain away most of life's ambiguities, the same attribute that makes conspiracy theories so attractive. One ex-fundamentalist who became an administrator of a Christian college says, "Fundamentalism grew out of an unpredictable world. In the middle of war, social upheaval and the emergence of new political and religious systems, people wanted something predictable. That's understandable, but the world will always be threatening and unclear."[20]

The strikingly inconsistency within these theories is that their attempts to create delineated explanations require that people adhere to extremely complex and unrealistic scenarios that disregard humanity's self-centered nature. For an actual New World Order to exist, there would have to be a cabal of accomplices so huge (yet as the same time so surreptitious), a maze of deception so complex and rigid and a mindset so overpowering (yet with dronelike obedience) that the whole scenario would seem impossible, even to those who possess suspicious minds. Such was the case with seasoned journalist Dick Reavis.

After he decided he wasn't getting the whole Waco story from FBI press releases, Reavis began interviewing followers of David Koresh after the tragedy. Reavis saw how the standoff drew the attention of the extreme Right. "These Constitutionalists began coming to Waco to demonstrate. After it was all over, they started to help the survivors of Waco get settled in."[21] Reavis says he knows why the conspiracy theories about Waco began to flourish:

> A lot of that material is not true. The problem is, when there's not enough knowledge, conspiracy theorists come along to fill in the gaps. Some of the things that happened there may never be explained, but a conspiracy theorist thinks everything can be explained, and in this case, their explanation is based on a general mistrust of government.[22]

Journalist Gordon Witkin believes that the appeal of conspiracy theories originates from something more fundamental:

> They reflect a primary need. In a world where everything seems to be changing incomprehensibly fast, conspiracy theories satisfy a hunger for logical explanations, for order. It may be twisted, but it's order nonetheless—and more attractive than the explanation that events unfold randomly. Conspiracy thinking allows people to avoid confronting the idea that sometimes, well, stuff happens.[23]

Fellow conspiracy critic Sanford Pinsker believes that these theories reveal a similar fundamental flaw: "The imagination seeks a Truth deeper than truth, a Reality more patterned, more coherent, than the messy affair that brought a president [Kennedy] and an Oswald to Dealey Plaza."[24] In this vein, conspiracy theories are akin to the highly marketed Psychic Friends Network. Both claim to provide a patterned and coherent world if only one is willing to submit to their leadership and claims of exclusive knowledge, which are accompanied by a customary and reasonable price tag. Both create a kind of crystal ball but with one telling difference; conspiracy theories usually appeal to the head and intellect while psychic readings often appeal to the heart and feelings. They are a kind of wrestlemania tag team that is capable of twisting the ears of those who are willing to pay for the newest tape or book on how to strategize and survive economic hell on earth, and of those who will gladly pay two dollars a minute to find out if love is in the future.

But some, such as Robert Brown, editor and publisher of *Soldier of Fortune* magazine (not exactly a pro-centralized government publication), are not as gracious in their assessment of the endurance of conspiracy theories. He says that the conspiracy community does not "want reasonable explanations . . . because they don't fit their preconceived notions."[25]

The apostle Paul wrote that there are innate ambiguities in life: "Now we see but a poor reflection as in a mirror; then we shall see face to face. Now I know in part; then I shall know fully, even as I am fully known. And now these three remain: faith, hope and love. But the greatest of these is love" (1 Corinthians 13:12-13). Conspiracy theories gain much of their popularity from their promise to explain many of the mysteries of life. But in their quest to explain, they create a simplistic, two-dimensional world that represents more a work of fiction than the real world. Even worse, the fear and paranoia they create are antithetical to faith, hope and especially love.

This desire to explain away life's complexities is even greater during times of sweeping change. Dave Frohnmayer, the 1990 Republican candidate for Oregon governor and now president of the University of Oregon, says that this type of cultural whiplash has bred a new tribalism:

> The end of the Cold War and the evaporation of a monolithic external Communist threat has released new energies for tribal-style nationalism around the world. Religious fundamentalism of all stripes is resurgent. Massive changes in the world economy, including the globalization of corporations, have disrupted old industries and dislocated local workers. Employees with white collars are just as threatened as those wearing blue.[26]

Frohnmayer says that the result is insecurity, which isn't always rational. "People look for scapegoats, and they find them across the political spectrum. They begin thinking in terms of 'us versus them.'"

This public insecurity, combined with Machiavellian political opportunism, "is one of the most serious threats facing us today."[27]

While ridding the world of painful ambiguities, Christian conspiracy theories attract adherents for another reason: they are a way of laughing in the face of a culture that seems to have ridiculed fundamentalist thought. By saying that today's conspiracies are signposts of the end as foretold in the Bible, Christian conspiracy theorists are able to kick sand in the eyes of a world that mocks them. They are the ones in tune with the secret rhythm of life, and history will validate this understanding sooner than most think.

Such a desire does lead to twisted ends and dangerous consequences, but it is nonetheless attractive. It is similar to the gravitation of some Europeans before World War II toward fascism when faced with the encroaching threat of communism. There's a conspiracy theory for every ambiguity in search of a scapegoat.

Communal, Isolated Lifestyle

Some will argue that popular Christian conspiracy theorists do not intend to lead anyone down the destructive path created by cult leaders and conspiracy theorists such as David Koresh, and I agree. But cult leaders such as Koresh have made use of the end-times conspiracy theories found in more mainstream prophecy circles.

The Davidians held to antigovernment conspiracy theories that were fueled by their complicated eschatology. According to one former Davidian,

When [Branch Davidians] start to get information that would normally indicate, or should indicate, "Well, wait a minute, this is wrong, this is false, something's funny here," instead they interpret it by running through their processing system and figure a way out of the dilemma. They'd work it out to where they'd think, "No, this is okay. This is God's doing. God works in mysterious ways."[28]

The Davidians, driven by an intense and complicated view of end-times prophecy, believed that their showdown with the federal government was a sign of the times around them. They believed that the forces found in the outside world were evil and that they would eventually have a showdown with the federal government, which was part of an end-times conspiracy against them. According to their eschatology, this would be the beginning of Armageddon.

Those who study cultic behaviors and ideas divide the field into three components: sociological, psychological and theological. From a sociological perspective "the primary indicator of a group's cultic nature is complete withdrawal from society into a communal, isolated lifestyle."[29] The Weaver family fled to an isolated section of Idaho in part because of the end-times speculation of Hal Lindsey. James "Bo" Gritz, a kind of patron saint in the conspiracy community, has formed his own isolated enclave in the Pacific Northwest for fellow conspiracy believers. When translated, its name means "Almost Heaven."

Religious experts who study cult leaders and behavior have discovered sixteen commonly observed habits. *At least* six of them are exhibited within the conspiracy community:[30]

1. *Isolation of members—psychologically as well as physically—from individuals outside the group whose ideas and philosophies are contrary to those promoted by the group.* Christian conspiracy publications often warn their readers that they cannot get the truth from any publication outside their own official sources of information. These publications are not referring to a form of media bias. They believe that the mainstream press is part of Satan's covert conspiracy to bring about worldwide oppression.

2. *The use of fear and intimidation against members who desire to leave the group, or former members seeking to break ties with the group.* As mentioned previously, a woman who left a group of conspiracy theorists—a group that claimed to be Christian—threatened to kill her because she might reveal to the government their identities and location in Florida. At least one militia cell in America that is propelled by antigovernment conspiracy theories has been charged with murder when a defector was found dead.

3. *The promotion of an "ends justifies the means" philosophy within the group.* The most tragic example of how conspiracy theories create

such a mindset is found in the New World Order fears and anger of terrorist Timothy McVeigh and his accomplice, Terry Nichols.

4. *An "us vs. them" mentality that stresses the group's unique hold on truth and demonizes anyone who opposes that alleged truth.* Oppose these theories on a Christian radio station and watch the accusations come rolling in.

5. *A siege mentality that dismisses all criticisms of the group from outside sources as unwarranted "persecution."* Not only was this mindset found among the conspiracy-saturated Branch Davidians, it is found in the rhetoric of people such as Christian conspiracy preacher Chuck Missler. When Christian journalist and cult expert Richard Abanes exposed how Missler had quoted anti-Semitic sources in his zeal to prove the existence of a New World Order conspiracy, Missler accused Abanes (whom he once characterized as a non-Christian, then as someone from the "Christian left") of carrying out a smear campaign against the brethren. Louis Farrakhan has used similar arguments to dismiss meaningful criticism.

6. *An elite attitude that is drilled into members, which states that those outside the group are spiritually lukewarm—or entirely lost.* As one who has crossed swords with numerous Christian conspiracy theorists during my talk show, I cannot remember how many times I was dismissed as a spiritual greenhorn. If I were only more in tune with God and his cosmic truths, they implied, I would know deep within that these conspiracies are real and are all part of God's divine plan during these "last days." To some I was spiritually lukewarm and to at least one not even a Christian.

These traits are troubling enough, for a "surprising number of truly Christian churches, groups, and independent ministries are cultic from a psychological perspective." More important, religious groups that are cultic from a psychological or sociological perspective "are vulnerable to evolving into a cult from a theological perspective."[31] One of the characteristics of a cult, when interpreted from a theological perspective, applies all too well to Christian conspiracy theories: "Any religious movement which claims the backing of Christ or the Bible, but distorts the central message of Christianity by 1) an additional revelation, and 2) by displacing a fundamental tenet of the faith with a secondary matter."[32]

This "additional revelation" continually originates from contemporary and popular end-times preachers. As Chuck Swindoll and other Christian leaders realize, this is a community that often thrusts its new revelations *on* the Scriptures rather than promoting ideas *from* Scripture. One belief that is growing in popularity is that a "secret code" that reveals detailed accounts of future events has been hidden—until now—in the Bible.

There is no better example of "displacing a fundamental tenet of the faith with a secondary matter" within the Christian conspiracy community than its devotion to a subjective view of eschatology that serves as its theological engine. "Theological cults tend to distort . . . doctrinal issues as well, often going well beyond the various Christian positions that are biblically feasible, especially concerning eschatology."[33] To devout Christian conspiracy theorists, end-times prophecy becomes a religion in itself. Yet as Chuck Swindoll and others warn, it has the ability to "consume a person's mind" and bring about tragic ends.

Though popular Christian conspiracy theorists from within the evangelical/fundamentalist community do not officially list a particular view of the end times as an essential of the orthodox Christian faith, many speak and write as if it were. It is often *the* consuming issue worthy of their newsletter, latest book or sermon. As a former Christian conspiracy theorist told me, his Christian faith was increasingly driven by a New World Order/end-times prophecy impulse.

A Christian's view of eschatology has always been considered a secondary matter. It was never meant to be the sole subject of study or, for that matter, the primary motivator of faith. Yet when people question the Christian conspiracy community's view of prophecy, they are often met with hostility, as if it were an essential of the faith.

Christian conspiracy theories do not (at least not yet) promote a single leader, though many did rally behind Pat Buchanan for president in 1994. But they do share other red flags that are commonly associated with cultic groups that do rally behind a specific leader and that destroy the lives of those within their influence. One of a cult's most attractive qualities is that it attempts, often by means of new revelations, to provide clearly delineated answers to life's persistent problems. Christian conspiracy theories offer the same charming remedies.

Nietzsche's Prediction

It is possible that America's predisposition toward conspiracy theories was predicted during the late 1800s by the German philosopher and social critic Friedrich Nietzsche (1844-1900). He is best known within evangelical/fundamentalist circles for his statement "God is dead." Nietzsche saw that humanity no longer lived as if God were relevant to daily life, as if God had anything meaningful to say to his creation. In this way humanity had "killed" God, but in killing their belief in God people had killed their ability to rid themselves of the eroding influences of sin and guilt.[34]

Nietzsche predicted that as a result culture would become more pagan, secular and gloomy, giving way to rising skepticism, which would be fostered by the world's leading thinkers in the twentieth century. These leading thinkers were, like Nietzsche, secular intellectuals, those "who believe they can refashion the universe by the light of their unaided reason."[35] Historian Paul Johnson argues that unlike their religious predecessors who more than two hundred years ago felt constrained by the precepts of tradition with its established moral code, these secular intellectuals did not feel bound by a corpus of revealed religion or truth and hence "were not servants and interpreters of the gods but substitutes. Their hero was Prometheus, who stole the celestial fire and brought it to earth."[36] With this surrogate fire, secular intellectuals such as Rousseau, Marx and Sartre pronounced a harsh and condemning judgment upon both churches and clergy. And with this fire they have set the modern world ablaze with hitherto unseen misery and destruction. Johnson confirms Nietzsche's prediction of rising gloom and despair during this century when he concludes:

> For a variety of reasons, social engineering [the driving impulse on behalf of secular intellectuals] has been the salient delusion and the greatest curse of the modern age. In the twentieth century it has killed scores of millions of innocent people, in Soviet Russia, Nazi

Germany, Communist China and elsewhere. Social engineering . . .
was pioneered by Rousseau, systematized by Marx and institution-
alized by Lenin.[37]

Nietzsche helped grease the rails of this slide perpetrated by the
heartless tyranny of ideas that is unbalanced by the virtues of religion.
But he did not wear rose-colored glasses when analyzing its effect. He
predicted that this new secular worldview would lead to contempt for
humanity for this reason: since people no longer believe in God, they no
longer can believe in truth, beauty and ultimate redemption. Fallible
humans with their fickle minds and fluctuating hearts would now rule.
Consequently humanity would condemn itself and its institutions, limp-
ing through the twentieth century in search of new standards that never
satisfy.[38]

As Johnson explains, humanity has already toppled the institution of
religion as a medium of goodness and importance and replaced it with an
alliance with government, a kind of secular savior. But now a growing
number of Americans are turning their backs on government because of
their affinity with conspiracy theories. It seems government too has failed
them, so for the last few decades Americans have begun to "kill" the
secular prophets of government. Author Tom Wolfe argues that other
secular prophets, namely science, the arts and entertainment, are also
under attack from a culture that once was willing to truckle to their leading
but have now grown hostile toward their inability to please their souls.

Nietzsche may not have predicted the rise in conspiracy thinking that
occurred toward the end of the twentieth century, but he did predict rising
skepticism and pessimism, which have fertilized conspiracy theories
across the political spectrum, especially in economically beleaguered
communities. When contempt for other people rises, it is often a matter
of time before a political, religious or racial conspiracy theory is born.

Scapegoat for Societal Troubles

Much has been written about the conspiracy community since the rise in
awareness of America's patriot movement. Some have purported that it

is the latest manifestation of white male disenfranchisement. Reports have made it appear as if being a conspiracy disciple is yet another option to alleviate midlife crisis, similar to buying a Harley. Though this is a simplistic analysis, it does contain a grain of truth.

Some conspiracy disciples have checked out of life, angry and frustrated in a country that offers so much promise but so little realization. Many believe that they are working harder for less. Shifting global economies, in which high-paying jobs have been replaced by either cheaper labor or high technology, haven't helped. Opposing such a shift was one reason conservative Pat Buchanan received such glowing reviews from the patriot community.[39]

One reason farmers and ranchers joined the Freemen of Jordan, Montana, was that they found themselves in dire financial straits and wanted to blame their problems on someone else. Bob Fletcher, cofounder of Militia of Montana, said his slide into the world of conspiracy hit full speed when he ended up on the losing end of a business deal. Instead of chalking it up to experience when his Georgia-based toy company went under or questioning his prior decision to form a partnership with someone of questionable character, he blamed his misfortune on a veiled government conspiracy somehow connected to the Iran-Contra scandal.

Terry Nichols is a disheartening example of how conspiracy theories attract those who are down and out. He started his patriot lifestyle when he joined a group that helped farmers hold on to their land by fighting the government and the banks. According to journalist Jeffrey Toobin,

> Nichols's life was a catalogue of failure. He was a flop as a farmer, a real-estate salesman, and soldier, and also as a husband—first to an American woman five years his senior and then to a Filipina mail-order bride eighteen years his junior. "The young ones are easier to train," Nichols told his second wife, who was seventeen when they married.[40]

She has since returned to the Philippines. She and Nichols had a two-year-old son who suffocated in a plastic laundry bag in 1993.

Such is the age-old blame game, except that today it has an end-times theological twist. In the 1980s my generation blamed our parents for our angst and unhappiness. Today the blame has switched to the government, with the backing of some within the church.

A Witnessing Tool

Some Christians promote end-times conspiracy theories because they believe them to be a "witnessing tool." By this they mean that the theories provide an opportunity to share the good news that through Jesus Christ sins are forgiven for those who believe. For example, the Christians may be in a conversation with a non-Christian when the topic turns to current events. Since they believe that such events are orchestrated by the hand of God in order to bring about the imminent end of this present world, they begin to "show" how the events fit perfectly into Bible prophecy. If this idea is new to the non-Christian, it may lead to further questions and discussion, which may lead to a presentation of the gospel.

I have talked to people who say they came to or renewed their faith in Christ because of Bible prophecy. But I have yet to speak to people who accepted Christ as their Savior through end-times conspiracy theories.

For some, being a spokesperson for Christian conspiracy theories carries with it evangelical motives. But renown atheist Stephen Jay Gould in his book *Questioning the Millennium* claims that these theories are yet more proof that faith equals gullibility—an age-old equation promoted by atheists and other skeptics that in this regard rings true. Augustine, the Christian theologian of the fourth and fifth centuries who accepted the doctrine of Christ's second coming, argued against detailed speculations in regard to Christ's return. He warned against embracing apocalyptic claims so that "we [not] fall into a panic over present happenings as if they were the ultimate and extreme of all things . . . [and] be laughed at by those who have read of more and worse things in the history of the world."[41] The church endorsed this view at its Council of Ephesus in A.D. 431.[42]

Moreover, Christian conspiracy theories are not a good witnessing tool because, when viewed in their entirety, they are far from admirable. They inadvertently borrow information from anti-Semites and breed fear, paranoia and even hatred, as well as other social ills. In addition conspiracy theories in general are tools in the hands of calculating politicians and others who extract their political utility for questionable and often deplorable gain.

> The single case in modern history in which one might say that the paranoid style has had a consummatory triumph occurred not in the United States but in Germany. It is a common ingredient of fascism, and of frustrated nationalisms, though it appeals to many who are hardly fascists and it can frequently be seen in the left-wing press. The famous Stalin purge trials incorporated, in a supposedly juridical form, a wildly imaginative and devastating exercise in the paranoid style.[43]

Conspiracy theories derive some of their political utility from their ability to create a stark *us* (the forces of good) versus *them* (the forces of Satan) mentality, which has been used skillfully by dictators such as Saddam Hussein. The skillful use of fear, an effective short-term motivator, results in two conditions beneficial to those who traffic in conspiracy theories: as with Louis Farrakhan, it galvanizes their support base by motivating supporters to defend themselves *through* their leader, "who brings with him the promise of redemption and victory,"[44] and it helps generate financial gain.

As program director of KDOV I once helped to sell more than 125 copies of an interview with a well-known Christian conspiracy theorist. Yet when we interviewed drug czar William Bennett, who offered sober but hope-filled answers to complex issues that were void of any conspiracy thinking, only five listeners ordered copies. I believe that this same fearful drive is at work when conveniently priced books, videos and tapes are sold through Christian conspiracy newsletters.

The profitability of conspiracy theories has been evident for decades. In the 1960s New Jersey preacher and Christian conspiracy theorist Carl McIntire raised money through donations solicited on his religious broadcasts and through his publication, *Christian Beacon*. By the middle of the 1960s both organizations were collecting more than $3 million a year.[45]

During the late 1990s, Jim Benson, editor of *American Survival Guide: The Magazine of Self Reliance,* said that his circulation of sixty thousand magazines per month was double what it had been four years earlier. He admitted that one reason was the publication's playing on the fear that guns may be taken from people by the "Klinton" administration: "If we take guns off the cover, sales plummet."[46]

One reason Thomas Nelson Publishers, the largest Christian publisher in the United States at $300 million a year, is "growing at a double-digit rate is the success of a book entitled *Beginning of the End: The Assassination of Yitzhak Rabin and the Coming Antichrist.*" Written by preacher and conspiracy theorist John Hagee, this book, which is now in its seventh printing and is circulating among patriot and militia circles, promises to be the company's bestselling book ever.[47]

Perhaps the clearest contemporary use of fear and urgency within the Christian conspiracy community is found in the computer of Don McAlvany. Each issue of *McAlvany Intelligence Advisor* (MIA) takes his devoted readers on a tour of disasters about to happen if they don't follow his advice, which includes financial investments through his organization. In early 1990 he wrote, "MIA believes that the next five years will be the most dangerous period since just before World War II and could be setting the stage for World War III in the early to mid-1990s."

In November 1991 he said, "This writer has a growing sense of urgency that a whole series of crises are about to manifest themselves in America: financial, social, . . . political, etc." The year 1992, he said, was supposed to be the year of "Danger, Deception and Depression." Under his "Final Thought" category in May 1993, he warned, "This writer believes that very tumultuous times (financially, socially, and politically) lie ahead for America, Europe, South Africa, and much of the world between now and the year 2000."

Contrary to McAlvany's urgent alarms of economic disaster, America in the 1990s experienced sustained economic growth. McAlvany's alarmist claims are similar to statements made by fellow Christian conspiracy theorist Billy James Hargis, who sent out fundraising letters asking for $1,000 donations to fight the "darkness and conspiracies all about us."

One letter asked, "Will 1983 Be The Year America Is Destroyed By The Soviets?" Hargis asked his followers to send money to buy full-page ads in the *National Enquirer* warning of the Communist conspiracy. He promised those who made donations that "God [will] bless you as you have never been blessed in your life."[48]

According to one expert on gold coins, whom I'll call David,[49] McAlvany and his telemarketing company make a substantial profit. "McAlvany encourages his readers to not buy gold bullion because he says the government will come and confiscate it." But David, who has been dealing with gold for more than seventeen years and who attends an evangelical church, says that the real reason McAlvany frowns on bullion is because its markup is small when compared to gold coins. Indeed, one advertising insert in McAlvany's newsletter begins, "Attention Precious Metals Investors: 'First I Suggested It. . . . Then I Strongly Encouraged It. . . . Now I'm Seriously Advising You: Switch Your Gold Bullion Immediately Into U.S. $20 Gold Coins.'"[50]

David says that McAlvany exploits the novice conspiracy theorist with extreme markups. McAlvany will often sell a twenty-dollar gold piece for seventy-five dollars more than coin shops charge, sometimes more. "They make a whole lot of money. The people who are really into conspiracy theories know that you can get gold coins for much less from a coin shop."

David believes that McAlvany's newsletters are designed to take the reader on a tour of crisis and fear. But while he has his audience captive, McAlvany provides the reader with a solid solution—buy gold coins from him at a premium price—and people respond. He says that one gold coin supplier cannot keep enough coins in stock after the release of an especially motivating McAlvany newsletter.

Coin collecting is a harmless hobby for many people. But Christian conspiracy theorists believe it is a path to economic salvation. Since they believe that paper currency is backed by nothing and that the Federal Reserve has the power and will to collapse our economy, businesses that sell gold and other types of coins become a kind of sanctuary for them. David says that he has yet to meet an owner of a coin shop who did not believe that America's monetary system is crooked and who did not adhere to at least one conspiracy theory.

David has watched people walk away from the Christian faith because of these theories. "As they get deeper and deeper into this stuff, they put down their Bible and pick up law books. They freak out and stop trusting and following God." Given how convincing these theories can be, David says that if it weren't for God's grace and sound Bible study, he too might have walked away from the faith.

Satan's to Blame

Christian conspiracy theorists claim that their message is about revealing a good God's perfect plan for the world. But if you look at the content of their message and what they spend most of their time "revealing," they are really in the business of "exposing" their subjective and often tantalizing view of Satan and his evil plans. The best contemporary example of fraudulent claims about Satan is the debunked life of Mike Warnke.

Warnke claimed to be a satanic high priest who had fifteen hundred followers in three cities. Warnke claimed that "he had unlimited wealth and power at his disposal, provided by members of Satanism's highest echelon, the Illuminati. And then he converted to Christ."[51] He was a favored speaker within the evangelical culture for almost twenty years. "A generation of Christians learned what they knew of Satanism and the occult from [Warnke's book] *The Satan Seller*. The book sold, by the author's own reckoning, three million copies in twenty years."

But in the early 1990s two reporters from *Cornerstone* magazine, a gutsy Christian publication based in Chicago, unraveled the tall tales of Warnke, exposing them as raw and often unsophisticated fabrications. Reporters Jon Trott and Mike Hertenstein say that one reason the evangelical/fundamentalist community was so ripe to accept Warnke's claims that Satanists had infiltrated the media, law enforcement and other realms of influence was the belief that occultism will accelerate in the end times. This was essentially the message of Hal Lindsey's second book, *Satan Is Alive and Well on Planet Earth*.

Lindsey's linking of undocumented stories of Satanists with modern philosophy seemed another *Reefer Madness*-style attempt to scaring people into the author's conclusions. Worse, there was a tendency for the sensational elements to distract attention from more subtle evils. The "gory story" approach reduced Satan from a cunning deceiver to a comic-book character. . . . Hal Lindsey's second book was another huge success.[52]

This book and the financial success it garnered helped Zondervan Publishing Company to expand and enlarge the company's chain of Family Bookstores. "Zondervan wasn't the only religious publishing company to strike gold in End Times or Satan books."[53] Describing a Christian Booksellers Association Convention during the early 1990s, *Publishers Weekly* noted that it featured "books that are driven by fear— fear of what the educational system is doing to your children, fear of what the Antichrist is going to do in a couple of years, fear of what the 12 steps are going to do to the rest of the Church."[54]

Another observer commented that most CBA books during that particular convention were "nothing more than a feeble and reactionary attempt to formulate an apologetic against a vague and undefined enemy. . . . Some Christian publishers thrive on perpetuating this paranoia by marketing the latest call to arms in the ongoing competition to discover the focus of evil in the world."[55]

At this convention numerous self-professed experts claimed to have identified the groups plaguing America and the conspiracies they were implementing. However, "none seemed to work quite as advertised—a situation that may have been too bad for book buyers, but was just fine for the book business."[56]

Conclusion

The reasons for the increasing popularity of conspiracy theories are as complex as humankind's fears, hopes and dreams. But some of the reasons, which are often a mixture of both secular and religious impulses, are known. They include how some evangelicals and fundamentalists view the world through filters that have made them susceptible to these theories and their destructive ramifications.

Those who decide to oppose Christian conspiracy theories should realize that their opposition will put them at odds with many tenets held dear within fundamentalism. The price for such opposition is great, according to former ordained Baptist minister and militia leader Norman Olson: "There are people taking names now and people in the media will stand charges with the tyrants. Spreading news is a sacred gift of God and if you don't deliver, the people will come knocking at your door."[57]

As many former fundamentalists know, to defect from this powerful religious and political subculture is to be ostracized socially and economically, and even from your own church. Perhaps this is the main reason many church leaders will not speak out against the dangers of Christian conspiracy theories. One caller to *The Paul Thomas Show* said, "It's politically incorrect to oppose them. Too many of the people sitting in the congregation believe in these conspiracies. They're afraid to rock the boat."

10

Toward a Solution

The LORD spoke to me with his strong hand upon me,
warning me not to follow the way of this people.
He said: "Do not call conspiracy everything that these people call conspiracy;
do not fear what they fear, and do not dread it.
The LORD Almighty is the one you are to regard as holy,
he is the one you are to fear."
Isaiah 8:11-13

What's wrong with the world is me.
G. K. Chesterton

There is no snare set by the fiend for the mind of man more dangerous
than the illusion that our enemies are also the enemies of God.
Ruskin

As the previous chapters reveal, Christian conspiracy theories have the ability to change a person's life. They are as real to those who believe them as the Trinity is to Christians. They are an addendum to their faith tied tight to popular end-times prophecy. They are the very reason some have fled for the hills, denounced their government and joined the militia nearest them. Some in the church are becoming more aware of their bitter fruit, but those who propagate such theories have done little to amend, curtail or modify their speculative message.

Moving toward a solution depends on a realization of what these conspiracy theories feed on, such as blatant superstition and the desire to blame the world's problems on a certain group of people. Part of the solution also includes acknowledging that the Christian conspiracy community harbors legitimate concerns.

Families whose peace and joy have been taken away by sincere yet dangerous speculation will find them restored only when they accept certain truths: that the evil of the end times demands no conspiracy; that superstitious beliefs are perilous; that the truth needs to be spoken in love; that end-times messages need to be tempered; that legitimate concerns need affirmation; that the real enemy must be recognized; that complaints must be about something real; that hope and joy can be restored.

The Evil of the End Times Demands No Conspiracy

Despite claims made by the Christian conspiracy community, there are many different interpretations of prophetic information found in the Bible. All have strengths and weaknesses. Numerous Christian authors have argued that key prophesies in both the Old and New Testament have already been fulfilled. Their view is often at odds with today's popular belief that key prophecies have yet to be fulfilled. Consequently some argue that the best solution to the problem of Christian conspiracy theories is to refute their eschatology. But given how rigid many Christian conspiracy theorists are in regard to their view of end-times Bible prophecy, it is unlikely that this view will change.

Instead, we need to point out that a person can still adhere to the belief that this is the "terminal generation" without also adhering to wild and speculative conspiracy theories. To put it simply, there is no need for a conspiracy to bring about the evil described in popular end-times prophecy. In fact, a conspiracy is needed to bring about good. (Christian fellowship is part of this conspiracy of good in a world that gravitates toward evil. C. S. Lewis argued that when people attend church, they are partaking in a centuries-old conspiracy, with the Bible as their coded message.)

The evil that was the Third Reich came to power accompanied by cheers from many Germans. No conspiracy led post-World War I Germany to adore Hitler and accept the infamous leadership of Julius Streicher, Ernst Roehm, Heinrich Himmler, Carin von Kantzow Göbbels and Hermann Göring. According to Daniel Jonah Goldhagen, ordinary Germans embraced the Third Reich's leaders and their blazing anti-Semitism.

Goldhagen argues that contrary to early rumors after the war, average

Germans such as those in police battalions who were too old to join the army were willing to round up Jewish women, men and children and blood-stain their uniforms by shooting them at close range. Or perhaps they would set them on fire. He points out that though the "police" were given the option to be excused from murdering Jews, few took it. Some proudly sent photos home, such as one from Police Battalion 101 that shows an officer taunting Jewish captives. His fellow Germans are in the background, with wide smiles of approval.[1]

I have talked with a German woman who was a young girl when Hitler rose to power. Today, despite the black-and-white pictures and chilling testimony and libraries of paperwork that document the atrocities of the Holocaust, her reverence for her Führer remains solid. She speaks about all the good Hitler did for her country: employment where there was poverty, food where hunger reigned, nationalistic pride where there was bitter humiliation after World War I. But when probed about her thoughts on the Holocaust, how millions of Jews were executed for being Jewish, she glibly responded, "Oh, Hitler didn't kill them all. There's plenty of them left."

Hannah Arendt defined such a terse defense of the Holocaust perpetrated by Hitler and his men as the "the banality of evil." This banality turned genocide into another government program that allowed people such as Eichmann to hide behind paperwork and workloads, allowing them to abdicate personal responsibility while bolstering their defense.

There is no United Nations conspiracy that makes this woman defend the "banality of evil." There was no conspiracy that made Hitler's rambling manifesto *Mein Kampf* outsell all books in Nazi Germany other than the Bible. During Hitler's first year as chancellor it sold a million copies, making him the most prosperous author in Germany. No conspiracy made this Nazi bible commonplace within German homes. "Few households felt secure without a copy on the table."[2] Germans felt obligated to give a copy to the groom and bride at weddings, and nearly every schoolchild received one on graduation day. By the time World War II began, six million copies had been sold in Germany.

The importance of such gravitation toward evil cannot be overstated.

The Christian conspiracy community cannot produce any event or entity—whether it be GATT, NAFTA, Ruby Ridge, Waco, the United Nations, talk of a New World Order—that can rival the evil found in the rise and fall of the Third Reich and the popular appeal it held for millions who were drawn to the charisma and character of its leader.

No conspiracy made the Nazi bible a bestseller year after year. Germans gladly displayed the book on coffee tables as a badge of nationalist pride that comes with the privilege and prestige of political and economic power. Certainly the Third Reich held secret meetings, but its plan of Aryan supremacy, military expansion and burning hatred of Jews was spelled out in black and white throughout the country. It was a plan present in children's school desks, in honeymoon luggage and in the homes of millions of ordinary people. In it Hitler wrote,

> The Aryan gave up the purity of his blood and, therefore, lost his sojourn in the paradise that he had made for himself. He became submerged in a racial mixture and gradually lost his cultural creativeness. Blood mixture and the resultant drop in the racial level is the sole cause of the dying out of old cultures; for men do not perish as a result of lost wars, but by the loss of that force of resistance which is continued only in pure blood. All who are not of good race in this world are chaff.[3]

This "chaff" included Jews:

> I began to see Jews and the more I saw, the more sharply they became distinguished in my eyes from the rest of humanity. . . . Later I often grew sick to the stomach from the smell of these caftan-wearers. . . . Was there any form of filth or profligacy, particularly in cultural life, without at least one Jew involved in it? If you cut cautiously into such an abscess, you found, like a maggot in a rotting body, often dazzled by the sudden light—a kike![4]

During Hitler's demented last days, he wrote of the same conspiracy that the racist segment of the militia believes in:

> It is untrue that I or anybody else in Germany wanted war in 1939.
> It was wanted and provoked exclusively by those international
> statesmen who either were of Jewish origin or worked for Jewish
> interests. . . . Further, I have never wished that after the appalling
> First World War there should be a second one against either England
> or America. Centuries will go by, but from the ruins of our towns
> and monuments the hatred of those ultimately responsible will
> always grow anew. They are the people whom we have to thank for
> all this: international Jewry and its helpers. [5]

The Third Reich, born January 30, 1933, boasted a type of New World
Order with a thousand-year reign. But it lasted twelve years and four
months—proof that the bulging rhetoric from inflated leaders does not
guarantee their longevity. As demonstrated by the Third Reich, evil does
not require a conspiracy to grow and prosper. Ordinary people will gladly
do its bidding.

It was ordinary Hebrews who, defying their Lord's command, created
a golden calf and other idols at the foot of Mount Sinai. I do not recall
reading in Scripture that such idol worship was orchestrated by, say, the
Freemason/Illuminati Order. Rather, like the children in William Gold-
ing's *Lord of the Flies,* the Hebrews, a microcosm of all humanity,
conspired against their own good. We do the same today without the aid
of "international bankers" or the host of other supposed cabalists.

Superstitious Beliefs Are Perilous

C. S. Lewis argued that there are two problems with evil: one is to deny
that it exists; the other is to become preoccupied with it. Christians who
believe in grand conspiracies are likely to find evil around every corner.
Even end-times writers Peter and Paul Lalonde warn against such a
destructive practice:

> Superstition plays a big part in the mark-of-the-beast tales. Many
> otherwise solid believers would never write a check number 666 for

fear of damning their souls to eternal punishment. Others will skip over page 666 in a large book for fear some antichrist spirit would jump from the page and snare them.[6]

The Lalonde brothers also admit that some prophecy buffs have sensationalized certain issues: "This, unfortunately, has contributed to prophetic apathy rather than prophetic awareness."[7]

Another example of end-times superstition hit the church rumor mill in the early 1980s. According to the Lalonde brothers, the rumor insisted that the U.S. government issued social security and other types of retirement checks with a notice that the check could be cashed only if the "bearer had a mark on his right hand or on his forehead."[8] But none of the alleged recipients kept the check or a photocopy of it.

"The beast" interpreted as the computer put Christian conspiracists on night watch as well. Hidden someplace in Brussels, the story goes, is a computer big and powerful enough to keep track of everyone in the world. I have met a number of people who, once they knew I was writing a book on conspiracy theories within our culture at large and the church in particular, said they knew about the computer in Brussels and believed that it was a fulfillment of Bible prophecy. It was reported that an entire town in Sweden had received the mark of the beast. According to the Lalondes, they found no proof of this accusation.[9]

Many remember the Procter & Gamble affair. The U.S. company allegedly supported the Satanist church. Proof, said the accusers, was found in the company's former symbol. Consistent with the conspiracy community's obsession with symbolism, they said the thirteen stars and the man-in-the-moon symbol were proof of its satanic support. The couple who began these rumors were brought to court and had to pay damages to the company. Even the Lalonde brothers say there was no proof that the company used satanic symbolism or that a Procter & Gamble executive appeared on national television admitting that the company gave financial support to the Satanist church, another damaging rumor.[10]

In the late 1980s the Gothard Basic Youth Conflicts (IBYC) seminars traveled throughout the country. An information packet from the seminar states that the then-popular Cabbage Patch dolls were demon inspired. A letter from the Gothard organization states that during the seminar parents revealed startling concerns about the seemingly benign dolls. "These parents reported strange, destructive behavior and symptoms that could be directly traced to the purchase of the dolls and which ended when the dolls were removed and/or destroyed." Part of the organization's concerns came from the realization that the dolls were advertised to come from the "enchanted Cabbage Patch" and that children were encouraged to enter a written pact to "love a doll with all his/her heart." The letter states that such a pact is a violation of the First Commandment.[11]

The following letter was written by a seminar attendee who takes Christian superstition to disturbing levels:

> Dear Bill and staff,
>
> I attended for the third time the IBYC Seminar in Sacramento, April 1989. My husband and daughter, age 16, also attended.
>
> During one portion, you talked about the evil influence of Cabbage Patch Dolls. I have 2 daughters, each having one doll. We destroyed them, and for 3 days now our 5 year old, Stacy, has improved in her eating. We had noticed 2 years of alarming lack of weight gain (We've had her doll for 2 years) and in September we made a concerted effort to add weight to her. She has put on one pound, now weighing only 33 pounds at age $5^1/2$.
>
> In addition, our 16 year old daughter has come back under our authority, admitting that she has engaged in premarital sex for $1^1/2$. years—the same time as having her Cabbage Patch doll!
>
> Realizing that getting rid of something will not be the only step to take—we pray for continued spiritual protection that more evil spirits might not come in to take the place of the two we threw out. (1 John 1:9)
>
> Sincerely, [Name withheld]

I have children, and none owns a Cabbage Patch doll. Yet they have gone through times when they wouldn't eat much. And blaming a doll for a daughter's premarital sex poses many problems. This "devil-made-me-do-it" mentality may lead people to justify dangerous mistakes once they are grown up. Even some within the end-times conspiracy community realize that many within the church are highly susceptible to the ailments of superstition. Combine these superstitions with fear and paranoia—two of Christian conspiracy theory's most potent byproducts—and a mighty group can be mobilized. The direction they march, however, is toward precipitous cliffs.

In 1692 an infamous American community believed that all events could be explained with supernatural answers. The failure of a crop or even the stubbing of a toe could be solved by an inflamed and prevalent view of good versus evil, similar to that of Manichaeism (see chapter nine). This is the view that led to the Salem, Massachusetts, witchcraft hunts, where twenty people were executed because of a superstitious view of "evidence." The similarities between the "Salem Witchcraft Trials . . . and the 'contagious hysteria' of satanic panic in the 1980s are disturbing. The role of evangelical Christians and their own media in fanning the flames is even more so. Witch hunts have never rid the world of evil, but instead have provided the most universally recognized examples of evil."[12] We should add to this list of examples the Oklahoma City bombing.

This same "satanic panic" exists today because the evangelical/fundamentalist community has given evil too much due. It has taken the fraudulent testimony of Mike Warnke and the fiction of people such as Frank Peretti and applied it to today's complex world too literally and too thickly. (It is no coincidence that Peretti, who renders almost too vividly the war between good and evil, is a favored speaker at conferences that emphasize Christian conspiracy theories, such as the conspiracy-friendly Steeling of the American Mind conferences.)

Secular skeptics sneer at the orthodox Christian belief that actual evil exists. But the Christian conspiracy community has fallen into an equal but opposite mistake: it finds evil everywhere, much as the Christian brothers and sisters in Salem did.

The journalists who exposed Warnke say that the Christian community accepted him and his stories unconditionally. "He walked in these doors during a time of great openness, especially to *supernatural* claims. People were eager to listen, eager to believe, eager to grant authority."[13] These journalists also wonder if sin may have prompted these people to believe the Christian conspiracy theorist:

> Mike Warnke represented the promise of secrets revealed. In the face of a quickly changing world, this fearful audience longed for inside information, magic formulas of faith. . . . Yet seeking solace in secret formulas was always forbidden by God—not because this shortcut worked, but because it did not. Mere knowledge of good and evil was never enough to satisfy humanity's longing or calm its fears.[14]

Speak the Truth in Love

Only months after my debut as a talk show host, I found myself ridiculing Christian conspiracy disciples. I saw the fear and pain they were spreading, and I couldn't help but unload. I thought everything they said at every moment was wrong, even stupid. Now years later I see how wrong I was. Many are truth seekers, people who live serious, deliberate lives. My early ridicule of them and the media's unwillingness to look at the people beneath the fear have only hardened their resolve.

There was a time when I could count on a handful of conspiracy disciples to call and heat the airwaves with debate. But once my ridicule matured, they simply stopped calling. It became increasingly clear what I had done. My ridicule was producing a unique hybrid of bitter fruit. To many, I wasn't just questioning their political views, I was questioning the core of their beliefs, ridiculing their religion. These theories were more than the fervent merger of end-times speculation and current events. They were an addendum to their faith.

The antidote to ridicule, of course, is to speak the truth in love, an arduous task. When our station was taken off the air to build a new station at a different frequency, I had time to sit and reflect on what my message was doing. I stopped seeing conspiracy disciples as two-dimensional. I began to see them as fathers and mothers of small children, who want desperately to protect them in a world where random, faceless violence is increasing. I began to see them as people who are sick of seeing government work against them.

My on-air debates became much more meaningful. During one show, I invited a well-known conspiracy theorist to discuss current events on the spur of the moment. When I called him at home, he told me he would be glad to do the show but that he planned to spend the morning with his daughter. I asked him if he could do the show for half an hour. "I would, Paul, but that would be one less half-hour I would be able to spend with my daughter." This family man cares deeply about his wife, his beautiful children and his country. He is not detached from reality. In many respects, our country would be better off if there were more fathers like him.

I hope that those in the press who see an easy score when covering this community realize what their scorn can do. The media should criticize the propensity of the conspiracy theorists toward violence and expose the dangers of their beliefs. But in speaking these truths, critics must remember that ridicule will drive them further underground, producing the type of fruit our culture cannot afford to harvest.

Temper End-Times Messages

It is easy and even justified to look back at Hal Lindsey's failed predictions with sadness. Some I have spoken to express a deep disgust. Others border on contempt for his message now that they have witnessed its bitter fruit. Indeed, there is a clear link between Lindsey's work and the Weavers' flight to Ruby Ridge. But Christians must keep in mind that it was and is the church at large that has made Lindsey into one of its most influential leaders. His popularity is likely to grow, not wither, even in light of his false predictions and the conspiracy theories they fertilize.

Lindsey and many who have repeated his interpretation of Bible prophecy have both strengths and weaknesses in their position. Lindsey should be commended for his opposition to dominion theology's inclination toward anti-Semitism. However, Lindsey and the many other pop end-times preachers he has produced need to temper their message with the knowledge that across this country are people of great action and great anger who will use their message for destruction.

Many of these preachers command a strong following. They radiate such a charismatic confidence that they, in subtle ways, are able to ridicule those who disagree with them without making it seem so. They leave the strong impression that because they are accurate about Christ's plan of salvation for all humankind they must also be correct about their view of end-times prophecy, current events and the conspiracies that they have identified. When they mix their accuracy about the essential doctrines of the historic Christian faith with their own speculation about history, international politics and international economies all in the same sermon, they make it difficult for many within the church to sift biblical truth from human speculation. More often than not, Scripture's authority is devalued in the process.

There will always be different views regarding the last days. Christians can put differences aside and agree to disagree, but end-times preachers must actively oppose these damaging conspiracy theories that are so popular within the church. People of great action and great anger are listening, and like Islamic fundamentalists they are eager to give their anger theological justification.

End-times preachers must understand that their tongues and pens and Web sites contain spiritual nitroglycerin. As Chuck Swindoll knows, no other topic within Christianity has the ability to obsess a believer more for ill than end-times prophecy. His warning is worth repeating: "There's something captivating with the prophetic message that seems to consume a person's mind, and often very bright people get into this subject and it's like drilling a well deep into their lives and they can't get out of the well they dig."[15] Bruce Barron, congressional aide to Rick Santorum (Republican of Pennsylvania), warns, "As Christians seeking to give an effective, credible witness for the Kingdom of God, we should base our public-policy advocacy on verifiable facts and sound logical arguments, not hearsay, suspicion, and unverifiable conspiracy theories fueled by our own end-times expectations."[16]

Affirm Legitimate Concerns
"We must address the concerns and frustration that lead some ordinary people, people who are not criminals or neo-Nazis, to consider joining

militia groups," says Montana senator Max Baucus.[17] When President Clinton went to Montana in June 1995, he spoke out against the dangers of a militia but also spoke with a Montana rancher, Tom Breitbach. Clinton asked the rancher why ordinary people might listen to the conspiracy theories offered by the militia.

The answer was simple, and one our nation must heed: "As [people] feel more pressured economically, they feel more desperate, and become willing to resort to desperate measures." Baucus writes, "Most casual militia members are not Nazis or criminals. But they are angry. Angry about slow income growth, economic pressure on working families, and some of Washington's decisions on bread-and-butter issues."[18]

The senator cited what at first seemed to be yet another costly but well-intentioned government regulation: "Back in February [1995], some loggers in the Flathead Valley in northwestern Montana called me up. They said that OSHA, the Occupational Safety and Health Administration, had ordered them to buy steel-toed, chain-saw-resistant boots to protect their feet. They had two weeks grace, and after that it was no boots, no work.

"Well, steel-toed boots may sound good in Washington. But in Montana, they can make the job more dangerous, not less. On a cold day they make your feet go numb. When your feet go numb out on a steep hill, you can slip and fall. And that's no joke when you're holding a live chain saw.

"Because these loggers acted so fast, I was able to get to the Secretary of Labor and stop the regulations. But the fact is, nobody at a desk in Washington should be telling people in the Flathead what kind of shoes to wear. And to threaten someone's job . . . is an outrage. You can expect people to be mad about it."[19]

To conspiracy disciples such indiscriminate regulations are not the product of government oversight or incompetence. They are tremors of the New World Order. It is difficult to admit, but America owes the conspiracy community at least a backhanded compliment. This community has kept examples of government error and abuse alive long enough to bring about real change.

As most forgot about the unwarranted behavior of law enforcement at

Waco and Ruby Ridge, the conspiracy community doggedly kept it alive. They raised valid issues and placed them before the American people. They wrote their congressional representatives to demand an investigation. The result, in part, was a fundamentally new approach to dealing with civil unrest. The peaceful resolution with the Freemen of Jordan, Montana, is a telling example of how the conspiracy community successfully helped reclaim certain liberties for all Americans, even those who are dangerous.

Recognize the Real Enemy

We need look no further than our own noses if we wish to place blame for the problems of the world. As Christian thinker and author G. K. Chesterton wrote, "What's wrong with the world is me." We solve the problem of irresponsible conspiracy theories and the ailments they claim to resolve by taking responsibility for our own actions.

We must realize that one reason we do not have enough money in the bank is that most Americans live beyond their means, not that the government is trying to break us. That our children are less educated today than they were twenty years ago is not because of a socialist conspiracy to make them dumb but because many parents do not value learning.

One reason premarital sex is rampant is that our young people long to fill the void left in their families by churchgoing moms and dads who are so busy climbing the corporate ladder that they neglect to nurture their children's souls. Or worse, these kids have never seen genuine marital bliss and so do not wait. Their Cabbage Patch doll is not responsible.

Drugs come to America not because of a CIA/New World Order conspiracy but because Americans want them. Television fare is rotten because we are getting what we demand. Inside each of us beats the heart of Cain.

Complain About Something Real

Columnist Cal Thomas, a member but critic of the Christian community, says there is nothing in Scripture that commands those who seek to follow God to demand their rights. . . . There are many Christians in other parts of the world who might gladly change places with American believers. In other nations they face torture, discrimination and murder. Here, "suffering" is limited to occasional slights from reporters and cartoonists.[20]

Thomas says that this may be because American Christians have it too easy and wouldn't recognize real persecution if they saw it. "[Christians] relax in a subculture of their own making and are outraged when the world criticizes them. But they have refused to engage the world in sufficient numbers to make their influence felt in the very institutions they lambaste." This refusal to engage their culture is in part the result of their end-times theology. As Thomas says,

Many Christians refuse to equip themselves to compete on territory that once believed their views contributed to the general welfare. . . . Is it any wonder American institutions have suffered from spiritual deficiency anemia? If Christians don't like being persecuted by intellectual snobs, let them enter law school, academia, the film industry and journalism and change these and other fields from within.[21]

Conservatives such as Thomas, as well as others less conservative, have worked long and hard to show that Christianity deserves a seat at the table when questions of the world's problems are discussed. But Christian conspiracy theories are threatening to make Christianity appear as if it has few answers. Indeed, the bulk of popular Christian writing about the future gives the answer not to be concerned because the end is at hand. It may be possible that such a "Christian" message has led some to reject Christianity as a weak and feeble religion, unable to help in time of need, which, ironically, is what the church says about secular answers.

Conservative Christians need to stop straddling the fence regarding the influence these theories are having. They must decide whether they are battling a conspiracy or a consensus of ideas. When people battle against a consensus—a package of widely held beliefs—they try to change a culture's perception about issues. But when people war against a conspiracy, they are usually prone to rely on some form of violence if law enforcement and the courts do not expose their version of the truth.

Employing violence to change perception, as has happened with the abortion issue in America, is the worst possible option. It works directly against the cause. Stereotypes are fortified, and the battle to help unborn children is dealt a major setback because such violence turns public perception against the cause. Fighting against a "conspiracy" when it is really a consensus leads to ineffective and dangerous strategies because it misidentifies the opposition. Time, passion and resources are misspent, leading to lost opportunities in the war of ideas. This is yet another reason for conservative Christians to oppose conspiracy theories.

Restore Hope and Joy

One reason I wrote this book was to help restore hope and joy to the lives of those who adhere to these theories and those who have loved ones who have slipped into the murky waters of Christian conspiracy theories. I have developed what I call a conspiracy spectrum. This spectrum is defined by the intensity of a person's belief.

On the left end of the spectrum are those who believe that these theories are probably true, but the individuals are not likely (at least at this point in life) to pay much attention to them. Then there are those in the middle, who believe that these theories are the fulfillment of Bible prophecy. They are on many, if not all, of the mailing lists for Christian conspiracy magazines and buy the latest book that allegedly exposes these New World Order plots. On the far right end are the hardcore Christian conspiracy disciples. These theories have greatly changed their lives. They live in rural areas and are proficient with guns and other weapons. They and their families are prepared to live without aid from society for at least two years thanks to a stockpile of food, some of which is immersed in a kind of nitrogen gas. It gives the nuts and other foods of survivalists a chemical aftertaste, but it will keep the food edible for decades.

At the turn of the millennium, some of these people will sell their rural enclaves where food is concealed in fake panels and opt for more mobile living. They will convert large buses into motor homes and equip them with solar panels and banks of car batteries to store the precious electricity. Some of these end-times road-warrior-like vehicles carry enough fuel to drive at least a thousand miles and water that can last for months if it is not squandered on showers. This is helpful in order to escape from regions such as the West Coast that will suffer the devastating earthquakes that the Bible warns about, which they believe will usher in the tribulation.

These are the people who once went regularly to church, where many of them learned about the last days and the end-times conspiracies that shroud the globe. But today they are likely to hold only family devotions or small group Bible studies among like-minded conspiracists. As was the case with Randy and Vicki Weaver, these devotions are increasingly dedicated to aligning current events with apocalyptic scenarios that conspiracists believe are found in the Bible.

They spend an increasing amount of time studying and arguing about the peripherals of the faith as opposed to the basics of the faith, the teaching that the apostles and other early disciples were willing to die defending. Understanding the original intent of the Constitution, as interpreted by fellow conspiracy theorists, is of utmost importance to these people. Their Bible study gives way, subtly at first, to a study of an antiquated view of law and government. But the Bible is still important to them, especially new and "mysterious insights" into the sacred text, such as the increasingly popular hidden "Bible Code" belief. They are likely to embrace new revelations and a kind of paranormal Christianity that embraces the likelihood that alien encounters have been recorded and predicted in the Bible. Or they are even more extreme, believing that the coming antichrist will have alien connections.

Those who want to help friends or loved ones who are hardcore Christian conspiracy disciples must be realistic. These disciples have a complex theological justification for what they believe, and they see their political and social enemies as God's enemies too. Because conspiracy disciples believe they have a special understanding of how the world *really* operates, their friends or loved ones may also have to battle an odd manifestation of pride. Some conspiracy disciples see their belief as a sign of spiritual maturity, since they view themselves as truly in tune to what God is doing in the world. They may view those who question them as spiritual greenhorns, people who are not ready for, cannot handle or perhaps do not want to know God's prophetic plan or his "greater mysteries."

Making the attempt even more difficult is their belief that most in the popular media are either directly or indirectly part of the New World Order conspiracy. So when a person quotes one publication or another in an effort to show inherent weaknesses in their arguments, a friend or loved one is likely to dismiss the evidence as part of the conspirators' master plan. This dismissal results from the conspiracist's belief that he or she has all the information necessary. "He has little hope that his evidence will convince a hostile world. . . . He is not a receiver, he is a transmitter."[22]

Judging from the angry and abusive mail and calls I have received over the years, Christian conspiracy theories are an odd kind of security blanket. When a person attempts to unravel it piece by piece, conspiracists are likely to tolerate a few tugs but will soon lash out when the blanket begins to slip and unravel. They are likely to assign evil intentions to the rescuer.

These are difficult words to read, and they are difficult to write because I know too well the mindset of Christian conspiracy theorists. They believe that all of history is an orchestrated, evil and overarching conspiracy against them and the forces of good. Yet one reason someone should study history is to learn how things *do not* happen. Hofstadter asserts,

> It is precisely this kind of awareness that the paranoid fails to develop. He has a special resistance of his own, of course, to such awareness, but circumstances often deprive him of exposure to events that might enlighten him. We are all sufferers from history, but the paranoid is a double sufferer, since he is afflicted not only by the real world, with the rest of us, but by his fantasies as well.[23]

Conclusion

People the world over have done the bidding of conspiracy theories for more than a thousand years. Americans since their war for independence have shown a potent affinity for them, and the evangelical/fundamentalist community in particular has fed them for the latter half of the twentieth century. These conspiracy theories, a swirling mixture of secular and religious impulse and speculation, are adults now: adults who are strapping and virile and reproducing by the day. Magic bullets and panaceas, which are the allure of these handsome theories, will not be useful in combating them. And they will be with us always, like viruses and plagues and the poor. But they can be contained in part by the solutions offered in this book and in this chapter. The solutions will need to be implemented on a daily basis, which is to our advantage, for as Abraham Lincoln wrote, "the best thing about the future is that it comes one day at a time." These theories have taken our culture and our churches one convincing message at a time throughout a span of days both spectacular and lackluster. We will help to solve the problems they create in the very same way.

Postscript

A Likely Scenario for How This Will End

I am often asked what will happen to the far-Right conspiracy community as we enter a new century. There will be more isolated skirmishes between them and all aspects of society, not just with the federal government. We will likely hear of other fatal acts of domestic terrorism—reports preceded by the words "We interrupt this program for a special news bulletin."

The most chilling lesson from the Oklahoma City bombing and the court trials of Timothy McVeigh and Terry Nichols was how easy it was for these men to assemble a powerfully destructive bomb. One journalist who covered both trials wrote, "They assembled most of the ingredients for their bomb without breaking any laws. It was ridiculously easy to buy ammonium-nitrate fertilizer and racing fuel and then to rent a truck. . . . The main reason that McVeigh and Nichols didn't get help was that they didn't need it."[1]

As the lawlessness of the far-Right conspiracy community increases, they will begin to butt heads with average Americans. This has already happened with the Freemen of Jordan, Montana.

A neighbor who is a rancher in that wide-open country has been grazing his cattle for years on federal property that the Freemen claimed was theirs. The Freemen threatened to kill the rancher or any other who trespassed on the stolen land. The rancher didn't budge, for he knew he had little time to fatten his cattle in that cold, unforgiving country. To listen to the Freemen for even a few months could have spelled financial ruin.

They also placed a Freemen-created lien against the home of Reverend Jerry Walters, who publicly exposed and criticized the group's racist theology. This is further evidence that the enemies of some in the patriot movement are not the government but those who disagree with them.

Self-professed patriots in many other obscure towns across America will begin declaring war on their neighbors as well as on the federal government. Though some patriots are motivated by an inflamed ideal of preserving their interpretation of the Constitution and its original intent, others will use the movement as an excuse for lawlessness of many kinds. After all, when Freemen attempt to defraud banks, businesses and public agencies of millions of dollars, threaten to murder a federal judge and steal television equipment, how can such lawlessness possibly reinstate the original intent of the Constitution?

True confessions from federal agencies that were too quick to treat Americans as enemies have helped ease some of the fears in the Christian conspiracy community. But overall they have not been swayed because we live in a special time in history—the turn of a millennium—which is to them an apocalyptic finish line. As the clock ticks toward the end of one century and into the beginning of another, revelation about the "last days" is fused to speculation, most with the best of intentions.

Then there is the possibility of outright war. Since the Christian conspiracy community believes that the American political system is part of the grand conspiracy, they are forced to work outside the existing political framework in their quest to obtain real political change. Contrary to their rhetoric, that system is the most powerful in the world. If they cross it, the U.S. government will crush them, and crush them utterly.

In spite of all the locker-room bravado, these militia leaders must know that, like my grandfather fighting against the British on behalf of the Irish in the Easter Rising of 1916, they are fighting the enemy with mere shillelaghs and pitchforks. Though they see themselves as a blessed, ragtag, holy army, they will soon realize that the holy wars of the Old Testament are over and done with, never to be resurrected or blessed by the hand of God.

Finally there is another, more realistic scenario. The counterculture of the 1960s also had its battle cries, manifestos and complex conspiracy theories. But where is it today? Some "kept the faith," but most moved on. The movement fell under its own weight, crushed under consuming talk of revolution and the fear and paranoia delivered by drugs and antigovernment/corporate-America/CIA conspiracy theories. It was a movement, true to its youthful roots, that promised to end in a bang but instead limped and whimpered along, a parody of its heady idealism.

The patriot movement and the Christian conspiracy community that feeds and fuels it will suffer ailments similar to those that felled the 1960s counterculture. I say similar because there are two profound differences: its consuming theological underpinning and the fact that most in the movement are not motivated by transient youthful passions. But harboring thoughts of revolution wears on people, whether they are eighteen or forty-eight. Eventually the impelling force that makes revolutions crest is the same that brings them tumbling down.

The convoluted history of conspiracy thinking reveals that these theories come in successive and episodic waves, which rise as much from societal impulses, such as shifting values, fears and, at times, hatred, as from Bible prophecy, either real or fabricated. We'll find no comfort from this truth, especially when we consider how McVeigh and Nichols are seen by some as heroes, not villains. And heroes amass followers.

Contrary to the claims of the various conspiracy theorists, we are the generation of the false alarm, triggered by those in the crowd-making business. Today's Christian conspiracy community is yet another wave in a sea of distrust and revolution that will rise, crest in fleeting glory, then fall to be replaced by yet another out at sea, still forming.

Notes

Chapter 1: Conspiracy Theories Are Everyone's Business

[1] Gary Kah, *En Route to Global Occupation* (Lafayette, La.: Huntington House, 1992); William T. Still, *New World Order: The Ancient Plan of Secret Societies* (Lafayette, La.: Huntington House, 1990); Constance Cumbey, *Hidden Dangers of the Rainbow* (Shreveport, La.: Huntington House, 1982); Gary Allen, *None Dare Call It Conspiracy* (Rossmoor, Calif.: Concord, 1972); John A. Stormer, *None Dare Call It Treason* (Florissant, Mo.: Liberty Bell Press, 1964); Pat Robertson, *New World Order* (Dallas: Word, 1991).

[2] Untitled article, *Tuned In Magazine,* January 1996, p. 34.

[3] Undated letter from Don McAlvany, "The $10 Trillion Paper Pyramid Cover-Up."

[4] Interview with the author, February 1996, Ashland, Oregon.

[5] Chuck Missler, "As the Days of Noah Were," *Personal Update,* http://www.khouse.org/noah.html.

[6] George Johnson, *Architects of Fear: Conspiracy Theories and Paranoia in American Politics* (Los Angeles: Tarcher, 1983), p. 162.

[7] Michael Drosnin, "Excerpt: The Bible Code," http://www.simonsays.com/titles/excerpt.cgi?isbn=0684810794.

[8] Internet chat given by Michael Drosnin, found at http://www.simonsays.com/freshlink/chats/drosnin/drosnintrans.html.

[9] Ibid.

[10] Michael Drosnin, "The Rise of the Militia Movement," http://www.nidlink.com/~bobhard/militias.html.

[11] Louis Beam, *Leaderless Resistance,* as quoted by Tom Burghardt, "Leaderless Resistance and the Oklahoma City Bombing," http://nwcitizen.com/publicgood/reports/leadless.htm, p. 1.

[12] "Field Manual Section 1: Principles Justifying the Arming and Organizing of a Militia," *The Free Militia,* 1994, p. 78.

[13] Mike Tharp and William J. Holstein, "Mainstreaming the Militia," *U.S. News & World Report,* http://www.usnews.com/usnews/issue971421/21mili.htm.

[14] 1 Samuel 22; 2 Samuel 15; 1 Kings 2:28; 2 Kings 9:14; 10:9; 14:19;15; 21:23; 2 Chronicles 24:25-26; 33:24; Esther 2:21; 6:2; Psalm 2:1; 31:13; 56:6; 59:3; 64:2; 71:10; 83:3; 105:25; Isaiah 8:12; Jeremiah 11:9; Ezekiel 22:25; Daniel 2:9; Amos 7:10; Micah 7:3; Acts 4:27; 9:23; 23:12.

[15] Gordon Witkin, "Conspiracy's Twisted Appeal," *U.S. News & World Report,* June 2, 1997, p. 9.

[16] Strobe Talbott, "The Birth of the Global Nation," *Time,* July 20, 1992, p. 70.

[17] Ibid.

[18] Martin Sieff, "Family Ties: Strobe Talbott's Bumblings on the World Stage Are Best Explained If He's Nothing More than a Chip off the Old Block," *National Review,* September 25, 1995, pp. 80-81.

[19] Ibid.

[20] Kah, *En Route to Global Occupation,* p. 26.

[21]Max Baucus, letter to the Senate Subcommittee on Terrorism, Technology and Government Information, June 15, 1995.

[22]Roger O'Neill, "Oklahoma City Rescuers May Be Victims Now," *NBC News,* November 23, 1998, http://www.msnbc.com/news/217433.asp.

Chapter 2: The *Global* Not-So-New World Order Conspiracy

[1]B. J. Oropeza, *99 Reasons Why No One Knows When Christ Will Return* (Downers Grove, Ill.: InterVarsity Press, 1994), p. 110.

[2]Ibid.

[3]At Mount Vernon on July 4, 1918, President Wilson announced: "We believe . . . in a *new international order* [emphasis added] under which reason and justice and the common interests of mankind shall prevail. . . . Without that new order the world will be without peace and human life will lack tolerable conditions of existence and development. Having set our hand to the task of achieving it [the forming of the League of Nations], we shall not turn back." Herbert Hoover, *The Ordeal of Woodrow Wilson* (Washington, D.C.: Woodrow Wilson Center Press, 1958), p. 24.

[4]Paul Boyer, *When Time Shall Be No More* (Cambridge, Mass.: Harvard University Press, 1992), p. 65, as quoted by Oropeza, *99 Reasons,* p. 112.

[5]Oropeza, *99 Reasons,* p. 144.

[6]Walter C. Utt, "Illuminating the Illuminati," *Liberty,* May/June 1979, p. 17.

[7]Ibid.

[8]Ibid.

[9]Ibid, p. 19.

[10]Richard Hofstadter, *The Paranoid Style in American Politics and Other Essays* (New York: Vintage Books/Random House, 1967), p. 29.

[11]Utt, "Illuminating the Illuminati," p. 26.

[12]David Van Biema, "The Message from Mark Koernke," *Time Domestic,* June 26, 1995.

[13]Philip Lawler, "The U.N.'s 'Benevolent' Despots," *Wall Street Journal,* August 22, 1995. The irony in Lawler's critique is striking. Catholics are accused by some Christian conspiracy theorists of being part of the U.N./New World Order conspiracy.

[14]Ibid.

[15]Ibid.

[16]Ibid.

[17]Catherine Toups, "U.N. Faces Increased Scrutiny on 50th Anniversary," *Washington Times,* July 3-9, 1995.

[18]Ibid.

[19]"Stop the Press, President-Elect Clinton Attends Secret 'Renaissance Weekend,'" January 1993, http//www.rcfp.org/Clinton/cc1301.html.

[20]Don McAlvany, *McAlvany Intelligence Advisor,* November 1988.

[21]Texe Marrs, quoted in Oropeza, *99 Reasons,* p. 109. Marrs also believes that Promise Keepers is part of a New Age/homosexual conspiracy.

[22]Oropeza, *99 Reasons,* p. 109.

Chapter 3: The *American* Not-So-New World Order Conspiracy

[1]James W. Wardner, *The Planned Destruction of America* (Longwood, Fla.: Longwood Communications, 1993), back cover.

[2]Lamar Alexander, "Education's Conspiracy of Mediocrity," *Christian Science Monitor,* http://www.msnbc.com/news/118304.asp.

[3]Bruce Barron, "A Summary Critique: *En Route to Global Occupation*," *Christian Research Journal*, Winter 1993.

[4]Ibid.

[5]Michael Kelly, "The Road to Paranoia," *New Yorker*, June 19, 1995, p. 73.

[6]Testimony before the Senate Subcommittee on Terrorism, Technology and Government Information, June 1995.

[7]Peter Boyer, "Children of Waco," *New Yorker*, May 15, 1995, p. 39.

[8]Don McAlvany, "The Waco Massacre: 'Trial by Fire,'" *McAlvany Intelligence Advisor*, July 1993, p. 21.

[9]Oklahoma City Bombing Trial Transcripts, Tuesday, June 10, 1997, http://www.courttv.com/old/casefiles/oklahoma/transcripts/0610pm.html.

[10]Molly Ivins, "Militias, Cults See World Simplistically: Some Officials Add to Growing Paranoia," *Mail Tribune* (Medford, Ore.), May 14, 1985, p. 8A.

[11]Linda Thompson, Internet message, April 21, 1993.

[12]Special PBS *Frontline Report*, "Ten of the Most Frequently Asked Questions Concerning Waco," Joint Hearing of the Crime Subcommittee, July 1995, p. 4, http://www.pbs.org/wgbh/pages/frontline/waco/topten2.html#started.

[13]Ibid.

[14]Frontline Report: WACO/Dr. Nizam Peerwani, Interview Excerpts conducted August 1, 1995, http://www.pbs.org/wgbh/pages/frontline/waco/topten.html.

[15]Ibid.

[16]Maggy Reno, quoted in Boyer, "Children of Waco," p. 43.

[17]Mark England, "The Sinful Messiah—part 4," *Waco Tribune-Herald*, March 1, 1993; quoted in Kenneth R. Samples, *Prophets of the Apocalypse: David Koresh & Other American Messiahs* (Grand Rapids, Mich.: Baker, 1994), p. 234.

[18]Ibid., p. 58.

[19]Observer, quoted in Boyer, "Children of Waco," p. 42.

[20]Richard Read, "The Patriarch of Paranoia," *The Oregonian*, July 23, 1995, p. A19.

[21]Lawrence Myers, "A Closer Look," *Media Bypass*, December 1995, p. 35.

[22]Lawrence Myers, "OKC Bombing Grand Jurors Claim 'Cover Up,'" *Media Bypass*, November 1995, p. 46.

[23]Letter to the editor, *Media Bypass*, December 1995, p. 7.

[24]Ibid.

Chapter 4: The Militia's Religious Impulse
[1]"The Bleeding Border," *U.S. News & World Report*, February 24, 1997.

[2]Ibid., p. 41.

[3]"The Jewish Bible," *National Christian News* 31, p. 41, as quoted by Richard Abanes, *American Militias, Rebellion, Racism & Religion* (Downers Grove, Ill.: InterVarsity Press, 1996), p. 176.

[4]Pat Robertson, *The End of the Age* (Dallas: Word, 1995), quoted in Michael G. Maudlin, "The Bible Study at the End of the World, Part 1," *Christianity Today*, September 1, 1997, http://www.christianity.net/ct/7ta/7ta22a.html.

[5]Ibid.

[6]Testimony before the Senate Subcommittee on Terrorism, Technology and Government Information, June 15, 1995.

[7]Joe Maxwell and Andrés Tapia, "Militia Extremists Blend God and Country into a Potent Mixture," *Christianity Today*, June 1995, http://www.christianity.net/ctjun95mrw5T7034566b.

[8]Ibid.

[9]Ibid.

[10]Ibid.

[11]"Freemen surrender peacefully to FBI," June 14, 1996, http://www.cnn.com/US/9606/14/freemen.llp/index.html.

[12]Wynn Miller, "Montana 'Freemen' Clog Court System," *National Law Journal*, July 16, 1995, p. A09.

[13]Ibid.

[14]Joseph P. Mazurek, as quoted by Miller, "Montana 'Freemen' Clog Court System."

[15]Jerry Walters, interview with the author, June 1996.

[16]Ibid.

[17]Jerry Walters, interview with the author, June 1996.

[18]Jess Walter, *Every Knee Shall Bow: The Truth & Tragedy of Ruby Ridge & the Randy Weaver Family* (New York: Regan, 1995), p. 33.

[19]Ibid., pp. 28-29, 36-37.

[20]Ibid, p. 34.

[21]Ibid, p. 53.

[22]Edward Barnes, "A Rare Visit with the Rebel of Ruby Ridge," *Time Domestic*, May 29, 1995, p. 2 (http://www.pathfinder.com/time/magazine/domestic/1995/950529/950529.guncontrol.weaver.html).

[23]Walter, *Every Knee Shall Bow*, p. 7.

[24]James D. Tabor, *Why Waco? Cults and the Battle for Religious Freedom in America* (Berkeley: University of California Press, 1995).

[25]Transcript from *Frontline* Waco Report: "Is David Koresh Jesus Christ?" March 17, 1993. Excerpt of conversation between chief FBI negotiator Byron Sage and David Koresh concerning David Koresh's faith and whether he is Jesus Christ. The entire conversation lasted approximately an hour and ten minutes.

[26]Clint Van Zandt, interview with the author, August 1996.

[27]Special PBS *Frontline* Report, October 17, 1995.

[28]"Is David Koresh Jesus Christ?" excerpt.

[29]"Militia of Montana 1998 Preparedness Catalog, Documentation and Education Books," http://www.logoplex.com/resources/mom/docedbok.html.

Chapter 5: Old Lies on Life Support

[1]Anti-Defamation League, "Religion as Bigotry: The Identity Church Movement," special ed., October 1991, p. 2; quoted in Richard Abanes, *Defending the Faith: A Beginner's Guide to Cults and New Religions* (Grand Rapids, Mich.: Baker, 1997), p. 192.

[2]Robert Sessler, *To Be God of One World: The French Revolution Globalized* (Merlin, Ore.: Let There Be Light, 1992), p. 43.

[3]For a more detailed account, read Richard Abanes, *American Militias: Rebellion, Racism & Religion* (Downers Grove, Ill.: InterVarsity Press, 1996), pp. 137-47.

[4]Ibid.

[5]Henry Louis Gates Jr., "The Charmer," *New Yorker*, April 29 and May 6, 1996, p. 128.

[6]Abanes, *Defending the Faith*, p. 198.

[7]Ibid.

[8]Ibid.

[9]George Johnson, *Architects of Fear: Conspiracy Theories and Paranoia in American Politics*

(Los Angeles:Tarcher, 1983), p. 114.

[10]Ken Klein, *The False Prophet: Evil Architect of the New World Order* (Eugene, Ore.: Winterhaven, 1992), pp. 87-88.

[11]Den Fujita, *Jewish Business Methods: Controlling the Economy of the World,* as quoted in "The Resurgence of Anti-Semitism," *New Dimensions,* June 1992, p. 14.

[12]Ibid.

[13]James Wardner, *The Planned Destruction of America* (Longwood, Fla.: Longwood Communications, 1993), p. 186.

[14]Richard V. Pierard, "It Happened," *Christianity Today,* March 9, 1992, p. 20.

[15]Gates, "The Charmer," p. 125. The word *cabal,* a group secretly united to overturn or usurp, is related to the word *Cabalist,* a student or devotee of the Jewish cabala, an esoteric doctrine or mysterious art. This connection is more evidence that anti-Semitism is often at the root of the belief that elite groups control world affairs.

[16]Malcolm X, "Alex Haley Interviews Malcolm X," *Playboy,* May 1963.

[17]Louis Farrakhan, quoted in Harold Brackman, "Farrakhanspiracy: Louis Farrakhan and the Paranoid Style in African-American Politics," *Skeptic* 4, no. 3 (1996): 40.

[18]Quoted in ibid.

[19]Documented in Abanes, *Defending the Faith,* p. 198.

[20]Ibid.

[21]*Los Angeles Times,* quoted in ibid., p. 199.

[22]Craig Hulet, "All the News That's Fit to Invent," *Soldier of Fortune,* August 1995, p. 57; quoted in Abanes, *Defending the Faith,* p. 116.

[23]Abanes, *Defending the Faith,* p. 201.

[24]Ibid.

[25]Johnson, *Architects of Fear,* p. 115.

[26]Ibid., p. 116.

[27]Louis T. Beyers, quoted in Abanes, *Defending the Faith,* p. 201.

[28]Abanes, *Defending the Faith,* p. 201.

[29]Johnson, *Architects of Fear,* p. 113.

[30]William Guy Carr, *Pawns in the Game* (Lakeland, Fla.: American Press, 1956), p. 1; quoted in William Chandler Baum, *The Conspiracy Theory of Politics of the Radical Right in the United States* (Iowa City: University of Iowa Press, 1971), p. 10.

[31]William Guy Carr, *The International Conspiracy* (undated pamphlet), p. 4; quoted in Baum, *Conspiracy Theory of Politics,* p. 12.

[32]William Guy Carr, untitled article, *News Behind the News* 2, no. 9 (July-August 1958): 2; quoted in Baum, *Conspiracy Theory of Politics,* p. 13.

[33]Ibid.

[34]Mike Hertenstein and Jon Trott, *Selling Satan* (Chicago: Cornerstone, 1993), p. 103.

[35]Carr, *Pawns in the Game,* pp. 162, 164; quoted in Hertenstein and Trott, *Selling Satan,* p. 103.

[36]Hertenstein and Trott, *Selling Satan,* p. 103.

[37]Abanes, *Defending the Faith,* pp. 179-80.

[38]Ibid.

[39]Don McAlvany, "Coming Persecution of Christians," August 27, 1993 (Christian Conference, taped message); quoted in Abanes, *Defending the Faith,* p. 203.

[40]Hans Schmidt, "Schindler's List—Is ZIONIST PROPAGANDA!" *Criminal Politics,* February 1994, p. 21.

[41]*Criminal Politics,* February 1994, back cover.

Chapter 6: Big, Monolithic & Anti-Christian

[1] James W. Wardner, *The Planned Destruction of America* (Longwood, Fla.: Longwood Communications, 1993), p. 118.

[2] Ibid., p. 128.

[3] Richard Abanes, *Defending the Faith: A Beginner's Guide to Cults and New Religions* (Grand Rapids, Mich.: Baker, 1997), p. 107.

[4] Ibid.

[5] Michael Coffey and Terry Golway, *Irish in America* (New York: Hyperion, 1997), p. 102.

[6] Taken from an interview of Jeff Mapes, political reporter for the *Oregonian*, by Paul Coughlin, July 1996.

[7] Chris Williamson, political reporter for KTVL-10, interview with author, July 1996.

[8] Gary Wean, "Conspiracy to Control the Members of the House of Representatives," *Contact: The Phoenix Project,* February 11, 1997, p. 10.

[9] Linda Thompson, quoted in Abanes, *Defending the Faith,* p. 109.

[10] Carey Kinsolving, quoted in Andy Butcher, "God and the Evening News," *Charisma,* August 1994, p. 37.

[11] Peggy Wehmeyer, quoted in ibid, p. 39.

[12] Vanderbilt University study, quoted in ibid.

[13] Butcher, "God and the Evening News," p. 39.

[14] Charles Krauthammer, "Will It Be Coffee, Tea or He? Religion Was Once a Conviction, Now It Is a Taste," *Time,* June 15, 1998, p. 92.

[15] Ibid.

[16] Ibid.

[17] Ibid.

[18] Ibid.

[19] Ibid.

[20] Dick Reavis, *The Ashes of Waco: An Investigation* (New York: Simon & Schuster, 1995), quoted in Jeff Baker, "In Lonely Pursuit of the Story Behind Waco," *Oregonian,* July 23, 1995, p. C5.

[21] Susan Ladd and Stan Swofford, "Electronic Outline: Computers Link Patriots," *News & Record* (Greensboro, N.C.), June 26, 1995, Internet edition at http://www.-infi.net/nr/extra/militias/m-electr.htm, quoted by Richard Abanes, *American Militias: Rebellion, Racism & Religion* (Downers Grove, Ill.: InterVarsity Press, 1996), p. 104.

[22] Richard Turner, "When Rumors Make News," *Newsweek,* December 30, 1996/January 6, 1997, p. 72.

[23] Jewelle Taylor Gibbs, *U.S. News Online,* http://www.usnew.com/usnews/issue/970602/2week.htm.

[24] Karenna Gore, *Apology Not Accepted,* http://www.slate.com/Tangled Web/97-05-15/Tangled Web.asp.

[25] Ibid.

[26] Richard Hofstadter, *The Paranoid Style in American Politics and Other Essays* (New York: Vintage Books/Random House, 1967), p. 36.

[27] Ibid.

[28] George Johnson, *Architects of Fear: Conspiracy Theories and Paranoia in American Politics* (Los Angeles: Tarcher, 1983), p. 137.

[29] Robert H. Welch Jr., *The Blue Book of the John Birch Society* (Belmont, Mass.: Western Island, 1961), quoted in ibid.

[30]Hofstadter, *The Paranoid Style*, p. 37.
[31]Ibid.
[32]Turner, "When Rumors Make News," p. 72.
[33]Ibid.

Chapter 7: Conspiracies from Both Right & Left

[1]Jeffrey Toobin, *New Yorker*, January 12, 1998, p. 8.
[2]CNN/Time poll, June 1997. Other results found that 64 percent said that aliens have contacted humans, half said they've abducted humans, and 37 percent said they have contacted the U.S. government. The poll has a margin of error of plus or minus 3 percentage points.
[3]"In Egypt, Media Fans' Rumors of Di's Murder," MSNBC, November 3, 1997, http://www.msnbc.com/news/120150.asp.
[4]Ibid.
[5]Richard Hofstadter, *The Paranoid Style in American Politics and Other Essays* (New York: Vintage Books/Random House, 1967), p. xi.
[6]Ken Klein, *Storm Warnings* newsletter, January/February 1995, p. 1.
[7]*Flashpoint: A Newsletter Ministry of Texe Marrs* 95, no. 10 (October 1995): back cover.
[8]William T. Still, *New World Order: The Ancient Plan of Secret Societies* (Lafayette, La.: Huntington House, 1990), p. 7.
[9]Ibid., p. 8.
[10]Ibid., p. 9.
[11]George Johnson, *Architects of Fear: Conspiracy Theories and Paranoia in American Politics* (Los Angeles: Tarcher, 1983), p. 85.
[12]Ibid.
[13]Michael Coffey and Terry Golway, *Irish in America* (New York, N.Y.: Hyperion, 1997), p. 143.
[14]Lyman Beecher, *Plea for the West* (Cincinnati, Ohio: n.p., 1835), pp. 47, 62-63; quoted in Hofstadter, *The Paranoid Style*, p. 21.
[15]Quoted in Sister Paul of the Cross McGrath, *Political Nativism in Texas, 1825-1860* (Washington, Tex.: n.p., 1930), pp. 114-15, from *Texas State Times*, September 15, 1855; quoted in Hofstadter, *The Paranoid Style*, p. 9.
[16]Jedidiah Morse, quoted in Hofstadter, *The Paranoid Style*, p. 19.
[17]Daniel G. Reid, Robert D. Linder, Bruce L. Shelley and Harry S. Stout, eds., *Dictionary of Christianity in America* (Downers Grove, Ill.: InterVarsity Press, 1990), p. 801.
[18]Ibid.
[19]Dave Hunt, *A Woman Rides the Beast* (Eugene, Ore.: Harvest House, 1994), p. 65.
[20]Ibid., p. 465.
[21]Reid et al., *Dictionary of Christianity in America*, p. 801.
[22]Johnson, *Architects of Fear*, p. 88.
[23]Historian J. Higham, quoted in Reid et al., *Dictionary of Christianity in America*, p. 801.
[24]Johnson, *Architects of Fear*, p. 88.
[25]Ibid., p. 87.
[26]Ibid.
[27]"Talk of the Town: Sean Lennon Has a New Record—and a Theory About His Father's Murder," *New Yorker*, April 20, 1998, p. 45.
[28]Research Catalog, *Prevailing Winds*, no. 3 (1996): 80-95.
[29]Joan Bokear, *Fundamentalism and the New Right* (n.p., n.d.), p. 89.

[30]Alex Constantine, "Operation Mockingbird: The CIA and the Media," *Prevailing Winds*, no. 3 (1996): 17.

[31]Jerry Mander and Edward Goldsmith, eds., *The Case Against the Global Economy, and For a Turn Toward the Local* (San Francisco: Sierra Club Books, 1996), back cover, cloth ed.

[32]Ibid., p. 92.

[33]Larry Abraham and Franklin Sanders, *The Greening of America* (Atlanta: Soundview, 1993), p. 239.

[34]Ibid., epilogue, p. 1.

[35]Ibid., p. 84.

[36]J. DeParle, "Talk Grows of Government Being Out to Get Blacks," *New York Times*, May 2, 1990, pp. B6-7, as quoted by Harold Brackman in "Farrakhanspiracy, Louis Farrakhan and the Paranoid Style in African-American Politics," *Skeptic* 4, no. 3 (1996).

[37]Brackman, "Farrakhanspiracy," p. 38.

[38]ABC News, *Turning Point*, June 21, 1997.

[39]"James Earl Ray Dies at Age 70," MSNBC, http://www.msnbc.com/news/160382.asp.

[40]Alex Haley, "A Playboy Classic: Alex Haley Interviews Malcolm X," *Playboy*, May 1963, p. 2, http://paul/spu.edu.~sinfein.malcx_in.html.

[41]Ibid.

[42]Brackman, "Farrakhanspiracy," p. 39.

[43]Ibid.

[44]Henry Louis Gates Jr., "The Charmer," *New Yorker*, April 29 and May 6, 1996, pp. 125-28.

[45]*Warren Duffy Show*, KKLA, California, February 14, 1997.

[46]Gates, "The Charmer," pp. 126, 128.

[47]Sanford Pinsker, "America's Conspiratorial Imagination," *Virginia Quarterly Review* 68, no. 4 (Autumn 1992): 625.

[48]Daniel Pipes, *Conspiracy: How the Paranoid Style Flourishes and Where It Comes From* (New York: Free Press, 1997), p. 163.

[49]Naomi Wolf, *Beauty Myth: How Images of Beauty Are Used Against Women* (New York: William Morrow, 1991), pp. 10, 13.

[50]Pinsker, "America's Conspiratorial Imagination," p. 625.

[51]Ibid., p. 620.

[52]Leon Jaroff, "Did Aliens Really Land?" *Time*, June 23, 1997.

Chapter 8: A Healthy View of End-Times Prophecy

[1]Chuck Smith, *Future Survival* (Word for Today, 1978), p. 20, http://village.ios.com/~dougg/calvary/cc2ndcom.htm#dsdehock.

[2]C. Marvin Pate, quoted in Jeffery Sheler, "Dark Prophecies," *U.S. News Online*, http://www.usnews.com/usnews/issue/971215/15prop.htm.

[3]Hal Lindsey, *The Late Great Planet Earth* (Grand Rapids, Mich.: Zondervan, 1970), p. 54.

[4]Hal Lindsey, *The 1980's, Countdown to Armageddon* (New York: Bantam Books, 1981), back cover; quoted in Richard Abanes, *Defending the Faith: A Beginner's Guide to Cults and New Religions* (Grand Rapids. Mich.: Baker, 1997), p. 94.

[5]Smith, *Future Survival*, pp. 17, 20.

[6]*End Times* (Word for Today, 1978), p. 35, http://village.ios.com/~dougg/calvary/cc2ndcom.htm#dsdehock; *Snatched Away* (Word for Today, 1976, 1980), pp. 23, 45, http://village.ios.com/~dougg/calvary/cc2ndcom.htm#dsdehock.

[7]B. J. Oropeza, interview with the author, *The Paul Thomas Show*, KDOV radio station,

Medford, Ore., October 4, 1994.

[8]Jim Keith, *Black Helicopters over America* (Lilburn, Ga.: IllumiNet Press, 1994), p. 84.

[9]"Japanese TV Cartoon Sets Off Seizures: More than 600 Hospitalized After Watching Popular Show," MSNBC, http://www.msnbc.com/news/130751.asp.

[10]Chuck Missler, "As the Days of Noah Were," *Personal UPDATE*, http://www.khouse.org/noah.html. A portion of a Web site—http://www.idt.net/~dougg/calvary/calvary.htm—has been devoted to similar statements by Missler.

[11]Letter from Zondervan Publishing House to *Christian Bookseller*, March 1994.

[12]Os Guinness, *Fit Bodies, Fat Minds: Why Evangelicals Don't Think and What to Do About It* (Grand Rapids, Mich.: Baker, 1994), p. 63.

[13]Ibid., p. 65.

[14]Ibid., p. 67.

[15]Richard Abanes, *Defending the Faith: A Beginner's Guide to Cults and New Religions* (Grand Rapids, Mich.: Baker, 1997), p. 94.

[16]Paul Fattig, "Land Grabber Won't Give Up," *Medford Mail Tribune*, April 15, 1995, p. A3.

[17]Daniel Junas, *Militias in America: The Real Story* (Vital Film & Video, 1995); quoted in Abanes, *Defending the Faith*, p. 102.

[18]Mark Koernke, *A Call to Arms* (Real World Productions, 1993); quoted in Abanes, *Defending the Faith*, p. 102.

[19]Des Griffin, quoted in Johnson, *Architects of Fear*, p. 69.

[20]James Colins, "The Burden of Proof," *Time*, May 26, 1997, p. 34.

[21]Robert P. Lightner, *The Last Days Handbook: A Comprehensive Guide to Understanding the Different Views of Prophecy* (Nashville, Tenn.: Thomas Nelson, 1990), pp. 180-81.

[22]Ibid.

[23]Chuck Swindoll, "Let's Be Realistic About the Present," *Insight for Living*, 1993.

[24]Wendy Murray Zoba, "Future Tense: How Do We Live Under the Shadow of 'the End?'" *Christianity Today*, October 2, 1995, pp. 22-23, http://www.ctcurrmrw5TB0185919.

[25]Ibid., p. 23.

[26]Ibid.

[27]Ibid.

[28]Ibid.

[29]C. S. Lewis, *The Joyful Christian* (New York: Macmillan, 1977), p. 71.

[30]Stefani Kopenec (Associated Press), "Waco Fire Still Burns in Memory: Anniversary of Tragedy Draws Near," *Mail Tribune* (Medford, Ore.), April 18, 1996, p. 5A.

Chapter 9: Why Conspiracy Theories Are So Prevalent & Attractive

[1]Richard Hofstadter, *The Paranoid Style in American Politics and Other Essays* (New York: Vintage Books/Random House, 1967), p. xi.

[2]Ibid., p. xii.

[3]Ibid., p. 4.

[4]Ibid.

[5]Thomas Cahill, *How the Irish Saved Civilization* (New York: Doubleday, 1995), p. 49.

[6]Joe Maxwell and Andrés Tapia, "Militia Extremists Blend God and Country into a Potent Mixture," *Christianity Today*, June 1995, http://www.ctjun95mrw5T70-34566b.

[7]Hofstadter, *The Paranoid Style*, p. 30.

[8]Ibid., p. 32.

[9]Norman Cohn, *The Pursuit of the Millennium* (London: n.p., 1957), pp. 309-10 (see also pp.

58-74); quoted in Hofstadter, *The Paranoid Style,* p. 38.

[10]Timothy Dwight, "The Duty of Americans in the Present Crisis," speech given on July 4, 1798; quoted in Hofstadter, *The Paranoid Style,* p. 13.

[11]Hofstadter, *The Paranoid Style,* p. 31.

[12]Ibid.

[13]William Guy Carr, *Pawns in the Game* (Lakeland, Fla.: American Press, 1956), quoted by William Chandler Baum, *The Conspiracy Theory of Politics of the Radical Right in the United States* (Iowa City: University of Iowa Press, 1971), p. 62 (italics added).

[14]Stefan Ulstein, *Growing Up Fundamentalist: Journeys in Legalism & Grace* (Downers Grove, Ill.: InterVarsity Press, 1995), p. 11 (italics added).

[15]Ibid.

[16]George Johnson, *Architects of Fear: Conspiracy Theories and Paranoia in American Politics* (Los Angeles: Tarcher, 1983), p. 147.

[17]Ibid.

[18]Ibid.

[19]Ibid.

[20]Ulstein, *Growing Up Fundamentalist,* p. 33.

[21]Jeff Baker, "In Lonely Pursuit of the Story Behind Waco," *Oregonian,* July 23, 1995, p. C5.

[22]Ibid.

[23]Gordon Witkin, "The Twisted Appeal of Conspiracy Theories," *U.S. News & World Report,* http://www.usnews.com/usnews/issue/970602/2week.htm.

[24]Sanford Pinsker, "America's Conspiratorial Imagination," *Virginia Quarterly Review* 68, no. 4 (Autumn 1992): 624.

[25]Richard Abanes, *Defending the Faith: A Beginner's Guide to Cults and New Religions* (Grand Rapids, Mich.: Baker, 1997), p. 85.

[26]Dave Frohnmeyer, "New Tribalism," *Old Oregon,* Autumn 1992, p. 17.

[27]Ibid., p. 18.

[28]Abanes, *Defending the Faith,* p. 15.

[29]Ibid., p. 33.

[30]Ibid., pp. 38-39.

[31]Ibid., p. 40.

[32]Gordon Lewis, *Confronting the Cults* (Grand Rapids, Mich.: Baker, 1975), p. 4; quoted in Abanes, *Defending the Faith,* p. 41.

[33]Abanes, *Defending the Faith,* p. 41.

[34]Speech by Tom Wolfe, "The End of the Century and the Spirit of the Age," delivered at Brown University, January 1997.

[35]Paul Johnson, *Intellectuals* (New York: Harper & Row, 1988), p. 340.

[36]Ibid., p. 2.

[37]Ibid., p. 340.

[38]Wolfe, "End of the Century."

[39]For Buchanan to be the choice of most patriots for president is an interesting study in the inconsistencies of the conspiracy community. Buchanan's Catholicism caused some to question whether he was also part of the conspiracy. According to Dave Hunt's *A Woman Rides the Beast* (Eugene, Ore.: Harvest House, 1994), it is a papal conspiracy that will usher in the New World Order. Some anti-Catholic conspiracy theorists believe that the papacy will attack Protestantism and promote idol worship of Mother Mary through New Age religion. This anti-Catholic sentiment, which has a long history in conspiracy thinking, hurt Buchanan's

campaign. Christian militia leader Dean Compton said he had to search deep within his soul in order to support Buchanan. He said that if Buchanan had showed any sign of being lock-step with the Vatican, he would have withdrawn his support immediately (Compton, interview with the author, Ashland, Ore., February 1997).

In 1968 Buchanan helped put together a coalition of voters to help Richard Nixon win the general election. In 1980 he helped Ronald Reagan obtain his landslide victory. Given his political history as a trusted aide to two American presidents, it is somewhat amusing that Buchanan would become the conspiracy community's premier choice for president. According to Christian conspiracy theorist William Still, Nixon was planning to overthrow America with a militia takeover and suspend the Constitution. Reagan has been accused of similar "acts of treason."

[40] Jeffrey Toobin, *New Yorker,* January 12, 1998, p. 9.

[41] Jeffrey L. Sheler, "Dark Prophecies," *U.S. News & World Report,* http://www.usnews.com/usnews/issue/971215/15prop.htm.

[42] Ibid.

[43] Hofstadter, *The Paranoid Style,* p. 7.

[44] Ibid., p. 35.

[45] Johnson, *Architects of Fear,* p. 153.

[46] Jim Benson, quoted in Mike Tharp and William J. Holstein, "Mainstreaming the Militia," *U.S. News Online,* http://www.usnews.com/usnews/issue/970421/21mili.htm.

[47] Tharp and Holstein, "Mainstreaming the Militia."

[48] Billy James Hargis, quoted in Johnson, *Architects of Fear,* p. 155.

[49] The expert wishes not to be named for fear of reprisal.

[50] Don McAlvany, "Attention Precious Metals Investors" (full-color advertisement), *McAlvany Intelligence Advisor,* no date given.

[51] Mike Hertenstein and Jon Trott, *Selling Satan* (Chicago: Cornerstone, 1993), p. 3.

[52] Johnson, *Architects of Fear,* p. 155.

[53] Ibid.

[54] William Griffin, "CBA in Orlando," *Publishers Weekly,* August 16, 1991; cited in Os Guinness and John Seel, eds., *No God But God* (Chicago: Moody Press, 1992), p. 68; quoted in Hertenstein and Trott, *Selling Satan,* p. 156.

[55] Kim Riddlebarger, "This Present Paranoia," in *Power Religion: The Selling Out of the Evangelical Church?* ed. Michael Scott Horton (Chicago: Moody Press, 1992), p. 268; quoted in Hertenstein and Trott, *Selling Satan,* p. 156.

[56] Ibid.

[57] Abanes, *Defending the Faith,* p. 226.

Chapter 10: Toward a Solution

[1] Daniel Jonah Goldhagen, *Hitler's Willing Executioners* (New York: Knopf, 1996), p. 245.

[2] William Shirer, *Rise and Fall of the Third Reich: A History of Nazi Germany* (New York: Simon & Schuster, 1960), p. 81.

[3] Adolf Hitler, *Mein Kampf,* American ed. (Boston, 1943), p. 296, quoted in ibid., p. 87.

[4] Ibid.

[5] Ibid., p. 1124.

[6] Peter and Paul Lalonde, *Racing Toward . . . the Mark of the Beast: Your Money, Computers and the God of the World* (Eugene, Ore.: Harvest House, 1994), p. 198.

[7] Ibid., p. 195.

[8]Ibid., p. 196.

[9]Ibid.

[10]Ibid., p. 197.

[11]Undated packet of information entitled *Information on Cabbage Patch Dolls,* from Bill Gothard's BasicYouth Conflicts seminar. The packet includes numerous letters from other concerned parents who had attended at least one of the seminars.

[12]Mike Hertenstein and Jon Trott, *Selling Satan* (Chicago: Cornerstone, 1993), p. 401.

[13]Ibid., p. 403 (italics added).

[14]Ibid., pp. 403-4.

[15]Chuck Swindoll, taped message entitled *Let's Be Realistic About the Present* (Anaheim, Calif., 1993).

[16]Bruce Barron, "A Summary Critique: *En Route to Global Occupation and the New World Order,*" *Christian Research Journal* reprint, Winter 1993, p. 2.

[17]Max Baucus, letter to the Senate Subcommittee on Terrorism, Technology and Government Information, June 15, 1995.

[18]Ibid.

[19]Ibid.

[20]Cal Thomas, "Christians Complain Too Much," *Mail Tribune* (Medford, Ore.) April 17, 1996, p. 10A.

[21]Ibid.

[22]Hofstadter, *The Paranoid Style,* p. 38.

[23]Ibid., p. 40.

Postscript

[1]Jeffrey Toobin, "The Plot Thins: The Oklahoma City Conspiracy That Wasn't," *New Yorker,* January 12, 1998, p. 9.

Index